Revitalising The Waterfront

Revitalising The Waterfront

INTERNATIONAL DIMENSIONS OF DOCKLAND REDEVELOPMENT

Edited by

B.S.Hoyle D.A.Pinder
and M.S.Husain

Belhaven Press
(a division of Pinter Publishers)
London and New York

© B.S. Hoyle, D.A. Pinder and M.S. Husain

First published in Great Britain in 1988 by
Belhaven Press (a division of Pinter Publishers),
25 Floral Street, London WC2E 9DS

British Library Cataloguing in Publication Data

A CIP catalogue record for this book is available from the
British Library

ISBN 1 85293 047 0

Library of Congress Cataloging-in-Publication Data

Revitalising the waterfront: international dimensions of dockland
   redevelopment / edited by B.S. Hoyle, D.A. Pinder and M.S. Husain.
      p.   cm.
   Includes index
   ISBN 1-85293-047-0
   1. Urban renewal. 2. Waterfronts. I. Hoyle, B.S. II. Pinder,
David. III. Husain, M.S. (M. Sohail)
HT170.R48 1988   88-26219
307.1'4—dc19   CIP

Printed and bound in Great Britain by
Biddles Ltd, Guildford and King's Lynn

Contents

List of figures

List of tables

Notes on contributors

Roger Bristow is Special Lecturer in Urban Studies in the Department of Planning and Landscape, University of Manchester. After taking Geography at Cambridge and following a spell in the port industry, he has been researching and teaching at Manchester since the 1970s. Most recently he has written widely on Hong Kong and other Far Eastern planning matters, and is currently working on property cycles in Hong Kong and Malaysian planning systems.

Andrew Church is a Lecturer in Geography at Birkbeck College, London University. He is completing a PhD thesis on the economic regeneration of London Docklands after being a postgraduate student based jointly at Queen Mary College, London University and the London Docklands Development Corporation. He has published several journal articles and book chapters on the redevelopment of London Docklands. Other current research activities include work on economic change in South East England for the South East Regional Research Laboratory (SERRL), based jointly at the Birkbeck and LSE Geography departments, and the analysis of regional wages in Britain.

Michael Clark is a Senior Lecturer in Geography in the School of Construction and Surveying, Lancashire Polytechnic, Preston. He holds BA (Sussex) and PhD (Wales) degrees. His main research interests are in planning, with special reference to large-scale coastal developments and the landward implication of maritime technological change. Dr Clark is a member of the Council of the Town and Country Planning Association and a former Secretary of the Geography and Planning Study Group of the Institute of British Geographers.

Gene Desfor is an Associate Professor in the Faculty of Environmental Studies, York University, Canada, where he has taught since 1973. His current teaching focuses on development processes – both in urban industrialised and Third World contexts. He has recently completed research on the late-nineteenth and early-twentieth-century history of

Toronto's waterfront development. He holds a PhD degree in Regional Science from the University of Pennsylvania.

Arwel Edwards studied at the Universities of Wales, California and Durham. He first worked for The British Council in Pakistan but then returned to lecture in the Department of Geography at University College, Swansea, on regional economic policy and planning in the USA. He has undertaken research and consultancy work in South Wales on economic impact analysis, economic change, business and marina development. He is also Director of the Social Science Research Institute at Swansea.

Michael Goldrick is a graduate of the London School of Economics and currently an Associate Professor of Political Science at York University, Canada, where he specialises in the political economy of cities and labour. He was full-time alderman on the Councils of the City of Toronto and the Government of Metropolitan Toronto in the mid-1970s. Since then, he has maintained involvements with labour organisations and social policy groups.

Yehuda Hayuth is a Senior Lecturer in the Department of Geography, University of Haifa, Israel, and Director of the Wydra Institute of Shipping and Aviation Research. He studied for his MA at the Hebrew University of Jerusalem, and for his PhD at the University of Washington (Seattle). Dr Hayuth's experience includes work for the UN in Thailand and research for the US Office of Coastal Zone Management. He was an Assistant Professor at the University of Rhode Island and has served as a visiting academic at the London School of Economics.

David Hilling holds MSc (Wales) and PhD (London) degrees, and is a Senior Lecturer in Geography at Royal Holloway and Bedford New College, University of London. From 1960 to 1966 he was a Lecturer at the University of Ghana, Accra, during which time he travelled widely in West and Equatorial Africa before returning to London in 1966 as a Lecturer in Geography at Bedford College. He is a Member of the Chartered Institute of Transport. His special research interests are in maritime transport technology and associated problems of port development, both in developing and mature economies.

Brian Hoyle is a Reader in the Department of Geography, University of Southampton, and holds MA (Nottingham) and PhD (London) degrees. A Member of the Chartered Institute of Transport, Dr Hoyle is currently Secretary of the Transport Geography Study Group of the Institute of British Geographers, and a Corresponding Member of the Marine Geography Study Group of the International Geographical Union. He has held previous substantive university appointments at Makerere (Uganda) and

Aberystwyth (Wales); and has travelled extensively in tropical Africa, Southeast Asia, Australia and North America. His primary research interests lie in economic development, especially transport, with particular reference to the developing countries. He has written extensively on problems of port development and related issues, including urbanisation and industrial expansion.

Sohail Husain has been a Lecturer in the Department of Geography at Southampton University since 1976. A graduate of Nottingham University, much of his research has been focused on economic development in western Europe, and he has a particular interest in West Germany. Dr Husain's port-related research has been concerned with port development policies and structural change in the oil-refining industry, on which he has published several papers, some of these being the product of co-operative work with David Pinder.

Chris Law is a Reader in Geography in the University of Salford. His interests are in urban and regional development problems and planning, predominantly in Britain but also in other areas of western Europe and in North America. Mr Law has published books on British regional development since World War I and on the uncertain future of the urban core.

Roy Merrens is a Professor of Geography at York University, Canada. He did his undergraduate work at University College London and completed his PhD programme at the University of Wisconsin. A former Guggenheim Fellow and a Toronto Harbour Commissioner, he is the author of a number of books and articles published in Canada and the United States.

David Pinder, a graduate of Reading University, is an economic geographer with a particular interest in planning. He is a Senior Lecturer in Geography at Southampton University, and from 1982 to 1987 was Honorary Treasurer of the Institute of British Geographers. Since the early 1970s his research has concentrated on European economic and regional development issues. During an appointment in the Economic Geography Institute, Erasmus University, Rotterdam (1978–79), a major research focus was on conflicts in port–city relationships arising from environmental pressures. Although he maintains his Dutch interests, recent projects have been Europe-wide. Since the mid-1980s port-related research, undertaken in collaboration with Sohail Husain, has been primarily concerned with economic crisis and the restructuring of the European oil-refining industry.

Ray Riley is a Principal Lecturer in the Department of Geography, Portsmouth Polytechnic. His main fields of research are the geography of industry and regional development, urban history and urban conservation.

Particular regional interests are the Benelux countries and Portsmouth, a port economy more than normally controlled by external influences. These themes have been developed in a number of papers and books, most recently in a study of the geography of defence.

Dr Kenneth E. Rosing graduated in Geography at the University of Minnesota. After experience as a regional planner in the early 1960s he moved to England and was appointed Lecturer in Geography at King's College, London, in 1965. He took his PhD while in London, and moved to Erasmus University, Rotterdam, in 1971. He is now a Reader in Geography in Rotterdam, and his publications reflect a wide range of research, teaching and consultancy interests – from energy and urban studies to mathematical geography. He is currently concerned with inner-urban redevelopment in Rotterdam.

Louis Shurmer-Smith is a Principal Lecturer in the Department of Geography, Portsmouth Polytechnic. His main fields of research are in urban and regional development with particular reference to western Europe, especially France. Current research interests include political control and the urban planning process, and comparisons between the British and French experiences in the development and problems of medium-sized towns.

John Tunbridge is an Associate Professor of Geography at Carleton University, Ottawa, where he arrived in 1969 via Cambridge, Bristol and Sheffield Universities, and originally from the London Docklands. His prime research interest is in urban conservation issues. His interest in waterfront revitalisation stems from involvement with urban heritage, and from directing field courses in Boston.

Iain Tweedale, at the time of writing his chapter, was a research officer in the Social Research Unit of the Department of Sociology at University College, Cardiff, where he worked mainly in the field of training and vocational education. He is currently completing a PhD thesis on the redevelopment of Cardiff docklands and now works as an economist with the Welsh Development Agency.

Preface and acknowledgements

Waterfront revitalisation is currently a subject of widespread interest in many parts of the world. In this context, an international seminar on change and development at the port–city interface entitled 'Waterfront redevelopment and the cityport economy' was held in the Department of Geography, University of Southampton, in November 1987. The seminar was based on the initiative of members of the Department's International Development Research Group and arose (as did an earlier seminar held in 1979 on problems of cityport industrialisation) from long-established interests within the Department in urban development and port studies. The object of the meeting was to create a forum for the discussion of the problems of the port–city interface, and the implications of these problems for waterfront redevelopment and cityport economies.

The literature on waterfront redevelopment already contains numerous case studies. The Southampton seminar was designed to move towards an integrated systematic approach to the topic through the juxtaposition of ideas, methods of analysis and results based on a wide range of port cities. Over fifty participants came from fourteen countries and included economists and geographers, representatives of port managements and development companies, planners and political scientists. Papers were presented on contextual and methodological issues, on recent and current research, and on policies and planning experience. While the experience of members of the seminar was derived primarily from North America and Western Europe, contributors also presented evidence from Australia, the Middle East, Latin America and South and East Asia.

Selected papers presented at the seminar have been extensively revised and edited for the present volume, the structure of which is outlined in the Introduction. The policy of the editors has been to work closely with authors whose contributions were seen particularly to illuminate, within a balanced structure, three essential aspects of waterfront revitalisation: contextual elements, contrasted policies, and planning issues. Numerous additional papers presented on these and related themes are in course of publication elsewhere.

The support of the Economic and Social Research Council, the British

Council, the Nuffield Foundation and the Government of Canada for the seminar is appreciated and gratefully acknowledged. It is a pleasure also to record our gratitude to the contributors for their co-operation in the preparation of this book, and to the large number of authorities in ports and cities around the world without whose assistance the research on which this volume is based could not have been accomplished. Individual authors have acknowledged, where appropriate, their indebtedness to sources of research funds. Some of the maps and diagrams were prepared or amended in the Cartographic Unit of the University of Southampton, under the direction of Mr Alan S. Burn; others were submitted by authors in a finished condition, thus accounting for some variation in cartographic style. We also record our appreciation of the substantial help – secretarial and organisational – provided by Mrs Maralyn Knight, Mrs June Gandhi and Mrs Tina Birring – in connection with the conference and with the preparation of this book.

Department of Geography   B.S Hoyle
University of Southampton   D.A. Pinder
April 1988   M.S. Husain

Introduction: Phoenix on the waterfront

The port-city interface is widely recognised, and has been identified in the literature, as an area in transition. Geographers and economists, politicians and planners, port authorities, port users and property developers are all keenly aware of development issues relating to this interface that confront cityports through the advanced world and, increasingly, in developing countries too. These development issues have been generated by technological change in the maritime field, by evolving patterns of world trade, by new levels of environmental regulation, and by changing relationships between ports and cities.

Against this background, and given the far-reaching implications of the processes involved, intensified research into the nature and consequences of change at the port–city interface is now overdue. Several important areas for investigation can readily be identified. For example, the impact of the economic recession of the 1970s and 1980s clearly requires evaluation, as does the influence of the environmental movement on port development in the late twentieth century. However, perhaps the most striking development in recent years has been the rejuvenation of previously moribund and decaying waterfront areas. Throughout the world, but especially in advanced countries, there has been a spectacular transformation of many such localities that was in most countries almost inconceivable twenty years ago. This wave of revitalisation, impressive and apparently successful though it may appear, in fact poses many physical planning, economic and socio-economic challenges, and it is on these that the present volume focuses.

Much has already been written about port cities in transition, and about the particular political or planning problems associated with the waterfront-redevelopment movement. In North America, where waterfront revitalisation became well-established in the 1970s, the movement has engendered a substantial literature in the fields of architecture, planning and urban design. This trend has also become very apparent in Western Europe in the 1980s, especially in the United Kingdom, and it is now spreading rapidly elsewhere in the world. Political scientists, geographers and economists have not been slow to record and comment on the changes taking place in specific areas and locations.

Yet, despite this wave of interest and activity, and despite the significance of waterfront revitalisation for cityport economies and populations, the field is far from fully researched. What is particularly evident is that no integrated, systematic overview of the revitalisation movement has yet appeared. The present volume aims to fill this gap. Based on the juxtaposition of ideas, methods of analysis and experience derived from a wide range of port cities in advanced and developing countries, its purpose is to stimulate discussion on a comparative basis, focusing especially upon present-day issues and their implications for future cityport development – physical, economic and social.

The book is divided into three parts. The first is concerned with frameworks for the analysis of waterfront revitalisation. Approaches appropriate to the understanding of forces generating redevelopment are examined; and the social, environmental and economic implications of these forces are considered at the local, national and international scales. In the first chapter, Hoyle outlines dominant stages in the evolution of the port–city interface, from the intimate pre-twentieth-century spatial and functional association between port and city to the modern retreat from the waterfront and its consequent redevelopment. From this analysis a model of the forces and factors affecting the zone of conflict or co-operation at the waterfront is proposed. Hilling then extends Hoyle's argument by highlighting the impact of port decline on social and economic conditions in the maritime quarter. This chapter emphasises the inter-relationships of port and city, and stresses that revitalisation strategies address only one set of problems if they focus on derelict port zones to the exclusion of port-related inner-urban problems. Riley and Smith recognise the power of international forces in the processes of decline and revitalisation, but also argue that analysis and understanding are seriously impeded if the influence of local site factors, and of local attitudes, decisions and policies is ignored. Hayuth, meanwhile, views waterfront redevelopment largely in terms of the ecological, technological and economic systems affecting the transformation of the port–city interface, adopting a model-based approach to clarify the potentially confusing proliferation of revitalisation programmes.

In Part II attention turns to policy and practice. Waterfront redevelopment is essentially an advanced-country phenomenon best examined largely on the basis of North American and European experience. In the 1960s and 1970s, the United States and Canada were the cradles of the waterfront-redevelopment movement. Appropriately, therefore, Tunbridge offers a wide-ranging discussion of North American experience involving considerable policy variations applied at widely contrasting scales. There follows a chapter in which Desfor, Goldrick and Merrens discuss the specific case of Toronto, Canada, a cityport that provides a classic illustration of the variety of forces and scales involved in the process of waterfront revitalisation; analysing this interaction, they trace the evolution of strategy in a changing socio-economic context and assess the present-day outcomes.

Turning to Western Europe, Pinder and Rosing show how Rotterdam, the Netherlands, represents those cityports where local authorities have adopted a strong stance over the formulation of redevelopment policy. Market forces have been constrained within a clear framework, and policy has acquired an overt social dimension. Although deep socio-economic contrasts between pre-twentieth and twentieth-century Rotterdam have not been broken down, progress has been made towards social goals and, simultaneously, commercial pressures have been accommodated. Edwards' study of Swansea, UK, is also largely concerned with the role of local authority policy, although in this case the central concern is to demonstrate that a distinction must be drawn between the physical and economic achievements of revitalisation. The importance of this distinction emerges again in the context of several other chapters in Part II, and re-emerges later as a major issue in Part III.

Law argues that in many cityports the essential challenge is that of dealing with problems of port-generated land use and, simultaneously, with socio-economic problems that are derived from the handicaps of the inner-city environment. Once again, considerable attention is given to the role of public policy, but the contribution of private capital is also stressed, and it is argued that thresholds – beyond which reliance on public investment falls sharply – may be important in revitalisation processes. Meanwhile, the power of private capital is a central theme in Bristow's study of Hong Kong, where demand-led planning is clearly dominant. Processes controlling land-use changes in a free-market economy are identified, and consequences in terms of new land-use patterns are considered. This chapter also illustrates how the need for revitalisation is already spreading to developing countries.

Most contributions in Part III also deal with examples of decline and revitalisation but draw from them major issues relating to global forces and to the consequences of current planning policies and practices. Above all, attention focuses on the power of private investors in redevelopment processes and on socio-economic problems which, it is argued, are not usually addressed by demand-led planning strategies. Tweedale draws together and extends the arguments of Hilling, Riley and Shurmer-Smith, and Law by interpreting change at the port–city interface in terms of capital accumulation and economic restructuring. His chapter provides a highly critical assessment of the effects of these processes on inner-city communities.

Church also offers a critical evaluation of the physical and socio-economic outcomes of demand-led planning, in this case based on detailed work on the London Docklands. He emphasises the role of national and international forces in determining the outcome of revitalisation measures, and concludes that such measures must have social and economic dimensions, not simply physical ones, if they are to contribute to the solution of the inner-city problem. Clark, in a contribution concerned primarily with the assessment of planning processes, argues that official revitalisation proposals are often insufficiently rigorous, and that there is frequently too great a readiness to equate change with progress. Revitalisation strategies are creating physical and social environments for the twenty-first century, and they must therefore be formulated and evaluated in terms of long-term objectives rather than short-term expediency.

While recognising that redevelopment problems in older port areas are pressing, Pinder and Husain argue that these problems should not be allowed to obscure the fact that recent deindustrialisation has extended the redundant-space problem to newer port areas. This extension poses planning problems for which current strategies are unsuited, and points to the need for radically different approaches. This need is underlined by the continuing progress of deindustrialisation and industrial restructuring in many advanced countries. In the concluding chapter the editors identify dominant themes emerging from earlier chapters – particularly strategy evolution, the role of public-sector planning and the power of private capital – and integrate them in an explanatory model of waterfront evolution. This forward-looking synthesis demonstrates again the need for evaluation to focus on both the physical, ecological and socio-economic outcomes of change on the waterfront and, finally, leads to a research agenda for the 1990s.

Part I: Frameworks for analysis

1 Development dynamics at the port–city interface

Brian Hoyle

Introduction

The 1970s and 1980s have witnessed substantial changes in port–city relationships on a variety of scales and in several different dimensions. The modern seaport acts as a gateway rather than as a central place, and the evolution of maritime technology (involving particularly the widespread development of bulk terminals, container ports and ro-ro methods) has had the general effect of weakening the traditionally strong functional ties between ports and cities. The migration of port activities towards deeper water, as a consequence of technological change, has introduced in many ports around the world an unaccustomed separation of port and urban functions. The retreat from the traditional waterfront, usually but not invariably towards the sea, has introduced major problems, challenges and opportunities for port and urban authorities. The redevelopment of water-front zones, in the context of the changing economic character of port cities, represents one of the most widespread and significant of these opportunities.

The challenges presented by the new spatial and economic order which port evolution and urban redevelopment represent are considerable. Firstly, they involve a re-assessment of the locational requirements of ports and a rethinking of the ways in which they should be built. Secondly, they necessitate the redesign of substantial areas of coastal settlements in order to create better environments for people living and working in maritime quarters. Thirdly, they must provide new stimuli for the further develop-ment of regions and nations within which cityports are set. Critical factors in this process, however, include the timing of the response to technologi-cal change, both in ports and cities; the broad ecological environment within which these changes are set; and the economic and political influ-ences which underlie spatial and social change.

Three inter-related objectives of this chapter are, firstly, to review these trends and patterns in broad terms, with the aid of two simple models of cityport development; secondly, to comment critically on some relevant theoretical contributions to this field of study, devised mainly to explain observed changes; and thirdly, to draw attention to the need for progress in the development of theory, and in the analysis of a wider range of case-study material from advanced and less-developed countries, in order to identify promising avenues for further research. The French Mediterranean port complex of Marseille–Fos is used as a classic illustration of historical and contemporary trends and patterns.

Geographical studies of the port–city interface

In the past, geographical studies of port cities have tended to focus attention either upon the patterns and problems of urban land use, interpreted chronologically or spatially, or upon the development and characteristics of port facilities and trade structures. Only relatively recently has attention been directed specifically to the problems and policies associated with the port–city interface and to the problems posed by the retreat from the waterfront and the consequent need to redevelop abandoned areas. Similarly, in recent decades there has been an increasing emphasis in port studies on comparative approaches and on the identification of common structures, mechanisms and processes within port systems. While each port city retains its individuality within its own specific geographical, political, economic and technological environments, and as a result develops its own special complexities and problems, any individual cityport nevertheless represents to a greater or lesser extent the overall trends that characterise all such locations and which reflect global rather than local factors.

In retrospect, two papers from the early 1980s are worth renewed emphasis. Norcliffe (1981b) used the Heckscher–Ohlin hypothesis, based upon the locational implications of the varying labour and capital requirements of different industries, as a framework for an analysis of processes affecting industrial development in port areas in Canada. This hypothesis assumes that 'for any given industry there are fixed technical inputs which preclude the substitution of labour for capital and vice-versa', and postulates that therefore

a logical pattern of industrial location will result ... Industries which make intensive use of labour are located optimally towards the city centre, while those requiring large capital inputs in the form of extensive sites will favour suburban locations ... Industries which experience dramatic technological changes, generally in the form of greater capital inputs, are likely to relocate to areas within the urban region where their factor-input costs are minimized.

[Norcliffe, 1981b, 152]

Taking essentially an urban-industrial standpoint, Norcliffe identified four major processes within this context which, potentially, produce radical changes in waterfront areas. These processes are: capital intensification and job elimination by port industries; greater space consumption by port industries; land-use competition within port areas; and the growth, in port areas, of industries not directly related to the port. Norcliffe illustrated these processes by a variety of Canadian examples, and concluded that

in many large North American ports, recreational, commercial, residential and institutional land uses have become prominent on the central waterfront . . . There is much less evidence of this process in West European ports . . . [but] these changes are amongst many examples of the profound effect of technological change on the spatial organization of society.
[ibid, 164]

During the 1980s these processes have become widespread on the European side of the Atlantic and, indeed, in many other parts of the world. world.

A more wide-ranging overview of the port–city interface as an area in transition was provided by Hayuth (1982). Whereas Norcliffe's study is essentially land-based, Hayuth took a more comprehensive view of the conflicts and innovative forces involved from both the urban and maritime standpoints. He distinguished between the *spatial system*, which involves functional interlinkages and geographical proximity between port and city, and the *ecological system* which is concerned with environmental inter-relationships and social priorities. Hayuth underlined the role of technological change in the design and size of ships (Mayer, 1973; Slack, 1980), rendering many ports unsuitable for some trades and requiring the widespread introduction of larger-scale terminals on previously undeveloped land with access to deeper water. He also emphasised the revolutionary innovations in cargo-handling techniques, notably containerisation, that have produced new port land-use patterns, creating greatly increased space demands and thereby requiring locations well beyond the confines of many traditional port areas. At the same time, Hayuth argued – and these ideas are further developed in his contribution to the present volume (Chapter 4) – there has been in effect a parallel revolution in public attitudes towards environmental issues, particularly in relation to such matters as industrial pollution, coastal management and the location of new port-industrial developments (Hayuth, 1982).

Both these early papers were included in Bird's (1984) typology of port studies in which he distinguished *the retreat from the waterfront* as the most recent in a series of eight categories and overlapping phases of port study developed from about 1960. Beyond these useful attempts at generalisation, and in part underlying them, there are numerous discussions in the literature on the experience of specific port cities in the context of recent technological changes. Although it is fashionable nowadays to denigrate the study of individual ports or port-groups in favour of structured analyses based on wide-ranging models and theories, the study of present-day trends and problems is unlikely to progress very far in a broad context until an adequate body of case-study material has been built up.

Port geographers acknowledge that the description of changing waterfront land use is a well-established theme in the USA and in Canada, where early papers by Forward (1969), O'Mara (1976) and Slack (1975), together with official surveys organised by the Federal Government (Canada, Ministry of State for Urban Affairs, 1978), helped to develop an interest in this theme. McCalla (1983) postulated the emergence of separate and specialised areas of port-related and urban activity in cityport waterfronts, using the Canadian examples of Saint John (New Brunswick) and Halifax (Nova Scotia). Ley (1981) identified Vancouver's changing employment characteristics, involving the rapid growth of service sectors, as a major factor in increased land competition at the waterfront; and Wilson (1978) demonstrated that the surplus of underutilised and vacant waterfront land in Toronto is a net result of new methods of cargo handling, differential land costs and tax structures in relation to central and peripheral urban areas. These contributions illustrate some of the ways in which geographers have attempted to explore specific spatial aspects of the changing waterfront phenomenon. Many other references to work in this area, especially in a North American context, are introduced in later chapters in this book.

Port–city inter-linkages, past and present

Present-day waterfront trends and problems must clearly be considered from a variety of viewpoints. In historical terms it is useful to consider the evolution of port–city inter-linkages as a series of distinctive stages (Fig. 1.1). The basic association of port functions and urban economies in this context rests upon the convenience and importance of waterborne transport; in pre-railway eras, any city with direct access to a navigable waterway had a major advantage in commercial terms. But, as Konvitz remarked,

every coastal town did not become a city, nor did communities exist wherever there was a good harbour, nor did every port city have a good harbour; there are mysteries about why men have chosen to live in cities, to occupy certain sites, and to link their destinies to the movements of ships that cannot be entirely explained by economic, social or political events.

[Konvitz, 1978, xi]

In those coastal locations where favourable factors combined, however, there lay potential for enormous growth based on contacts with distant cultures, societies and economies (Konvitz, 1982). This remains generally true in modern times, yet the continuing prosperity of cityports today is increasingly less dependent upon their specific maritime trading links than upon their regional and national economic roles. Ports have become more noticeably national gateways, while cities have retained their regional and local functions. Herein lie the seeds of separation between port and city. Among British cityports, Southampton illustrates this point effectively:

Stage	Symbol ○ city ● port	Period	Characteristics
I Primitive cityport		Ancient–medieval to 19th century	Close spatial and functional association between city and port
II Expanding cityport		19th–early 20th century	Rapid commercial and industrial growth forces port to develop beyond city confines, with linear quays and break-bulk industries
III Modern industrial cityport		mid-20th century	Industrial growth (especially oil refining) and introduction of containers and ro-ro facilities require separation and increased space
IV Retreat from the waterfront		1960s–80s	Changes in maritime technology induce growth of separate maritime industrial development areas
V Redevelopment of the waterfront		1970s–90s	Large-scale modern port consumes large areas of land- and water-space; urban renewal of original core

Figure 1.1   *Stages in the evolution of the port–city interface*

the port acts as a major maritime gateway in relation to the UK national economic space as a whole, yet only a relatively small proportion of employment within the cityport is directly related to the port function (Witherick, 1981).

I   The primitive cityport

The great medieval Italian cityports – Genoa, Naples, Venice – were the first to develop a commercial system whereby the products of distant lands became the necessities and luxuries of urban life. The co-existence of a primitive port and city involved close spatial association and maximum functional interdependence. In medieval cityports the urban centre was dominated by merchants' houses and the waterfront represented the focal point of the settlement as a whole.

At Marseille (Fig. 1.2) the original urban core occupies a triangular site north of the Vieux Port, protected by hills to the south and by offshore islands. Founded as a Greek colony in 599 BC, Marseille has enjoyed from its origins an advantageous site as a port and as a city: a comparatively large and sheltered harbour, invisible from the open sea; and a defensive site for a settlement protected on two sides by water and on the third by marshy ground. These attributes, common in one form or another to many Mediterranean port cities, underpin the first and longest stage in the evolution of the modern port–city interface; in this specific case, a combination of particularly favourable factors helped to create and to preserve Marseille's predominance among French and Mediterranean cityports.

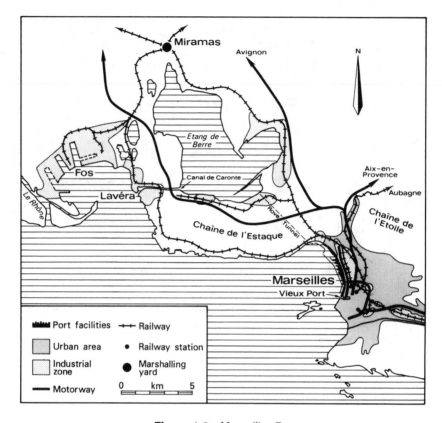

Figure 1.2 *Marseille–Fos*

The view of Marseille in 1602 reproduced as Figure 1.3 is among the oldest surviving attempts at an accurate reproduction of a cityport's physical appearance (Konvitz, 1978, 15, 190), for earlier views were often stylized, iconographic representations of reality. It provides an illustration of a classic interpenetration of land and sea, and a characteristic interdependence of urban and maritime activities, that have been associated with Mediterranean coastal settlements from the earliest times. Marseille is shown at a moment when it was beginning to emerge from the problems of the medieval period; then, the relatively shallow waters of the harbour had been reduced by infilling, and barriers known as *barquions* were set up at the foot of the steep streets of the town to prevent urban refuse from falling into the harbour. A narrow rudimentary quay had been built in 1511, and primitive piers added; by 1602 these had given way to a rather more substantial waterfront uniting city and port; but, as elsewhere at the time, the harbour and the sea were still separated by chains suspended across the entrance to prevent the entry of unwelcome vessels.

Figure 1.3 *Marseille, 1602 (Source: Konvitz, 1978, courtesy Newberry Library, Chicago)*

II   *The expanding cityport*

Rapid commercial and industrial developments in the nineteenth century forced many ports to break out of their traditional confines, and the seeds of port–city separation were widely scattered. At the same time, however, the expansion of port facilities exerted a marked influence upon patterns of urban land use. Marseille again provides a classic case study (Fig. 1.2). By the early nineteenth century, congestion within the Vieux Port had become so severe that the construction of artificial external basins was essential. In 1844 it was decided to begin the development of a series of basins towards the north – a controversial issue at the time, for the new port facilities could have been located towards the south, but one that effectively controlled subsequent patterns of industrial and residential land use in the expanding city. Factors affecting the rapid growth of port traffic at this time included the arrival of new means of communication (railways, steamships), the development of a French overseas empire (notably in North Africa) and the opening of the Suez Canal in 1869. These factors, together with the specific location of the new port facilities, produced a substantial concentration of industrial development in the northern parts of the nineteenth-century city, with residential and recreational forms of land use dominating the southern areas (Wolkowitsch, 1979, 1981).

Some of the expanding port cities of this period became effective instruments of exploitation and development in the colonial world, to which the European cityport model was exported with only limited adaptation to local circumstances. In West Africa, Dakar (Sénégal) and Lagos (Nigeria) represent respectively many characteristic features of French and British cityport traditions. Similar transplantations of European cultures in a cityport context may be found in Québec City, Boston and Buenos Aires; in the prosperous Chinese cityport states of Southeast Asia, Hong Kong and Singapore; and still further afield in Australia and New Zealand.

The initial selection in the late eighteenth and early nineteenth centuries of the sites of the capital cities of six Australian states (Sydney, Hobart, Brisbane, Perth–Fremantle, Adelaide, Melbourne), and the subsequent growth and development of those settlements, are directly related to the port function, the foundation stone upon which modern urban, regional and national economic development in that continent has depended (Bach, 1976; Bird, 1965, 1968; Forward, 1970). According to Bird, a common factor in the successful founding of these seaport capital cities was the 'proclaimed impulse', the political power imposed on a site and enshrined in a legal document.

None of the founders could have foreseen the present size of the settlements, nor the extent of the areas they now serve; and only an idea such as the proclaimed impulse can explain the continued success of the cities growing from the original site, despite the availability of the written reasons given by the founders themselves.

[Bird, 1986, 56]

Those reasons underlying the proclaimed impulse, however, included assessments of the water sites and land sites involved, of their potential for port and urban growth, and for forward and backward linkages from colonial coastal and commercial cores.

III   The modern industrial cityport

Increasing ship size and increasingly specialised industrial growth were major factors in nineteenth-century cityport change, and these factors continued in the mid-twentieth century to promote further port-city diversification. The need to establish facilities for the reception and refining of crude oil at some distance from traditional cityport core zones, and the introduction of technological changes (particularly containerisation) requiring extensive land sites, have together accelerated the separation of port–urban land uses and functions.

Marseille clearly illustrates these widespread trends (Fig. 1.2). The incorporation of the Etang de Berre (from 1919) and Fos (from 1965) in the area controlled by the Port of Marseille authorities represents the transformation of the traditional cityport into an industrial maritime complex on a vast scale. In one sense, the expansion of the traditional port to include the Etang de Berre and Fos is a natural outcome of the northward process of expansion towards the Rhône which began in 1844. In another sense, the Fos complex is an excellent illustration of an important global phenomenon: *a maritime industrial development area* (MIDA) dependent upon bulk transport, large-scale operation and investment, and planned and integrated development. MIDAs – or ZIP (Zones Industrielles Portuaires, as they are known in French-speaking areas) – are themselves an outcome of the revolution in maritime transport technology that occurred in the 1960s and 1970s, involving the introduction of very large bulk carriers for oil and ores, and the development of appropriate port facilities. The planned integration of port development schemes and industrial expansion programmes in this context has been a major feature of the changing economic geography of advanced and less-developed countries in recent years (Vigarié, 1979, 1981).

An entirely new port-industrial area has been developed at Fos since 1965, as a result of which Marseille–Fos now ranks as not only the largest French port in throughput terms but also as second only to Rotterdam amongst European ports. Fos is the largest Mediterranean MIDA, and perhaps the best example of this kind of integrated development; it is the principal French reaction to the revolution in maritime transport that has taken place since the early 1960s, and has been described as 'l'un des plus vastes chantiers de rénovation littorale d'Europe' (Vigarié, 1979, 230). Oil refining, petrochemical and steel industries have, together with port operation provided a framework for substantial new employment and induced a population increase within the Etang de Berre–Fos area of the order of half a million during the 1965–75 period.

Traffic through the Marseille–Fos port complex as a whole had increased by the early 1980s to over 100 million tonnes from the 1958 level of 56 millions. While the focus of port authority and administration remains very close to the ancient point of origin on the shores of the Vieux Port, the heaviest traffic flows (including an increasing proportion of containerised general cargoes) are handled at the most distant point, furthest from the original waterfront. The Provençal novelist Paul Guth wrote in the 1960s that 'on devrait parler de Marseille au pluriel, comme les Grecs parlaient autrefois des Athènes'. Today, the concept of a plurality of development points and zones within a vast but essentially problematic port-city planning region is essential to an understanding of the socio-economic and urban geography of the Marseille area today (Tuppen, 1984).

IV   Retreat from the waterfront

The retreat from the traditional waterfront has been largely induced by maritime technological factors, and the character and layout of modern port facilities are largely dictated by the requirements of ship-designers and ship-operators. The urban consequences of these trends, in terms of waterfront redevelopment and in terms of the wider contexts of local and regional socio-economic planning, have required the close attention of urban and other authorities confronted with the consequences of technological changes over which they have no direct influence or control. An important factor in this context is the attitude of communities generally or specifically involved in port-city development, particularly in an ecological context and in relation to the location and/or expansion of port-related industries. This question has been discussed, *inter alia*, by Hayuth (1982) and illustrated by Pinder (1981) in relation to Rotterdam.

The processes of port-city separation described above, and illustrated by the classic case of Marseille–Fos, have operated on a variety of scales over time and in a variety of spatial and technological contexts. As Bird's (1963) *Anyport* model underlined, ports located on estuarine sites have long displayed a tendency to move downstream towards deeper water, thus gradually introducing an enforced separation of port and city. The ultimate stage of this process reached today is represented by the large-scale development of MIDAs devoted, at least initially, to industries based on imported bulk commodities and occupying vast land and water sites often at a considerable distance from any associated city. The MIDA concept is the very antithesis of the medieval cityport, and represents in a sense the modern expression of an historically deep-rooted process; it also indicates how far the separation of port and urban functions has proceeded. In north-western Europe, examples of this phenomenon may be found at Antwerp, Rotterdam and Zeebrugge (Charlier, 1981), while in the Middle East and in Japan the concept of artificial island seaports has been developed, taking the separation of port and city to its logical extreme conclusion.

On a more modest scale than that of the West European superports, a common general trend in many advanced and less-developed countries is the development of an oil refinery, a container terminal and/or a bulk-cargo handling facility at some distance from an older port area. This process may be observed in many tropical African seaports, for example, including those of Kenya and Tanzania (Hoyle, 1983). Dar es Salaam (Tanzania) is a case where physical restrictions associated with the water site have led to the introduction of a single buoy mooring in a sheltered location outside the natural harbour to accommodate large crude-oil carriers. Unusually, both at Dar es Salaam and at Mombasa (Kenya), the development of port facilities during the twentieth century has moved upstream, away from the sea but within the confines of naturally deep-water harbours, rather than towards the sea in the manner of the *Anyport* model.

In contrast, Brisbane, the capital cityport of Queensland, has gradually abandoned its nineteenth-century city-centre wharves (located on a meander of the Brisbane river, some 20 km from the sea) in favour of down-stream developments including oil refineries. Extensive new container-handling terminals, together with coal-export and cement-import facilities, were developed during the early 1980s on the Fisherman Islands in Moreton Bay, at the mouth of the Brisbane River; and a seventh bulk-sugar handling facility was opened in 1985 as a further element in the rationalisation of the sugar-exporting system in favour of a limited number of specialised terminals (Hoyle, 1984). In New South Wales, the Maritime Services Board has developed an extensive series of container terminals and oil-handling facilities at Port Botany (Botany Bay), while continuing to maintain and redevelop the older-established port facilities of Port Jackson (Sydney Harbour). At both Brisbane and Sydney, nineteenth-century waterfront zones are undergoing rehabilitation – partly for recreational purposes, partly for commercial use, and partly to take advantage of opportunities to redevelop urban transport systems.

V Redevelopment of the waterfront

Some of the factors and processes involved in port-city inter-relationships, with special reference to the retreat from and subsequent redevelopment of waterfront zones, are summarised in Figure 1.4. Urban land uses are divided from port functions by the interface zone of decline and decay, often an area of conflict but sometimes marked by co-operation and competition. Port development, long inclined to migrate downstream, quits the traditional port-city core zone in favour of deeper water and more capacious bluecoast sites. Meanwhile port-based industries, no longer dependent upon the break-bulk function or on labour concentration, migrate to other urban zones and to greenfield sites beyond.

In the opposite direction, as waterfront sites become available, there is competition for the redevelopment of at least some of the most advantageous locations, both from land-based concerns (housing, restaurants, shopping complexes) and from maritime interests (marinas, recreation, water-based facilities). Within the redeveloping cityport core zone, and beyond, environmental controls are established in an attempt to harmonise development projects and reduce pollution risks; while the entire system is affected and in part controlled by overriding factors such as technological change, economic and political conditions at various scales, and national legislation.

The basic reason for present-day changes and developments in this sphere is, of course, the inability of most cityport sites either to satisfy the changing requirements of ports or to accommodate successive phases of urban growth. It is only in relatively small cityports, where urban growth has not been particularly rapid and where port facilities have not adopted every new technological innovation (but where the cityport economy as a

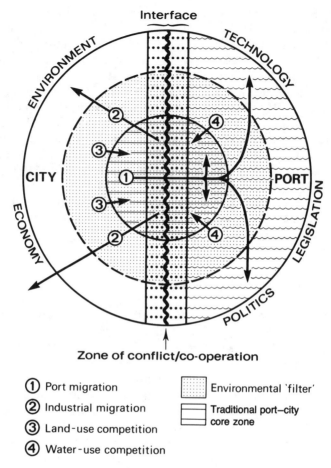

Figure 1.4   *Factors involved in port–city development*

whole nevertheless remains reasonably buoyant), that the traditional inti-
macy between port and city has been generally maintained. The retreat
from the waterfront has yielded the phenomenon of the 'abandoned
doorstep', the original land–sea interface zone which now emerges as a
spatial and functional vacuum, bereft of its traditional *raison d'être*, and
perceived as a zone of decay and potential conflict (Anderson *et al*, 1983;
Rose, 1986). This is often portrayed as a modern phenomenon, but (as the
case of Marseille shows) there are historical parallels within the earlier
phases of cityport development.

In advanced and less-developed countries alike there is today a growing
awareness of the challenges and opportunities associated with this now
widespread phenomenon, and of the need for careful and objective
analysis as a basis for policy formulation. For port authorities, the chief

difficulties are associated with the acquisition, planning and development of new port areas and facilities, generally on a much larger scale than in the past. A close association with industry is often a paramount consideration, and this may bring attendant problems of pollution or may introduce conflicts between contrasted forms of land use. For urban authorities, the virtual abandonment of older port areas, perhaps including the original waterfront close to the heart of the urban core zone, may offer unrivalled opportunities for redevelopment and may also bring great problems. The availability of extensive waterfront zones close to the urban core requires very careful consideration of the character and timing of appropriate redevelopment. Waterfront renewal is an expensive and sensitive process: skilfully done, it can bring new life into dead and dying urban areas, can create a wide range of new economic and social opportunities, and can provide a welcome antidote to the widespread tendency towards peripheral rather than central urban development.

Port–city relations have now become a major issue in many parts of the world in economic and political terms. The retreat from the waterfront has become a recognised trend; some of its consequences have become unacceptable, but some of its elements have led to exciting innovations. One result of this situation is that there is now a widespread *return* to the waterfront – a redevelopment of the 'abandoned doorstep' for new uses associated especially with recreation rather than with international trade. Globally, perhaps the best-known example is the Fisherman's Wharf area of San Francisco, where large derelict warehouses have been transformed into attractive shopping complexes and a rapidly decaying zone of great potential has become a major focus of activity and interest for residents and visitors alike. Virtually every North American city possessed of an urban waterfront on a river, a lake or the sea, has taken some steps towards the rediscovery and redevelopment of the interface zone; Seattle, Baltimore, Toronto and Vancouver are among those that have done so in a spectacular manner (Merrens, 1980; National Research Council, 1980; Norcliffe, 1981a; Price, 1987), but large numbers of others have done so in a more modest fashion.

In Western Europe, the Vieux Port at Marseille is now almost exclusively devoted to water-based recreational navigation; elsewhere in France, for example in Normandy, redevelopment schemes are receiving increased attention (Gay, 1986; Université Permanente . . . , 1986). In the United Kingdom considerable interest has been shown in this phenomenon in the 1970s and 1980s, particularly in relation to the long-standing inner-city crisis and to recent government initiatives in this sphere. National and local authorities have often been relatively slow to take up waterfront redevelopment opportunities (Clark, 1985). However, three major cityports – London, Liverpool and Bristol – have in different ways already achieved a remarkable transformation of some of their abandoned docklands, dilapidated warehouses, derelict waterfronts and substandard housing areas close to city centres (Gilman and Burn, 1983). Nothing yet quite compares with the dramatic changes that have already taken place under the umbrella of the London Docklands Development Corporation, where vast sums of money have been invested, new landscapes and waterscapes created, and social areas transformed (Church and Hall, 1986; Hall, 1982; Page, 1987). Numerous other cityports (including Cardiff, Dundee, Edinburgh, Glasgow, Hull, Manchester, Newcastle, Portsmouth, Southampton and Swansea) are following suit.

The renovation of decaying British docklands is perceived as a key element in the wider processes of urban renewal, and is central to the socio-economic and political objectives of accelerated job creation. Inevitably, these processes and objectives have proved controversial in economic, political and social terms (Budd, 1983; Hebbert, 1982). There is a sense, however, in which waterfront redevelopment in Britain has become the flavour of the decade, for planners and developers alike; yet there is a growing realisation that each specific location requires its own individual development solutions, both in terms of the particular geographical and economic associations of land and water uses, and in terms of the timing of changes and innovations in the context of the wider economic and political climate in which they are set.

Conclusion

The locational and functional separation of port and urban systems embodied in the retreat from the traditional waterfront is now a common phenomenon in many advanced countries and is becoming increasingly familiar in less-developed parts of the world. The problems posed by the redevelopment of the 'abandoned doorstep' have been approached in a variety of ways and on many different scales. However, a common sequence of stages of port-city development over time underlies the diversity of present-day situations and problems, and a common set of factors influences in varying ways the continuing evolution of cityports today. These stages and factors reflect particularly the balance between technological changes and ecological restraints, and between maritime perspectives and urban planning objectives, especially with regard to the contrasted spatial and locational requirements of port development and urban change. The analysis of development dynamics at any specific port–city interface requires an understanding of the broader trends within which local changes are set; and, in turn, the experience of each port city contributes towards the growing fund of practical information concerning the challenges and opportunities afforded by the processes of revitalisation and redevelopment on the waterfront.

References

Anderson, J., Duncan, S. and Hudson, R. (1983), *Redundant spaces in cities and regions* (London: Academic Press).

Bach, J. (1976), *A maritime history of Australia* (Sydney: Thomas Nelson).

Bird, J.H. (1963), *The major seaports of the United Kingdom* (London: Hutchinson).

—— (1965), 'The foundation of Australian seaport capitals', *Economic Geography*, 41, 283–99.

—— (1968), *Seaport gateways of Australia* (London: Oxford University Press).

—— (1984), 'Seaport development: some questions of scale', Hoyle and Hilling, *Seaport systems*, 21–41.

—— (1986), 'Gateways: examples from Australia, with special reference to Canberra', *Geographical Journal*, 152, 56–64.

Budd, A.J. (1983), 'Land-use conflict in Bristol's central dockland', *Developments in political geography*, ed. M.A. Busteed (London: Academic Press).

Canada, Ministry of State for Urban Affairs (1978), *The urban waterfront: growth and change in Canadian port cities* (Ottawa).

Charlier, J.J. (1981), 'Bruges to Zeebrugge: the emergence of a Belgian superport', Hoyle and Pinder, *Cityport industrialization*, 243–64.

Church, A. and Hall, J. (1986), 'Discovery of docklands', *Geographical Magazine*, 58 (12), 632–9.

City of Southampton (1985), *Lower town and quayside strategy* (Southampton City Planning Department).

Clark, M. (1985), 'Fallow land in old docks: why such a slow take-up of Britain's waterside redevelopment opportunities?', *Maritime Policy and Management*, 12 (2), 157–67.

Forward, C.N. (1969), 'A comparison of waterfront land use in four Canadian ports: St John's, Saint John, Halifax and Victoria', *Economic Geography*, 45, 155–69.

—— (1970), 'Waterfront land use in the six Australian state capitals', *Annals of the Association of American Geographers*, 60, 517–31.

Gay, F.J. (1986), 'La réutilisation des espaces portuaires en voie d'abandon', *Ports et mers: mélanges maritimistes offerts à André Vigarié* (Caen: Paradigme, Collection Transports et Communication), 261–72.

Gilman, S. and Burn, S. (1983), 'Dockland activities: technology and change', *The resources of Merseyside*, ed. W.S. Gould and A.G. Hodgkiss (Liverpool University Press).

Hall, J. (1982), 'Docklands in the metropolitan economy', *Town and Country Planning*, 51 (5), 120–2.

Hayuth, Y. (1982), 'The port–urban interface: an area in transition', *Area*, 14(3), 219–24.

Hebbert, M. (1982), 'The five problems of dockland redevelopment', *Town and Country Planning*, 51 (5), 129–31.

Hoyle, B.S. (1983), *Seaports and development: the experience of Kenya and Tanzania* (New York and London: Gordon and Breach).

—— (1984), 'Seaport systems and agricultural exports in a developing economy: the sugarports of Queensland, Australia', Hoyle and Hilling, *Seaport systems*, 361–89.

—— and Hilling, D. (eds) (1984), *Seaport systems and spatial change: technology, industry and development strategies* (Chichester: Wiley).

—— and Pinder, D.A. (eds) (1981), *Cityport industrialization and regional development: spatial analysis and planning strategies* (Oxford: Pergamon).

Konvitz, J.W. (1978), *Cities and the sea: port city planning in early modern Europe* (Baltimore and London: Johns Hopkins).

—— (1982), 'Spatial perspectives on port city development, 1780–1980', *Urbanism past and present*, 7 (2), 23–33.

Ley, D. (1981), 'Inner-city revitalisation in Canada: a Vancouver case study', *Canadian Geographer*, 25, 124–45.

McCalla, R.J. (1983), 'Separation and specialisation of land uses in cityport waterfronts: the cases of Saint John and Halifax', *Canadian Geographer*, 27, 49–61.

Mayer, H.M. (1973), 'Some geographical aspects of technological changes in maritime transportation', *Economic Geography*, 49, 145–55.

Merrens, R. (1980), *Urban waterfront redevelopment in North America: an annotated bibliography* (Toronto, University of Toronto/York University Joint Program in Transportation, Research Report No. 55).

National Research Council, Committee on Urban Waterfront Lands (1980), *Urban waterfront lands* (Washington, DC: National Academy of Sciences).

Norcliffe, G.B. (1981a), 'Industrial change in old port areas: the case of the port of Toronto', *Cahiers de Géographie du Québec*, 25, 237–54.

—— (1981b), 'Processes affecting industrial development in port areas in Canada', Hoyle and Pinder, *Cityport industrialization*, 151–65.

O'Mara, J. (1976), *Shaping urban waterfronts: the role of Toronto's Harbour Commissioners, 1911–60* (Toronto, York University, Department of Geography, Discussion Paper 13).

Page, S. (1987), 'The London docklands: redevelopment schemes in the 1980s', *Geography*, 72 (1) 59–63.

Pinder, D.A. (1981), 'Community attitude as a limiting factor in port development: the case of Rotterdam', Hoyle and Pinder, *Cityport industrialization*, 181–99.

Price, L.W. (ed.) (1987), *Portland's changing landscape* (Portland State University, Department of Geography, Occasional Paper No. 4).

Rose, E.A. (1986), *New roles for old cities: Anglo-American policy perspectives on declining urban regions* (Aldershot: Gower).

Slack, B. (1975), *Harbour redevelopment in Canada* (Ottawa: Ministry of State for Urban Affairs).

—— (1980), 'Technology and seaports in the 1980s', *Tijdschrift voor Economische en Sociale Geografie*, 71, 108–13.

Tuppen, J.N. (1984), 'The port-industrial complex of Fos: a regional growth centre?', Hoyle and Hilling, *Seaport systems*, 303–25.

Université Permanente d'Environnement, d'Architecture et d'Urbanisme de Normandie (1986), *Restructuration des espaces portuaires en milieu urbain*, Fécamp, Colloque Régional.

Vigarié, A. (1979), *Ports de commerce et vie littorale* (Paris: Hachette).

—— (1981), 'Maritime Industrial Development Areas: structural evolution and implications for regional development', Hoyle and Pinder, *Cityport industrialization*, 23–36.

Wilson, D. (1978), *Planning for a changing urban waterfront: the case of Toronto* (Toronto, York University, Department of Geography, Discussion Paper 18).

Witherick, M.E. (1981), 'Port developments, port–city linkages and prospects for maritime industry: a case study of Southampton', Hoyle and Pinder, *Cityport industrialization*, 113–31.

Wolkowitsch, M. (1979), 'Les rapports entre espaces portuaires et espaces urbains: l'exemple de Marseille', *Second colloque Franco-Japonais de Géographie: villes et ports* (Paris: CNRS, No. 587), 163–73.

—— (1981), 'Port extension as a factor in urban development: the case of Marseilles', Hoyle and Pinder, *Cityport industrialization*, 87–101.

2 Socio-economic change in the maritime quarter: the demise of sailortown

David Hilling

Introduction

The essential characteristic of the port is that it provides the interface between land and sea transport. At this interface cargo transfer takes place, and in older port areas there has emerged adjacent to it an urban functional zone in which the distinctive socio-economic features derive from their association with port activity. This port-related urban landscape may appropriately be termed the maritime quarter, although the name 'sailortown' (Smith, 1923; Hugill, 1967) is perhaps more evocative of the social spirit of such places.

It is significant that, while ports in general have attracted the interest of geographers and have resulted in a considerable literature concerned with their historical, economic and technical characteristics (Bird, 1984), the adjacent urban areas have been relatively neglected. The paucity of studies of the environmental and social aspects of ports has become generally apparent, and Hayuth (1982) has drawn attention to the neglect of the port –city interface. While there have been some studies on urban-waterfront land use (Forward, 1970), and although there is a rapidly growing literature on land-use change on the waterfront, the term 'waterfront' is frequently interpreted in a narrow sense, literally and geographically.

A rather broader interpretation was adopted by Kenyon (1968), who, in his study of nine American ports, was able to identify some of the hallmarks of port-related urban areas. Thus, they tended to be characterised by high population densities, high indices of functional admixture, low income, older housing stock with renters rather than owners, many multi-functional structures and multi-family households with high proportions of non-related individuals. In addition, manual workers made up the bulk of the employed population but with high levels of unemployment and high proportions of non-white people. Such areas were the havens of the sub-marginal, areas peripheral to the Central Business District (CBD) where the influence of the port was strong. It will be clear that the features identified by Kenyon typify inner-city problem areas and not just those associated with port activity.

Perhaps these port-associated urban areas were neglected in geographical studies just because they fall between the core interests of port and urban geographers. Whatever the cause, one aim of this chapter is simply to compensate for this neglect: sailortown is a fascinating urban quarter and deserves far greater attention than it has yet received. Beyond this, however, the primary aim is to demonstrate – by charting the rise and fall of sailortown's socio-economic system – the interdependence of port and city which once typified these districts. This interdependence, it is argued, was so far-reaching that any analysis of waterfront redevelopment problems which ignores it is seriously incomplete. Waterfront revitalisation, if it is to be comprehensive, cannot ignore the maritime quarters – and their populations – left stranded by the retreat of port activity.

The maritime quarter

As Smith (1923) noted and Hugill (1967) has amply demonstrated, maritime quarters were much the same the world over, their universal characteristics deriving from their common function in providing goods and services for the ships that called and the men that served them.

Some ship-servicing facilities had their location within the docks, but many more were to be found in the adjacent urban area. There was the need for stores of all kinds – meat, biscuits and other foods, fuel, rope, canvas, wire, furnishings, equipment, paint, charts – and frequently these items were manufactured on the spot. In addition there were the offices of the ship owners, brokers, agents, surveyors, insurers, financiers and commodity dealers.

The need for ship-servicing facilities is self-evident, while the need to satisfy the creature comforts of the seafarers can readily be explained by the character of the employment itself. Until the advent of the steamship, voyages were of.considerable duration, and even with faster ships the 'tramping' system meant that a ship and its men could spend months or even years away from the home port. While away, communication was at best difficult and at worst impossible, and many seamen in fact remained unmarried. Characteristically, seamen provided – and therefore had to purchase – their own bedding, equipment and clothing ('slop') and signed off after each voyage with some money in their pockets. They would often be forced to spend a long time ashore before signing on again, during which time they would require accommodation, food and entertainment. Not surprisingly, the boarding house and tavern became the centres for, and their keepers the organisers of, many of sailortown's activities, legal and illegal. In response, numerous religious and charitable organisations were established to protect the seaman ashore from the worst excesses of life in sailortown and provide welfare services.

Hugill (1967) has provided a non-academic, highly colourful and some would think rather exaggerated picture of Fiddler's Green, a composite, generalised model of world-wide sailortown. Yet many such areas were indeed larger than life. Charles Dickens (1860) described an area that he called 'Down by the Docks':

they board seamen at the eating houses, the public houses, the slop shops, the coffee shops, the tally shops, all kinds of shops, mentionable and unmentionable – board them, as it were, in the piratical sense, making them bleed terribly . . . the seamen roam in mid-street and mid-day, their pockets inside out, their heads no better . . . the daughters of wave-ruling Britannia also rove . . . scraping fiddles go in the public houses all day long.

All too often, sailortown became a notorious element in the urban landscape and a part of the town to be avoided by those with self-respect. Howard Spring (1972) provided a description of his boyhood Cardiff's maritime quarter which would be equally applicable to every large port, and certainly captured the ambivalent reaction of many to sailortown's special character. It was, he wrote, 'a warren of seamen's boarding houses, dubious hotels, ships' chandlers smelling of rope and tarpaulin . . . it was a dirty, smelly, rotten and romantic district, an offence and an inspiration and I loved it.'

The proximity of such areas to the docks is readily explained by the functional relationship between the two, and more fancifully by the claim that 'sailors abhor walking above all else' (Smith, 1923). Certainly it was often the case that sailortown was 'the street with the sea at the end of it' – the main thoroughfare to the docks. Ratcliff Highway (London), Bute Street (Cardiff), Union and Paradise Streets (Liverpool), Pacific Street (San Francisco), South Street (New York) and Grant Street (Bombay) are but a few of the best known. Around these principal streets, Hugill's 'Ships' Alleys', there usually spread a mass of associated side streets and back courts, the whole providing a high density of buildings and people, with the seemingly chaotic mixture of immensely varied land uses noted above.

The ultimate form of each maritime quarter was a function of the particular history and geography of the port concerned. London illustrates the way in which the form of the maritime quarter may change over time. There were certainly marginal quays on the Thames in Roman times and, from their origins in the vicinity of present-day London Bridge, they were gradually extended downstream and also on to the south bank of the river. While sea-going ships may have been accommodated at some of these quays, cargo was for the most part lightered to and from ships at moorings in the river. The port-related urban zone was a narrow and discontinuous fringe along the river with particular wharves, landing places and taverns providing focal points. Overall, 'the shape of the East End waterfront was entirely created by its manifold associations with the river' (Rose, 1951). It was reported that in 1560 there were no houses in Wapping, but forty years later the place was occupied 'thickly by seafaring men and tradesmen dealing in the commodities for the supply of shipping and seamen' (Besant, 1899).

As London's trade expanded, so the river became ever more congested and problems associated with the security of the cargo more acute. The new enclosed docks of the nineteenth century served both to increase port capacity and to provide greater security. Starting in 1802 with the West India Dock, there followed London Dock (1805 with later expansion), East India Dock (1806), St Katharine's Dock (1828), Shadwell Basin (1858) and Millwall (1869). With their high surrounding security walls these docks provided a far sharper separation of the cargo-handling areas and the general urban fabric than had hitherto been the case, and they also allowed massive expansion of trade and related sailortown activity. Already in the eighteenth century immigrants had been attracted into the Shadwell area and German, Dutch and Swedish churches had been established. At this time also the first black seamen arrived and, in some cases, settled. In 1817 it could be said of Shadwell that 'the population consists entirely of foreign sailors' (Banton, 1955). Wapping, Stepney, Limehouse and Poplar became great concentrations of ships' chandlers, taverns, boarding houses, tailor shops and pawn shops.

American ports certainly do not have the antiquity of London, but at many of them there developed sailortowns of world renown. In the case of New York the early nineteenth-century core of the maritime quarter included South Street, the East River from Battery to Chatham Square and lower Bowery, the parallel Water and Cherry Streets, and numerous other streets leading to the waterfront itself. Here was the greatest intensity of port-related activity of all kinds with South Street, 'the street of ships' (Hugill, 1967) having shipping offices, commercial houses, chandlers, and sail lofts interspersed with taverns and boarding houses. Here too was the early settling place for Irish, Polish, German and other immigrants, many employed on the waterfront and providing the cosmopolitan atmosphere which was characteristic of all maritime quarters. As port activity extended along the Hudson River side of Manhattan, so West Street assumed the features of a linear maritime quarter (Rosebrock, 1974). With time, maritime-associated activities spread in a patchy way over much of lower Manhattan.

Rapid development of the port of San Francisco after the 1848–9 goldrush provided all the ingredients for the development of what was to become the world's most infamous maritime quarter, the Barbary Coast. Ship arrivals were in hundreds, return cargoes difficult to find and ships often languished in port for months on end. Fortune hunters of all nationalities arrived in large numbers and prostitutes were shipped in by the thousand from New Orleans, the East Coast, Mexico, Peru and Chile. The Embarcadero and the grid of streets that developed north of Market Street became the maritime quarter, with Pacific Street and adjacent streets providing the core area. After 1860 this sailortown took on the name 'Barbary Coast' and, as San Francisco's large Chinatown developed, this merged with sailortown on its western side.

In New Orleans there was a fringe of maritime activity along the Mississippi waterfront but a considerable concentration – particularly of the services directed at seamen – in what is now known as the Vieux Carré, the area east of Canal Street and including such well known names as Basin Street, Bourbon Street, Rampart Street and the Storyville district. However, the boarding-house system was already in decline by the turn of the century, and slum clearance in the 1920s removed some of the worst features of the area.

By their very nature maritime quarters provide some of the earliest, and possibly best, examples of multi-ethnic communities. In them the maritime links provided the common cultural bond. Within the maritime quarters particular ethnic groups often occupied separate dwellings or zones, and it is reported of New Orleans that each national group of prostitutes had its own quarter (Hugill, 1967). Yet it was often the case that the boundaries with time became blurred and – by accident or design – there was considerable ethnic mixing. Indeed, maritime quarters were often proud of their uninhibited views on such cross-cultural liaisons.

These observations sustain the contention that studies of waterfront or dockland redevelopment will at best provide only partial understanding of the processes of change if they ignore sailortown and focus solely on the impact of relatively recent changes in cargo handling within the docks themselves. Indeed, as has already been hinted with respect to New Orleans, and as will be demonstrated in more detail in the case study which follows, socio-economic change in the maritime quarter pre-dated the cargo-handling revolution and was more evolutionary in character. Of greater significance than changes in cargo handling were gradual changes in the organisation of the shipping industry itself, and these affected all ports.

Each port is unique in its history and geography, and in each the evolution of the maritime quarter will take a different course. A more detailed study of Cardiff is not meant to provide a general model but rather to serve as a pointer to some of the processes involved. While it is not possible to reconstruct fully the activities and spatial extent of sailortown, commercial and street directories for Cardiff provide a basis for the mapping of selected indicators at different points in time. Commercial listings have been used to identify suppliers of ships' stores and equipment, marine surveyors, nautical instrument makers and suppliers, sail makers and rope makers. Street directories make possible the mapping of taverns, boarding houses, tailors and outfitters, and sailors' homes and missions. The picture that emerges is neither wholly accurate nor complete, the information base – which depended on the preparedness of individuals to report and therefore publicise their activities – is variable in quality. Even so the data are accurate enough to establish the principal features of this maritime quarter's development, internal evolution and eventual decline.

Cardiff – Tiger Bay

The derivation of the name 'Tiger Bay' is by no means clear but the term has been used with respect to at least three sailortowns – Georgetown (Guyana), Wapping (London) and Cardiff itself. Hugill (1967) suggests that the name was first used for London's Ratcliff Highway area because of the ferocity of its inhabitants, but Cardiff's Tiger Bay is probably the area that most readily comes to mind and must surely be classed as one of the world's great sailortowns in its time. It is of particular interest in that from origin to virtual extinction it had a life span of less than 100 years, and its demise was almost as rapid as its rise.

In 1801 Cardiff had a population of only 1,870 and its urban geography can have changed but little over many centuries (Carter, 1966). The small settlement was protected from the north by a castle and flanked on the west by a meander of the lower Taff River, on the banks of which was the town quay. This location is still marked by a Quay Street, although it is now some way from the river. As a port, Cardiff in 1830 was still insignificant in comparison with Newport to the east and Swansea to the west, and it was far surpassed as an urban centre by Merthyr Tydfil to the north. However, the completion of the Glamorganshire Canal in 1798 enlarged Cardiff's effective hinterland and the seaward end of the canal, behind a sea lock, provided more extensive port facilities. Trade increased from 10,000 tons in 1806 to nearly 350,000 tons in 1839 (Daunton, 1977). Then the opening up of the central part of the South Wales coalfield, increasingly important for its high-quality steam coal, and the gradual extension of the Taff Vale Railway from Cardiff to Merthyr (1841) and the head of the Rhondda valley (1856), brought a dramatic expansion of the port's trade. What the goldrush was for 'Frisco, the coal rush was for Cardiff. Growth was accommodated by the construction of a series of enclosed docks – the Bute West Dock (1839), the Bute East Dock (1855–9), the Roath Dock (1887) and the Queen Alexandra Dock (1907). Coal exports from Cardiff increased to 750,000 tons in 1851 and to a peak of 10.5 million tons in 1913.

This growth in port activity was associated with the rapid development of Cardiff's urban area and the emergence of Tiger Bay as a sailortown of world renown. For a time, Cardiff was the world's leading port of registry for tramp shipping. The Marquis of Bute, who was instrumental in the construction of the docks, also had the idea for a planned settlement to be located alongside them. This was to be a balanced community with high-income housing based on Mountstuart and Loudoun Squares and

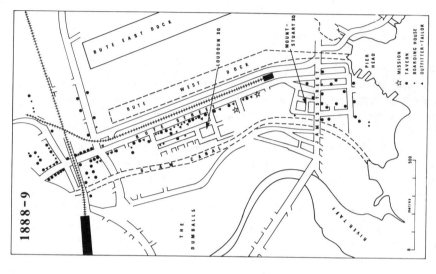

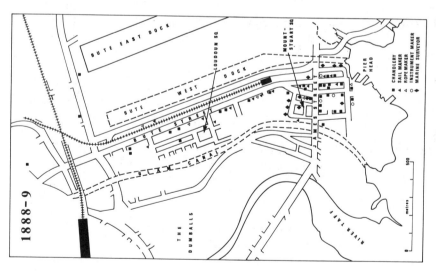

Figure 2.1   Commercial and social indicators of Cardiff's maritime quarter, 1888–9

extensive terrace housing for workers. Bute Street, to become Butey Street for seafarers, provided a north–south axis for the development, the whole being located to the south of the existing urban core area and flanked to the east and west respectively by the Bute West Dock and the line of the Glamorganshire Canal (Fig. 2.1a). What was to become known as Butetown therefore had a separate geographical and functional identity, and was further cut off from the urban core by the east–west line of the main London to South Wales railway – Butetown was very much the area 'Below the Bridge' (Evans *et al*, 1984).

The higher-income merchant group gradually withdrew from its part of Butetown and the residences were replaced by, or became, office accommodation, almost all of which was functionally associated with the port and shipping. For the rest, Butetown became Tiger Bay, the quintessential Fiddler's Green, and Bute Street ('Oriental Parade') the Ship Alley *par excellence*. In the words of Daunton (1977), 'it was an alien enclave . . . an odd mixture being cut off from the rest of Cardiff whilst part of a world-wide network of similar fringes to ports . . . a mysterious world which was impenetrable to outsiders.' Butetown attracted Lascar, Somali, Maltese, Chinese, West Indian and African seamen, each tending to have their own boarding houses and social gathering points. Many were transient but large numbers remained and made Cardiff their home port. Cardiff had the reputation of being a 'hard-up' port because it was almost entirely an exporting port and many ships arrived in ballast with skeleton crews having discharged elsewhere. Many of the seamen also arrived with little or no money after possibly prolonged periods on shore, having paid off at some other port.

The changing geography of Butetown emerges in the maps based upon the street and commercial directories (Wright's, 1888; *Western Mail*, 1913, 1932 and 1952). By 1888–9 the commercial aspects of the maritime quarter were firmly established towards the south of Butetown and, most particularly, to the west of lower Bute Street. There was also a dispersed spread of ship-related activities along Bute Street (Fig. 2.1). In contrast, while there were some sailor-related facilities such as taverns in the southern part of Butetown, the bulk of the boarding houses and tailors and outfitters were more densely spread along Bute Street, with an overspill north of the railway where the port and urban central-area functions merged. By 1888 the commercial functions were already taking over from the residential function in Mountstuart Square, where the large Coal Exchange building was opened in 1886. In the vicinity of the Square were many of the offices of ship owners, ship brokers, agents, foreign consuls and commodity sales agents. South of James Street there was a considerable amount of low-income housing interspersed with ship-servicing facilities, with a number of the buildings being multi-functional. The overwhelming importance of maritime-related employment for the residents of the area is well illustrated by the street directory for Adelaide

Street in 1888:

No. 2	Boatman	No. 13	Shipwright	No. 30	Pilot	
No. 3	Boatman	No. 14	Pilot	No. 32	Waterman	
No. 5	Waterman	No. 18	Mariner	No. 38	Hope and Anchor	
No. 6	Dockgate man	No. 20	Boatman		(Tavern)	
No. 7	Boatman	No. 22	Mariner	No. 41	Mariner	
No. 8	Rose Marie	No. 23	Boatman	No. 44	Outfitter	
No. 10	Boatman	No. 25	Mariner	No. 46	Mariner	
No. 11	Seaman	No. 26	Mariner			

It is perhaps as well not to speculate about who or what Rose Marie might have been!

While the boarding houses are identifiable from the street directories, there is no way of knowing for certain if the taverns provided residential, as well as drinking, facilities. Probably most of them did and many must also have provided other services. The Packet tavern was well known as the headquarters of the local prostitutes (Evans *et al*, 1984) but, beyond this, in 1860 Cardiff had 229 brothels (Daunton, 1977) while numerous cafes, bars[1] and boarding houses of Butetown must have provided a variety of services on the side including sex, gambling and drugs.

A significant element of any sailortown were the tailors' shops selling clothing both new and second hand, either directly to seamen or to ships' masters for the stocking of slop chests. Many of the tailors were by way of being general merchants (Hugill, 1967) and pawnbrokers' shops were frequent. In 1888 Bute Street had seven photographers, seventeen coffee shops and refreshment bars and six bootmakers. Boarding houses in the area can be identified specifically for Italian, Chinese and Arab seamen. The multi-ethnicity of the area is very apparent.

During the 1890s and early 1900s the trade of Cardiff was continuing to expand and with it sailortown. The ship-related functions had by 1913 (Figure 2.2) intensified in the Mountstuart Square and lower Bute Street area, but there is evidence of secondary concentrations in the south to the west of the Glamorganshire Canal and, further north, along its wharves. There was a particularly well-defined area of ship surveyors around Mountstuart Square, a principal focus of office activity where many of the buildings had multiple occupancy.

In 1913 the sailor-related activities were densely distributed along Bute Street with a spread into many of the adjacent streets such as Christina Street, Maria Street, Patrick Street and also Loudoun Square. There had also been a spread of boarding houses into the area south of James Street, and to counteract the prevailing evils of sailortown there were a number of organisations – missions, homes, a hospital – concerned with the welfare of seamen.

As a port Cardiff was essentially a product of the world demand for Welsh steam coal, with coal exports accounting for well over 80 per cent of

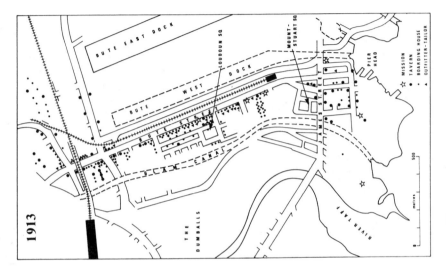

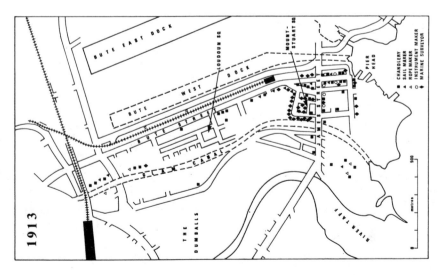

Figure 2.2 *Commercial and social indicators of Cardiff's maritime quarter, 1913*

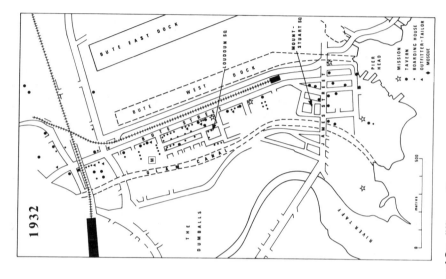

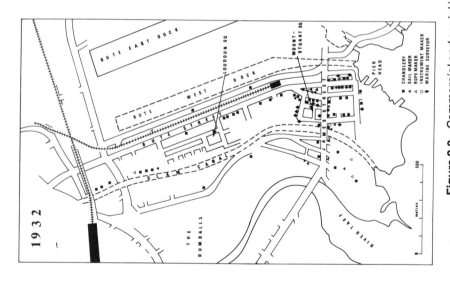

Figure 2.3   Commercial and social indicators of Cardiff's maritime quarter, 1932

Table 2.1 Maritime Cardiff – selected indicators

	1888–9	1913	1932	1952	1972	1986
Coal exporters	95	213	177	45	13	6
Ship brokers	123	184	143	52	26	7
Ship owners	82	136	187	56	13	1
Marine surveyors	14	38	27	4	1	?
Ship chandlers/marine stores	46	58	76	16	3	2
Sail makers	15	13	10	5	2	–
Rope makers	11	13	15	7	1	–
Chain and anchor makers	4	3	2	1	–	–
Nautical instrument makers	5	6	5	1	1	1

Sources: Compiled from *Western Mail* (various dates) and Wright & Co. (1888)

the traffic. The coal trade was badly affected by the 1914–18 war, lost markets were not regained and in many markets oil increasingly replaced coal. As the coal trade declined so did the port of Cardiff, and with it the diverse port-related activities (Table 2.1). The geographical expression of this decline is represented in Figure 2.3

Although past its peak as a port in 1932, the general pattern of the selected indices remains largely unchanged from 1913. However, there was a general thinning out, a trend that was particularly marked with respect to marine surveyors and services related to seamen. A number of the taverns had disappeared and there was a dramatic decline in the number of boarding houses, especially in the north, south of James Street and some of the streets west of Bute Street. By 1952 the contraction had been taken even further: ship-servicing functions had virtually disappeared from the north and along Bute Street, while the few remaining boarding houses were concentrated almost entirely along Bute Street and on Patrick Street. The marked change between 1932 and 1952 can, in part, be explained by heavy bomb damage inflicted on the area during the war, but also by significant changes in the organisation of the shipping industry which will now be discussed.

Factors in the demise of sailortown

The vitality of a maritime quarter will clearly be a function of the prosperity of the port with which it is associated. From a 1938 total of 6.8 million tons, Cardiff's trade after the war declined to 3.4 million tons in 1948 and 2.0 million tons in 1958. Coal exports ceased in 1963. With the redevelopment of some of the dock area previously devoted to coal handling, some new trade was attracted, but the closure of the East Moors steel works in 1978 removed a substantial part of the port's remaining base-load traffic. Despite some diversification into higher-value traffic (fruit, tobacco, grain, timber) and the return of a limited coal traffic, recession in the 1980s has held throughput at around two million tons a year.

With recent changes in the direction of British trade, Cardiff, like other west coast ports, now suffers from being on the wrong side of the country (Hilling, 1985). The Bute West Dock was closed in 1964 and has since been filled in, and the Bute East Dock ceased operations in 1970. The remaining facilities are seriously under-utilised.

Clearly the demise of Cardiff's sailortown was related to the general decline of the port and of industry traditionally associated with it. Even without this decline in the port, changes in the nature of employment at sea and shipboard life would certainly have resulted in serious erosion of demand for sailortown services. The formerly strong functional link between the docks and the adjacent urban area has been progressively weakened in most ports (Forsyth and Bankston, 1984) and this process was certainly started back in the last century. Many of the remaining port facilities, being demanding of space (Hilling, 1987) , are more remote from the congested urban areas where the ports had their origin. For example the new bulk handling terminals for oil are located well away from the core areas, and the seafarers calling at them may not actually visit the ports in any real sense of the term. Seamen spend far shorter times away from home, many more are now married and air transport provides a rapid means of returning home. There have been increasing opportunities to take wives to sea, ship board entertainment has become more diverse (bars, libraries, videos, swimming pools, saunas) and conditions of accommodation and catering have greatly improved. Seamen are less likely to have to provide all their own bedding, special clothing and equipment. Single-voyage signing-on is less common as seamen seek security, and methods of payment have become more sophisticated – it is less likely that the seaman will come ashore with a pocket full of money. It has even been suggested that, with sex now more readily available, recourse to prostitutes is less necessary (Hugill, 1967). All these factors have served to undermine the demand for shoreside facilities to cater for the seafaring fraternity.

Likewise, changes in ship maintenance and equipment have reduced the demand for the smaller suppliers of ships' stores of all kinds. Smaller crews and larger ships have reduced the feasibility of in-voyage maintenance, and sophisticated equipment may well be serviced by experts flown in for the purpose. The virtual elimination of the small ship-owning companies, the emergence of the large consortia, centralised purchasing and programmed maintenance have all contributed to the erosion – and in many ports the elimination – of the functional basis of the maritime quarter. No port has been immune from these universal changes. Moreover, the revolution in cargo handling, which has in recent years vastly reduced the need for dock labour, and in many ports has removed cargo handling from the traditional areas, has merely provided the *coup de grâce* for maritime quarters already in an advanced state of decline.

Vestigial sailortown

The former distinctive, thriving sailortown of Tiger Bay is no more and, as in comparable areas of San Francisco, New York, New Orleans, Hamburg or Shanghai, is now marked only by residual landscape elements (Figs. 2.4, 2.5). In Butetown most of the streets that formerly made up sailortown have themselves disappeared and the taverns, boarding houses and slop shops with them. Just a few of the once-notorious taverns have survived (for example, The Packet) and in a modernised form cater for the lunchtime excesses of office workers rather than the possibly wider needs of the off-duty sailor. Only their names now give hints of a possibly more interesting past. The Paddle Steamer in Loudoun Square and The Bosun in Angelina Street are relatively modern creations, so named in an attempt to invoke the atmosphere of the past.

The residual elements of the ship-servicing functions are now similarly few in number. In James Street there is one supplier of marine charts and nautical instruments; there are still several firms dealing in ships' provisions and stores; and on Dumballs Road there is an anchor and chain

Figure 2.4 *Residual elements of the maritime quarter, Cardiff: a sail loft, ship stores, part of the site of the Glamorganshire Canal, and a multi-ethnic population (Courtesy: Welsh Industrial and Maritime Museum, Cardiff)*

Figure 2.5   *Butetown, 1968: the old gives way to the new (Courtesy: Welsh Industrial and Maritime Museum, Cardiff)*

Figure 2.6   *Reconstruction of Loudoun Square, Cardiff, 1964 (Courtesy: Welsh Industrial and Maritime Museum, Cardiff)*

testing firm. Rather more of the business premises around Mountstuart Square have survived, and some are still devoted to firms associated with shipping.

Even where there has been considerable functional change and redevelopment, however, it is frequently the case that former maritime quarters retain elements of the ethnic diversity which was once their most distinctive feature (Fig. 2.4). In Tiger Bay the former association of particular streets with specific ethnic group (Maria Street – mainly Arab; Bute Street – mainly Chinese; George Street and Louisa Place – Spanish) has certainly become blurred, but current electoral registers still reveal a high proportion of names indicative of ethnic origins. Thus, family names indicative of Arabic origins make up over 20 per cent of the households in Maria Street, Hodges Street, Christina Street and Loudoun Square (Fig. 2.6). In what is left of Peel Street, Britain's oldest mosque and a newer Islamic Cultural Centre serve as further reminders of the origins of many of settling seafarers. Tiger Bay still prides itself on the multi-cultural aspects of its community life and can even boast an annual Mardi Gras festival (Evans *et al*, 1984).

Ports vary considerably in the chronology of sailortown's decline and in the extent to which the vacuum created by that demise has been filled by existing premises assuming new roles, by the redevelopment of complete sites, or by a combination of the two. While original sailortowns could never have been taken as tourist areas (Hugill, 1967), that is precisely what some of them have become. In the St Pauli district of Hamburg, sailortown was on the retreat from the Reeperbahn in the 1930s (Rudolph, 1980) and the tourists were moving in. In many respects the range of services on offer to the tourists is not very different from that once catering for seafarers, and the 'bleeding' of the gullible still goes on. Much the same is true of the Vieux Carré in New Orleans and of the Barbary Coast in San Francisco, but with the difference that redevelopment of the fabric has been less marked in the former than the latter. San Francisco's 'street of ships', the Embarcadero, is emerging as a linear zone of amenity and recreational land use, aspects of which (restaurants, bars and entertainment) would have been recognisable to seafarers.

Butetown as yet has made only tentative steps in this direction but the infilled Bute West Dock and adjacent area is in the process of redevelopment, as in many other ports, for a mix of commercial, residential, amenity and heritage functions. Appropriately, the Bute Road Station of the former Taff Vale Railway is to be the focal point of a Welsh Railway Centre, and in lower Bute Street is located the first phase of the Welsh Industrial and Maritime Museum.[2] But in Cardiff, the war and postwar redevelopment removed too much of the original fabric of the maritime quarter for there to be any effective reconstruction of an 'historic sailortown' along the lines of New York's South Street area. Many will think this no great disadvantage, with all too many places becoming dominated by their heritage industry and with little else to offer in the way of substantial economic activity. Is there a limit to the number of former seaports that can viably sustain maritime heritage industries?

Today the maritime quarter in Cardiff, or any other world port, is best viewed as a special case of the wider inner-city problem and the marginalisation of areas adjacent to CBDs from which traditional economic activities have been removed. Thus, Butetown originally possessed the range of characteristics noted by Kenyon (1968) as typical of American port-related urban areas, although recent redevelopment has reduced the population density and admixture of functions. While much of the older housing stock has been removed, renters still predominate, the employed population is still largely in manual jobs, unemployment is at a relatively high level and the proportion of non-whites in the population is high.

This concentration of disadvantaged groups in maritime quarters is a theme touched on by several of the chapters which follow and is treated as a major issue by Tweedale (Chapter 11) and Church (Chapter 12). All too frequently, recent redevelopment has created sharply defined socio-economic disparities in communities which were previously marked by a considerable degree of functional unity. As was indicated at the outset, the principal viewpoint adopted in this chapter is that the debate on waterfront revitalisation and social justice – if it is to be properly informed – requires a thorough appreciation of the rise and fall of maritime quarters as economic and social entities. To ignore their long-term dynamism, and focus simply on the uninhabited redundant space of docklands, is to ignore most of the social problems generated by port evolution.

Secondly, however, the chapter has also sought to create a much wider appreciation of sailortown as a historic urban feature. Undoubtedly there are some ports (Amsterdam, Hamburg, New Orleans, San Francisco) where the vestigial elements of sailortown, albeit with modifications, still provide a notion of what life might have been like in a more boisterous heyday. Perhaps in many more ports we shall have to settle for possibly artificial reconstructions of the past or echo the sentiments of the shanty-man outward bound from Liverpool when he sang:

> Farewell to Lower Frederick Street,
> Anson Terrace and Parkie Lane,
> I'm bound for California
> And may not see you again.   [Hugill, 1967]

Notes

1   Many of the taverns, characteristically for sailortowns, had names evocative of the sea and ships – Chainlocker, Packet, Ship and Pilot, Hope and Anchor, Cape Horn.

2   The Welsh Industrial and Maritime Museum is providing a valuable service in collecting and collating Butetown archival material of all kinds before that, like the fabric to which it relates, also disappears.

References

Banton, M.P. (1955), *The coloured quarter* (London: Jonathan Cape).

Besant, W. (1899), *East London* (London: Chatto & Windus).

Bird, J.H. (1984), 'Seaport development: some questions of scale', in B.S. Hoyle and D. Hilling (eds) *Seaport systems and spatial change* (Chichester: Wiley, 21–41.

Carter, H. (1966), *The towns of Wales* (Cardiff: University of Wales Press).

Daunton, M.J. (1977), *Coal metropolis – Cardiff 1870–1914* (Leicester: Leicester University Press).

Dickens, C. (1860), Report for *The uncommercial traveller*, quoted in J. Pudney (1975), *London docks* (London: Thames and Hudson).

Evans, C., Dodsworth, S. and Barnett, S. (1984), *Below the bridge* (Cardiff: National Museum of Wales).

Forsyth, C.J. and Bankston, W.B. (1984), 'The social and psychological consequences of a life at sea', *Maritime Policy and Management*, 11(2), 123–34.

Forward, N.C. (1970), 'Waterfront land use in six Australian state capitals', *Annals of the Association of American Geographers*, 60, 517–31.

Hayuth, Y. (1982), 'The port–urban interface: an area of transition', *Area*, 14(3), 219–24.

Hilling, D. (1985), 'The changing role of South Wales ports', *Cambria*, 12(2), 43–60.

—— (1987), 'Cargo handling technology and changing waterfront land use', *Journal of Shoreline Management*, 3, 23–37.

Hugill, S. (1967), *Sailortown* (London: Routledge and Kegan Paul).

Kenyon, J.B. (1968), 'Land use admixture in the built-up urban waterfront', *Economic Geography*, 44, 152–77.

Rose, M. (1951), *The East End of London* (London: The Crescent Press).

Rosebrock, E.F. (1974), *South Street* (New York: Dover).

Rudolph, W. (1980), *Harbour and town: a maritime cultural history* (Leipzig: Editions Leipzig).

Smith, C.F. (1923), *Sailortown days* (London: Methuen).

Spring, H. (1972), *An Autobiography* (London: Collins).

Western Mail (1913, 1932, 1952 and 1972), *Directory of Cardiff* (Cardiff: The Western Mail).

Wright and Co. (1888), *Directory of Cardiff* (Cardiff: Wright and Co.).

3 Global imperatives, local forces and waterfront redevelopment

Ray Riley and Louis Shurmer-Smith

Introduction

Couched as they are within a commercial setting, waterfront activities have traditionally been analysed within a least-cost framework concerned with the evaluation of economic, and sometimes political, forces as they bear upon particular port areas. Vessel characteristics, freight rates, port dues, handling costs and the impact of new technologies such as containerisation have all received a good deal of attention in explanations of the essential spatial unevenness of economic activity. The role of government has also been an issue, although its true significance has arguably not always been appreciated. However, the notion that spatial patterns are wholly the consequence of spatial variables has been recently challenged by researchers who argue that events at the local level are largely determined by economic and political policies and events at the national and indeed global levels, a structuralist thrust that has come to be termed the 'top-down' approach (Massey, 1984; Sayer, 1986). In other words, policies and events which lack an overtly spatial element may prove to be powerful determinants of spatial change.

Unfortunately, as Pickvance (1985) observes, the undoubted weight of government influence, and the strength of what Marxists see as the 'needs of capital', have led to the neglect of economic and political 'bottom-up' pressures from interests at the local or port level. The welding together of these two approaches promises much for many fields of geographical investigation – manufacturing, retailing and housing studies to name but three. But the physical characteristics of the locality (which have been seriously neglected by work on 'bottom-up' forces), and the influence of other local circumstances, are of such crucial significance for the analysis of waterfront redevelopment that any theoretical framework omitting these independent variables could hardly be deemed realistic. It is the purpose of this chapter to argue that an understanding of waterfront change may be furthered by bringing together 'top-down' and 'bottom-up' pressures, modified by physical site and situation constraints. Although the exemplification employed is largely drawn from the United Kingdom, it is contended that the very universality of the approach renders it suitable for the analysis of waterfront change in any port, irrespective of location.

The top-down approach

The international scale

That global events are of great significance to maritime transport and therefore to ports is widely accepted, but it is submitted that insufficient cognisance is taken of the sheer breadth of such events. The international trade cycle of boom and recession noted by Kondratiev (Hanappe and Savy, 1981) and Kuznets, and confirmed by product life-cycle theory and international trade theory (Freeman, 1986), goes some way to explaining the timing of port expansion and, since the 1970s, contraction. It is facile to assign particular causes to such macro events, but the OPEC oil price rises, imposed for an amalgam of economic and political reasons in 1973–4 and 1979–80 are generally regarded as a major contributory cause of the current recession. In encouraging the exploitation of North Sea oil, the price escalations reduced the demand for tanker capacity, for berths and for shipbuilding construction, thereby stimulating the generation of redundant space, not only at shipyards in the older ports, but also at tanker terminals. The assets of the oil majors are such that they are able to write off port structures without difficulty, the plethora of disused facilities at Milford Haven, for instance, bearing witness to the process. Rising prices also constrained final market demand for petroleum products, particularly heavy products, leading to a reduction of oil refinery capacity, with obvious implications for potential land-use change (Pinder, 1986; Pinder and Husain, Chapter 14).

Technological change is sometimes regarded as an autonomous variable, but not only is it subservient to economics – the objective is cost reduction and increased market share – its techniques are also internationally widespread. Thus the rapid increase in tanker size from the 1950s, which placed a premium on deepwater locations; the advent of the jumbo jet, which killed liner traffic and made liner berths and terminals redundant; the introduction of container vessels and the concomitant metamorphosis of many ports whose docks and warehouses became superfluous; and the use of roll-on-roll-off (ro-ro) ships for dual freight and passenger services, are global trends with powerful land-use implications. The advent of container ships and large bulk carriers has been conducive to the concentration of port activity and the concomitant availability of space for new development following the downstream migration of the new activities. The introduction of ro-ro traffic has worked in the same direction. With its modest requirements of a marshalling apron, link span and access to the motorway network – in place of costly cranage, extensive transit sheds and railway links – ro-ro technology might have presented many a small port with remarkably rapid growth opportunities, but at the same time it has been able to replicate the former function of entire dock systems in some older ports.

Rising standards of living, at least in the advanced nations, have led to substantial increases in disposable income. This has triggered social change in a number of directions. Perhaps the most obvious in the present context is the tourist boom, greatly assisted by the fall in the real price of the motor car. In Britain the result has been a dramatic upsurge in ro-ro facilities in ports on the south-east coast (Jones and North, 1982), with consequent space-demand implications elsewhere. A second development has been the channelling of leisure time into maritime activities and the emergence of considerable social cachet attaching to maritime living. This has created a demand for marinas in port areas, and more recently for housing, retail outlets, hotels, offices and even new transport systems – such as London's Docklands Light Railway and City Airport – as an integral part of such complexes. It is undoubtedly true that the social process of gentrification has injected new life into many old port areas, and in some instances the process has been associated with the construction of marinas (Tunbridge, 1987), even though – as Church (Chapter 12) and Tweedale (Chapter 11) argue – the outcome may not be ideal for all sectors in society.

Membership of politico-economic blocs such as the EEC may fairly be regarded as international in scale. For Britain one result has been a switch in the direction of imports and exports away from the rest of the world towards the EEC. Trade with the Community in 1972 accounted for 35.5 per cent of the total by value, but had risen to 50 per cent by 1986, bestowing advantages on ports in the south-east close to member countries, and adding to the momentum of ro-ro facilities provided by social change. No less than 70 per cent of the UK's ro-ro traffic was handled by ports in the south-east and East Anglia in 1986. The process has been encouraged by the spatial pricing ploicy of requiring continental purchasers of British goods to pay the sea – but not the overland – freight cost, a practice which inevitably causes them to select ports in south-east England for dispatch. The recent enlargement of the Community following the accession of Spain and Portugal ia almost certain to increase freight traffic through the south-western port of Plymouth, emphasising not only the random spatial impact of political events, but also the declining demand for waterfront facilities in ports located outside southern England.

Community industry policy has a bearing upon the activities of a number of ports. For example, the steel industry is seen to be unduly large in both the Community and world contexts. The Commission has long urged contraction, and both iron-ore imports and steel exports have fallen at least in part as a consequence, while in some instances tidewater-located steel-works have closed. Similarly the Community has urged the removal of capacity from the shipbuilding industry, a policy that has added to the speed of concentration. As with oil refining, rationalisation of steel and shipbuilding capacity has led to the emergence of a redundant land problem quite different from the widely recognised one of abandoned old port areas.

More imperceptibly, the existence of the EEC has contributed to the growth of the international economy by facilitating the mobility of capital and the internationalisation of services. There has been a concomitant increase in the size of the firm, causing multinationals to assume great importance. In practice major shipping lines have been international firms since steam navigation began, but this is not to diminish their importance within the framework being proposed. An early example of their locational flexibility was the decision by White Star and then Cunard to leave Liverpool in 1911 and 1919 respectively and base their transatlantic operations at Southampton, more conveniently placed in respect of London, the origin and destination of so much of their traffic. The emergence of Townsend-Thoresen, now trading as European Ferries after acquisition by P & O, as the leading passenger operator in Britain is a further case in point. Thoresen bought out the Dover firm of Townsend in 1963, shortly after the Norwegian operator arrived in the UK, and the new company's growth made a substantial contribution to the expansion of Dover. Conversely, however, in 1976 Thoresen greatly accelerated the process of waterfront abandonment in Southampton when the firm transferred its operations to nearby Portsmouth. One factor enabling shipping companies to migrate with relative ease is that they seldom own extensive shore facilities. This undoubtedly assists them in responding to restrictive union attitudes and other irritations. In the UK, for example, a number of firms have left in favour of more dynamic foreign locations such as Rotterdam and Antwerp, while similar reasons lie behind the departure of some companies from old-established ports to new ones, such as Felixstowe, with a more flexible ethos. Lastly, it is appropriate to note that bankruptcy among major shipping companies can induce far-reaching results. The collapse in 1986 of US Lines, a firm providing a worldwide service through twelve jumbo container vessels, removed substantial capacity from the market, and clearly caused a change in flows – and therefore land demand – through the many ports. Once purchased and integrated into the operations of other firms, the container ships will be used to establish trade flows, not all of which will replicate those of US Lines (*Financial Times*, 14 April 1987). In concluding this review of the impact of international capital upon waterfront change, it should be mentioned that the profitability of marina projects, which are an increasingly characteristic feature of port areas, is such that global enterprises involved in property development and construction engineering find them attractive propositions, and their participation has stimulated the speed of change.

The national scale

Whatever the strength of international constraints, national governments undoubtedly possess considerable room for manoeuvre; their actions may not always be explicitly spatial, but a specifically spatial impact may often be expected. Fears of reliance upon Middle Eastern refined products on the part of a number of West European governments gave rise to financial support for oil refinery construction in the UK and other European countries after the Suez crisis; in retrospect it is evident that this helped lay the foundation for the spate of refinery land abandonment that has swept the industry in the 1980s. Government funds have been devoted to motorway building, and although there has been a general reduction in the friction of distance there has inevitably been spatial differentiation, with poorly-served ports tending to lose economic impetus and gain surplus space. Also of potentially great significance is the UK government's decision to press ahead with the Channel Tunnel in co-operation with its French counterpart. One scenario generated by this project envisages the closure of Ramsgate, Folkestone and Newhaven with an associated loss of up to 20,000 jobs. The maintenance of a very much reduced ferry presence at Dover is also anticipated, through the introduction of six large vessels which will enable unit costs to be lowered (*The Guardian*, 24 October 1987). Both these developments would clearly generate substantial challenges in the context of waterfront redevelopment. Conversely, however, it might also be that ports in central southern England, beyond the shadow of the tunnel, would find that they had become highly attractive locations for expanded passenger ferry operations because the tunnel will be unable to meet total demand. This clearly demonstrates the potential for national decisions to have both positive and negative land-use effects.

Party political ideologies are at root aspatial, but again their execution in practice has a geographical impact. For example, the free-market ethic of Britain's present Conservative government led to the privatisation in 1983 of the British Transport Docks Board (BTDB). The latter's successor, Associated British Ports (ABP), has inherited 19 ports and has managed to make port operations pay. Arguably, in the absence of privatisation, land uses and trade flows in the 19 ports concerned would have been rather different. What is certainly true is that the turnround in ABP's finances is due in no small measure to rationalisation and a concerted move into the property market – as evidenced by the profitable Ocean Village project in Southampton. In a similar vein Britain's Ministry of Defence (MOD) has been encouraged to hive off for commercial development those areas in naval dockyards, and in the case of Chatham the entire yard, no longer regarded as cost effective within the current naval strategy. Portsmouth has been relegated to a second-grade repair and refit establishment as a result of the reorganisation, with a consequential reduction in the labour force from 8,000 to 2,000. Most of the surplus buildings are scheduled Ancient Monuments in the oldest part of the dockyard, and with financial support from the MOD, English Heritage and the National Maritime Musem, they look set to form the basis of a self-financing heritage area that is host to the *Mary Rose*, *HMS Victory* and *HMS Warrior* (Riley, 1987b). The switch from shipbuilding to tourism represents an unusual thrust, but it is one that has been effectively orchestrated from Whitehall. Local collaborative efforts have assisted these developments; they are 'bottom-up' pressures and are therefore dealt with later in the chapter.

While it is important to recognise the role of national policies and political philosophies in causing change on the waterfront, it is also necessary to acknowledge the influence these forces may have on the form of redevelopment which occurs. For example, Pinder and Rosing (Chapter 7) demonstrate the tight control exercised over development in Rotterdam and relate this to the Netherlands' strong tradition of urban planning. At the other extreme, Bristow (Chapter 10) details the outcome of a strongly free-market philosophy. Viewing the spectrum between these extremes, it is evident that in many places the pendulum has swung, or is swinging, towards demand-led planning, not least because of the enhanced power of capital in recessional conditions.

An outstanding example of this trend is provided by the UK. To a degree, British redevelopment strategy has attempted to revivify port activity, particularly through the creation of Free Port Zones (FPZs). In 1984 six were created, four of which were in seaports: Belfast, Cardiff, Liverpool and Southampton. The motivation for this initiative owed much to experience elsewhere. In the Hamburg FPZ 1,000 tenant companies have generated 20,000 workplaces (Husain, 1981; *Financial Times*, 14 April 1987) and other impressive instances of growth are well documented, especially in Southeast Asia (Pollock, 1981; Balasubramanyan and Rothschild, 1985). But Britain's experience demonstrates that the results may be disappointing – in Liverpool, the most dynamic FPZ, only 100 jobs had been generated by the end of 1986 – and this experiment should not be allowed to dominate the analysis. The main thrust of British planning in the 1980s has been to view port redevelopment as a dimension of the inner-city problem, and to pursue a policy of eliminating those constraints which, it is believed, deter private capital from spearheading the revitalisation of these areas. This line of thinking underpinned the designation of Enterprise Zones in 1979; two of these – Salford and the Isle of Dogs – are port-based and are discussed by Law (Chapter 9) and Church (Chapter 12). Most recently the Conservative party's philosophy of reducing restraints on enterprise has been extended through the creation of generously funded Development Corporations. The first of these was introduced for London's docklands (the LDDC, 1981), followed by Merseyside and Cardiff Bay in 1986. What is already apparent is that this liberalising strategy can achieve rapid change, as Church's discussion demonstrates. But it is necessary to recognise that redevelopment achieved in this way is not universally applauded. Controversy currently surrounds the issue of whether change should be equated with success (Clark, Chapter 13), while – as noted earlier – it is increasingly argued that gains accruing to capital entail major social penalties (Tweedale, Chapter 11; Church, Chapter 12). Political ideologies also have an impact upon port ownership, and through this on management style. An outstanding example in the UK context is the privatisation of the British Transport Docks Board and its purchase by Associated British Ports, a dynamic firm which is initiating complete reorganisation of water-front activities at many of its ports.

Not surprisingly there are numerous regulations initiated by central governments appertaining to port operations. For the most part they bear equally upon ports in each country, and it is only when there are significant cost differences between nations that the speed of waterfront change is affected. Of the European nations only Greece, Ireland, Sweden and the UK do not meet the cost of navigational aids from general taxation; light dues cost shipping companies using British ports some £46 million in 1986, thereby adding to other pressures towards contraction and redundant space (*Financial Times*, 14 April 1987). Because of their role in the defence of the realm, naval dockyard ports are subject to further con-straints. In the UK the Dockyard Port Act of 1865 confers wide powers on the Admiralty (now MOD) in respect of navigation and shoreline development, while the Crown Estates possess large land holdings in the vicinity of dockyards. Until well after the Second World War such control greatly inhibited commercial initiatives, and the more relaxed approach of the 1970s helps to explain the timing of the upsurge in waterfront change in some naval ports. This trend has been assisted by the MOD decision to allow commercial vessels the use of naval ports free of charge (Riley, 1987a).

In closing this analysis of 'top-down' pressures at the national scale, the role of firms whose activities are restricted to the nation should not be underestimated. Certainly shipping companies are always able to use the threat of departure elsewhere to lever improved agreements from port operators. That much of the refurbishment recently effected in the old ports has been undertaken by an amalgam of property companies, con-struction groups, financial consortia and manufacturing firms diversifying their portfolio, rather than by port authorities, simply underlines the crucial contemporary role of capital in waterfront redevelopment.

The bottom up approach: the local scale

Against this background it may appear that the scope for local initiatives may be attenuated, lending much support for the belief that aspatial government and corporate policies, together with wider societal changes, largely determine local events. Yet the execution of policy is essentially spatial and, while not dismissing 'top-down' influences, we argue that spatial outcomes in reality arise from the meeting of 'top-down' and locally generated 'bottom-up' pressures. Since localities have evolved in different ways, and have reacted distinctively through time to each aspatial 'layer' generated by government, capital and society (Massey, 1984), a series of unique regions has resulted, causing 'bottom-up' forces to vary widely from port to port. Local councils advised by their officers bargain, in effect, with forces from above *and* with local political opposition, the Port Authority itself (Suykens, 1985), stevedoring, shipping and waterfront manufacturing firms, developers, trade unions and environmental lobbies (Pinder, 1981).

Local authorities are also increasingly entering into corporatist-type relationships with private-sector firms, following the contracting availability of public finance and encouragement from governments. The trend was first noted in the USA in the 1950s when 'pro-growth' coalitions developed between city management, local business interests, property groups and even educational institutions. Spatial coalitions draw their support from a variety of social classes since the goal of economic development is shared. However, local economic policies are far from being an automatic response to local events; rather their precise form will reflect local economic structures, the nature of local political control and the power of individuals (Bassett, 1986). Our interpretation, therefore, is that local decision-makers are not always *reactive*, the meek recipients of others' policies. Rather they are capable of being *proactive*, influencing and possibly directing the nature of change. Indeed, their potential in this respect is so substantial that they might well be described as 'waterfront gatekeepers'. However, the strength of the actors concerned varies spatially and temporally, emphasising the likelihood of a series of unique spatial outcomes. What translates this likelihood into certainty is the infinite variation in coastal form which provides each port with a unique set of physical site constraints. Add to this a port's geographical situation in respect of the national core region, of competing ports and of trading links, and it becomes obvious that 'bottom-up' pressures do much to explain spatial unevenness, despite the power of higher scales in the hierarchy.

Both 'top-down' and 'bottom-up' forces are recognised in the literature, the former more so than the latter, but the role of the physical environment has not been related to them, doubtless because it is not regarded as a key issue in the distribution of human activities. But for port studies the notions of site and situation are crucial, and for many commentators they represent a start point, although this is not a position being supported here. Figure 3.1 indicates schematically how site and situation are at the interface of the bargaining position between the two sets of forces. 'Bottom-up' pressures are differentiated between ports (a) and (b). The former is proactive, is locally owned, has co-operative unions, and good working relationships exist between local actors. The site is propitious, thereby benefiting costs, and the situation in respect of proximity to other key ports is good. Local bargaining power is therefore

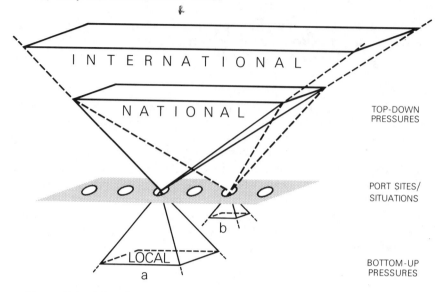

Figure 3.1 *A framework for the analysis of waterfront redevelopment*

considerable. On the other hand, port (b) is reactive, largely externally-controlled, union practices are restrictive, working relationships are only satisfactory, and the site and situation provide no special advantages. Here 'top-down' pressures are supreme.

Because uniqueness obtains at the local scale, exemplification of the power of 'bottom-up' forces is difficult if the aim is to present a representative cross-section of their influence. Such a goal is beyond the scope of this chapter, but the principles can at least be demonstrated through an examination of the Portsmouth case. Competition between Southampton and Portsmouth illustrates, among other things, the influence of situational factors in Portsmouth's emergence as the UK's second-ranking passenger terminal. The debate between, on the one hand, the city administration and the naval authorities and ferry companies on the other, highlights the interface between local and national actors. Lastly the strategies pursued by the city council underline the fact that waterfront redevelopment need not be confined to the leisure–tourism–recreation model, although the latter is of increasing significance in the city. Given the right conditions and motivation, redevelopment may be associated with new and highly profitable port activities. Locational relationships in this example are summarised by Figure 3.2, while Figure 3.3 identifies the principal 'top-down' and 'bottom-up' influences on the Portsmouth waterfront.

New commercial port development in Portsmouth is based on cross-Channel passenger and cargo ferry services developed since the mid-1970s. As was noted earlier, much of this traffic has been captured from Southampton, which has now lost its ferry-port function. Any explan-

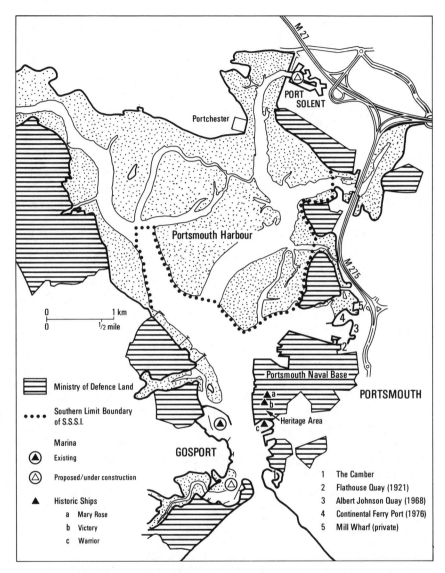

Figure 3.2 *Waterfront land uses around Portsmouth Harbour*

ation of the migration of ferry servies to Portsmouth must take account of global and national forces. The effect of the 1973–4 oil crisis was to enable Portsmouth to offer ferry companies substantial economies through a two-hour reduction in sailing time on a return cross-Channel sailing. The national strategy of maintaining and dredging the harbour for naval purposes gave Portsmouth a further cost advantage. National motorway policy also played a part. The M275, opened in 1976, leads directly to

Portsmouth's commercial port; in Southampton the early port area has yet to experience significant improvements in the road network. But it is also necessary to recognise that local leadership in Portsmouth played a crucial role. The firm Channel Stevedores secured a no-strike agreement with the local labour union which, having scant experience of port operation, had none of the traditional attitudes to work practices which blighted Southampton's quays. Most critical of all, however, was the initiative of the city administration in creating the conditions without which waterfront re-development for substantial commercial port purposes would have been impossible.

Here the key issue was the interface between the commercially minded city administration and the naval authorities which have been discussed elsewhere (Riley and Smith, 1981). Briefly, the Navy's long-standing inclination was to resist commercial development because of potential conflicts with military activities. As late as the 1960s, naval opposition forced the Thoresen company to abandon a plan to operate ferry services from Portsmouth; instead it was obliged to select Southampton. But the Navy's stance became less tenable as its contribution to the city economy declined through successive defence reviews, and in 1973 pressure from the city council was rewarded when a Harbour Revision Order was obtained to allow construction of modest ro-ro port facilities. In a particularly far-sighted fashion, the council suspended its Standing Orders and established a special port development group, led by a dynamic local councillor, which succeeded in completing the first phase of the project in only 300 days. Simultaneously, in an alliance of local interests, the charismatic director of Channel Stevedores opened up negotiations with St Malo Chamber of Commerce and secured agreement that Brittany Ferries would establish a Portsmouth–St Malo ro-ro route. Subsequently the council has undertaken a series of expansions – that in progress is the fifth – in the available wedge of waterfront driven between Ministry of Defence land.

Elsewhere in the harbour, at its northern extremity, the city administration has built on its new-found experience by encouraging, and greatly influencing, the £100 million Port Solent scheme. This combines a marina with housing, retailing, offices and a hotel, being akin to many waterfront redevelopment initiatives around the world. As with the commercial port, its very existence betrays the changing balance of power between national naval policy, national firms and local interests. As late as the mid–1960s the introduction of a major marina into a naval harbour would have been unthinkable. But Port Solent also illustrates the city administration's ability to negotiate effectively with external sources of capital. The council managed to secure a smaller office block than the developers, Arlington Securities, wanted; it also managed to contain shopping facilities to local needs, in contrast to the small hypermarket initially planned; and it has entered into a range of financial agreements with Arlington to ensure that at least a share of land-price rises caused by inflation moves into the city

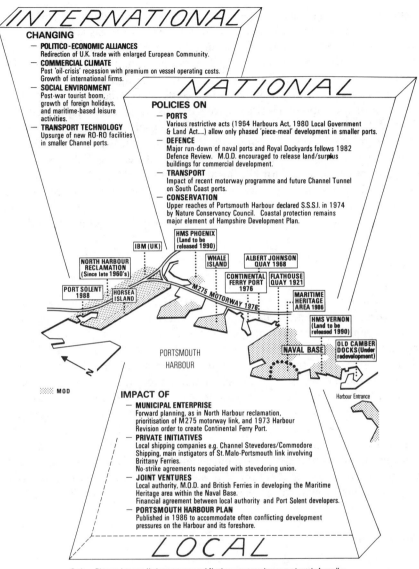

Figure 3.3 *'Top-down' and 'bottom-up' forces at work on the Portsmouth waterfront*

coffers. All this is indicative of the power of the council, and, of course, the desirability of the site.

Finally, in the 1980s the city has become an important agent of change in the exploitation of tourist opportunities presented by the reduction of dockyard activity. National pressures, referred to above, to retain the architecturally outstanding redundant buildings, coupled with decisions by national interest groups such as the Mary Rose Trust, whose patron is the Prince of Wales, and the Warrior Trust to base their vessels at Portsmouth, made the creation of a tourist resource a possibility. The precedent of public access to a naval dockyard had been established in 1922 when visits were permitted by the Admiralty to Nelson's flagship *HMS Victory*. With an eye to the generation of spending in the city, the council not only backed the idea of a dockyard Heritage Area but also financially supported the Portsmouth Naval Heritage Trust, set up to co-ordinate the work of the interest groups involved. Moreover, the council constructed a berth for *HMS Warrior*, the first armour-plated warship, at a cost of £1.3 million as a pump-priming initiative for the local economy (Riley, 1987b). Unquestionably the dockyard Heritage Area would have gone ahead irrespective of local authority support, but it is equally clear that its co-operation in the spatial coalition has added to the financial prospects of all concerned.

Conclusion

The thrust of this chapter is clear, and extensive reiteration is unnecessary. The power of global and national forces in initiating change, more particularly in generating redundant port space and, therefore, in creating the possibility of redevelopment, is not in dispute. Yet the study of revitalisation processes and strategies is seriously incomplete if it focuses on these forces to the exclusion of local socio-economic and political influences, local actors and site–situation parameters. As has been emphasised, the effects of these must vary from case to case, and the Portsmouth example is in no sense advanced as a model. However, the chapter does demonstrate the analytical benefits to be derived from merging the 'top-down' and 'bottom-up' influences to create a more balanced holistic framework, and it is argued that wider application of this approach will greatly increase our understanding of waterfront revitalisation processes worldwide.

References

Balasubramanyan, V.N. and Rothschild, R. (1985), 'Free port zones in the UK', *Lloyds Bank Review*, 158, 20–31.

Bassett, K. (1986), 'Economic restructuring, spatial coalitions and local economic development strategies', *Political Geography Quarterly*, 5 (supplement), 163–78.

Freeman, C. (1986), 'The role of technical change in national economic development', in A. Amin and J. Goddard (eds), *Technological change, industrial restructuring and regional development* (London: Allen and Unwin) 100–14.

Hanappe, P. and Savy, M. (1981), 'Industrial port areas and the Kondratieff cycle', in B.S. Hoyle and D.A. Pinder (eds), *Cityport industrialisation and regional development* (Oxford: Pergamon) 11–22.

Husain, M.S. (1981), 'Influences on development policy in the port of Hamburg', in B.S. Hoyle and D.A. Pinder (eds), *Cityport industrialisation and regional development* (Oxford: Pergamon) 223–42.

Jones, P.N. and North, J. (1982), 'Unit loads through British ports: a further revolution?', *Geography*, 67, 29–40.

Massey, D. (1984), *Spatial divisions of labour* (London: Macmillan).

Pickvance, C.G. (1985), 'Spatial policy as territorial politics: the role of spatial conditions in the articulation of "spatial" interests and the demand for spatial policy', in G. Rees *et al* (eds), *Political action and social identity, class, locality and ideology*, Explorations in Sociology 19, British Sociological Association (London: Macmillan) 117–40.

Pinder, D.A. (1981), 'Community attitude as a limiting factor in port growth: the case of Rotterdam', in B.S. Hoyle and D.A. Pinder (eds), *Cityport industrialisation and regional development* (Oxford: Pergamon) 181–200.

—— (1986), 'Crisis and survival in Western European oil refining', *Journal of Geography*, 85, 12–20.

Pollock, E.E. (1981), 'Free ports, free trade zones, export-processing zones and economic development', in B.S. Hoyle and D.A. Pinder (eds), *Cityport industrialisation and regional development* (Oxford: Pergamon) 37–46.

Riley, R.C. (1987a), 'Military and naval land use as a determinant of urban development – the case of Portsmouth' in M. Bateman and R. Riley (eds), *The geography of defence* (Beckenham: Croom Helm) 52–81.

—— (1987b), 'Urban conservation or private museum? Historic architecture in Portsmouth Dockyard', in R.C. Riley (ed.), *Urban conservation: international contrasts*, Occasional Paper No. 7, Department of Geography, Portsmouth Polytechnic, 4–7.

Riley, R.C. and Smith, J.L. (1981), 'Industrialisation in naval ports: the Portsmouth case', in B.S. Hoyle and D.A. Pinder (eds), *Cityport industrialisation and regional development* (Oxford: Pergamon) 133–50.

Sayer, A. (1986), 'Industrial location on a world scale: the case of the semiconductor industry', in A.J. Scott and M. Storper (eds), *Production, work, territory* (London: Allen and Unwin) 107–23.

Suykens, F. (1987), 'Administration and management at the Port of Antwerp', *Maritime Policy and Management*, 12(3), 181–94.

Tunbridge, J.E. (1987), 'Conserving naval heritage: its role in the revitalisation of North American urban waterfronts', in R.C. Riley (ed.), *Urban conservation: international contrasts*, Occasional Paper No. 7, Department of Geography, Portsmouth Polytechnic, 14–24.

4 Changes on the waterfront: a model-based approach

Yehuda Hayuth

Introduction

The longstanding traditional ties between cities and ports are gradually loosening. Historically, the geographical contiguity of cities and ports was dictated by transport technology and the nature of the trade. Most often, ports developed in close proximity to the centres of cities. In some cases, though, cities were established on sites that were conducive to the development of a port. Throughout history, the siting of ports has altered with the advance of shipping technology; this process became particularly evident when older ports could not accommodate the growing sizes of vessels. The Phoenician port-sites of the eastern Mediterranean survived long enough to accommodate the Crusaders' vessels many centuries later, but most of these seaports, adjacent to city centres, could not keep pace with and handle yet further development in ship technology, such as the steamship in the nineteenth century.

The establishment in the mid-1950s of outports in north-west Europe and the downstream development of port facilities in, for example, London (Bird, 1963) represent another trend of ports abandoning the centres of cities. The growing spatial and functional segregation between cities and ports greatly accelerated from the mid-1960s on, leaving a heavy impact on both the port industry and the traditional structure of port–urban interface areas. Two parallel developments also hastened the loosening of ties between the conventional seaport and the historical port city. On the one hand, there have been changes – technological, logistical and organisational – in the shipping industry and concomitant modernisation of port operations. On the other hand, there has been a transformation in the attitudinal change of the public toward coastal areas in general and urban waterfronts in particular. The discussion in this chapter, guided by the model drawn as Figure 4.1, provides a basis for retrospective and prospective analyses of trends taking place at the urban waterfront.

Containerisation and intermodality

Characterising the 1970s and 1980s has been the spectacular increase in the size and draught of ships, rendering many older ports unusable. During this period, furthermore, the methods of handling cargo have been drastically modified and new transportation concepts introduced. In particular, two interrelated concepts – containerisation and intermodality – have greatly affected not only port operation and port structure, but also the traditional functions of ports.

The huge oil tankers and the large bulk carriers gradually began to disappear from the urban waterfront scene. The conventional oil and bulk terminals at these sites are limited in alongside draught; equally important is the fact that they lack the extensive land areas for storage that are required to serve the very large ships. However, the closest ties, both functionally and spatially, between cities and ports, occurred in the area of the general cargo trade. Unitisation, especially containerisation, was introduced in order to improve port productivity and speed up the turnaround time of ships in ports. The physical and organisational aspects of ports were not left unaffected by the general cargo-handling innovations (Hilling and Hoyle, 1984). Specialised cellular vessels and new kinds of terminal facilities accompanied the entry of ports into the containerisation era. Large, high-speed gantry cranes, having a lifting capacity of thirty tons or more, replaced the conventional loading/discharging gear that could only lift between three and five tons. Straddle carriers and bridge cranes became the dominant handling-machinery in yard operations, instead of the conventional forklift.

The functions of a port are aligned to the services it performs for ships, cargoes and land-transportation modes. If, however, the concept of the transport system, of which these components are a part, undergoes change, it is highly probable that the very function of the port will be affected. Traditionally, the chain of trade by ocean transport was interrupted only in the port. Inbound and outbound cargo had to be stored in warehouses, silos or tanks before being loaded on or unloaded from ships. Containerisation, however, made possible the rapid movement of large volumes of general cargo through the port without any breaking of bulk at the port itself. For its part, the port was to function as a link in a transportation chain, rather than as an abrupt or lengthy stop in the end-to-end transport haul.

This development naturally reduced the importance of some conventional waterfront services, like warehousing; it also entailed a new system of port operation and management. These trends, initiated in the 1960s and given further impetus in the 1970s, greatly intensified in the 1980s under the impact of a new, multimodal phase of containerisation. Indeed, this decade may be termed 'the intermodal transport era' (Hayuth, 1987). The objective of intermodal transportation is to transfer goods in a continuous flow through the entire transport chain, from origin to final destination, in the most cost- and time-effective way. This is done by capitalising on the relative advantages of a different transport mode for various segments of the cargo movement. Close co-operation and co-

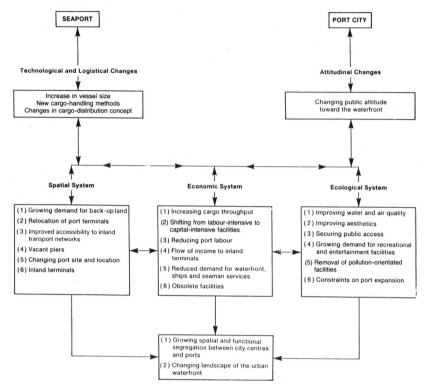

Figure 4.1 *Trends and developments at the port–city interface*

ordination among shipping lines, ports and all land-transportation modes
are essential for effective multimodal transport operation.

As this total, integrated transport concept matures into a significant
mode in the general cargo trade, seaports have had to struggle to maintain
their role in the modified transport chain. For one thing, they have had to
stretch their functional responsibilities beyond the traditional port domain.
Ports, like the other links in this chain, began to think in terms of a systems
concept. Containerisation had necessitated changes that were mostly technological in nature. Intermodality, however, requires primarily organisational changes, and this has led seaports to assume new functions. Inland
transportation, new marketing schemes, multimodal rates, improved
documentation and effective information systems comprise the new areas
of port involvement that now occupy port management.

Parallel with these changes in the maritime freight-transport industry,
the impact of which on the port–urban interface will be analysed later in
this chapter, another development with significant implications for the
urban waterfront began to take place: in the sphere of public awareness
and attitudes. Lack of public awareness of, and interest in, the environmen-

tal problems caused by seaports long characterised the attitude of many urban communities toward their city's port. In many cities, the urban waterfront consisted of unsavoury, run-down and neglected areas. As public concern over environmental issues generally began to grow, with it came increased pressure to improve the ecological structure of the cities as a whole – and the waterfront in particular.

The impact on the port–city interface of technological–organisational developments in shipping and ports on the one hand, and the public's attitudinal change toward its coastal areas on the other, may be analysed in three different, though related, dimensions: spatial, economic and ecological (Fig. 4.1). Each of these will now be discussed in detail.

Spatial dimensions

The physical layout and the land-use configuration of the conventional general cargo terminal are totally inadequate for container handling. With containerisation, the ratio between the length of a berth and the amount of back-up land needed for cargo handling has changed dramatically. The much higher throughput of containerised cargo, the need to store containers and plan the loading of a container vessel in the port 24–48 hours before the arrival of the vessel, the space needed to discharge imported containers and the additional terminal area required for container-marshalling, all combine to impose a demand for back-up space in ports that amounts to ten-fold, and more, than that used in the conventional, break-of-bulk system. Neither the traditional finger-pier, so common in many ports, nor any other configuration of a narrow apron and shedded storage area adjacent to the water can facilitate container handling. The once-sufficient one- or two-hectare terminals had to be replaced with terminals of 10 or 15 hectares or more. Most ports, however, could not find the necessary space within their existing boundaries. Expansion of port facilities became impossible when contiguous areas were built up or otherwise designated for non-port activities. Some container terminals, consequently, having found it difficult to operate at an existing urban waterfront port, were forced to relocate.

Indeed, the relocation of port terminals is one of the most notable changes that has occurred in ports during the last two centuries. This phenomenon is not restricted to specific ports in selected regions, and the examples below are drawn from many different parts of the world. For ports located along a navigable river, downstream reclamation of a new port site provides the solution for obtaining considerable new land-side space. The relocation of port facilities from the old docks in London to the new terminal in Tilbury, the development of the German port of Bremerhaven downstream from Bremen, and the constant crawling toward the sea of new terminals in the ports of Rotterdam and Antwerp, are among examples of major river-based cityports that have adopted this policy.

In other cases, port authorities have removed the centre of their port activities from the conventional site to an entirely new location. The huge container complex of Port Elizabeth in New Jersey that replaced the famous finger-piers lining mid- and downtown Manhattan presents a case from the Port of New York–New Jersey. In France, the growth of port activities in the western Mediterranean required the extension of the urban waterfront at Marseille to the more remote area of Fos (Chapter 1). The construction in Egypt of the new port of El-Dekheila, some fifteen kilometres west of the veteran port of Alexandria, represents an example from the eastern Mediterranean.

Another option exercised by ports in their search for extended back-up land is reclamation of land from the sea. The extent of such a practice may range from a relatively small project – such as the new 33 hectare terminal in the eastern section of the port of Haifa, Israel – up to the creation of an artificial island, like the ones constructed in different parts of the Pacific Ocean for the port of Seattle and for the port of Kobe, Japan (the latter one of the largest in the world).

The accessibility of ports to inland transport networks was recognised as a most important factor in port competition during the containerisation era. With intermodality, this issue has become vital (Hayuth, 1987). Since the intermodal system effectively makes ports one of the links in a total transport chain, the close co-operation and co-ordination of seaports with inland transport modes are prerequisites for the efficient flow of cargo. Indeed, the critical nature – for both port operation and inter-port competition – of this accessibility to major highways, railway lines and navigable rivers becomes obvious as one views the growing volume of trade leaving ports in Europe and the United States for destinations hundreds and even thousands of kilometres inland.

In Europe, railheads are commonly located within the port area; in the United States, by contrast, many ports lack their own rail terminals (Ashar, 1984). A major effort has been made by some of the largest ports on the west coast of the United States, such as Los Angeles, Long Beach and Seattle, to bring railheads as close to the waterfront as possible. The port of Tacoma (Washington State) provides a classic example of the considerable advantages accruing to a port able to provide immediate land-side transport. This port constructed an intermodal railhead adjacent to its container terminal in 1985, and more than tripled its volume of container traffic in just one year. It is not enough, then, for ports merely to find large back-up tracts for their port operations. These lands must be accessible to highways, railways or rivers. It is difficult to picture hundreds of thousands of containers manoeuvring through a city's congested downtown areas. This matter of land-side accessibility provides yet another reason why port cities have relocated terminal facilities away from their central area.

One of the most significant impacts on the characteristics of the port–urban interface is related to the use of obsolete port facilities left behind by the relocated port. The old urban waterfront in many instances has started to be penetrated by non-port activities. As a result, considerable alteration of land-use configuration, as well as of the overall atmosphere of the area, has occurred. The old finger-piers of the port of Seattle, for instance, have been transformed into a waterfront park, consisting mainly of public-oriented commercial enterprises, an aquarium and parking lots. At Fisherman's Wharf in San Francisco and Ports of Call in Los Angeles, attractive shops and restaurants have replaced abandoned or underused port facilities. Old wharves in Boston now form part of the Quincy Market, a major tourist attraction; here, too, one of the features is an aquarium, a section of which is located in a specially converted boat tied up at the dockside. The old colonial quay in Savannah has been renovated as a promenade, and the old Baltimore waterfront has experienced a substantial facelift so as to be able to offer a variety of urban land uses and an attractive marina. The professional periodical literature discusses in detail many such urban-waterfront land-use changes in the United States (see, especially, National Academy of Sciences, 1980).

In Europe, although the same types of development have taken place, they began somewhat later than in the United States. The large-scale renovation project in the London docklands and the smaller-scale 'Ocean Village' scheme in Southampton each combines new residential housing, commercial centres and marinas. Construction of residential quarters along part of the old section of Rotterdam's waterfront and the expansion of the maritime museum in a central urban-waterfront location in the port of Antwerp offer two further illustrations of these trends on the European continent.

The economic dimension

Seaports constitute major assets to their cities and regions. As major employers, as suppliers of services to vessels and their cargo, as junctions of commercial and industrial activities related to international trade, ports are large complexes with – potentially – enormous economic impact on their surrounding urban communities. The economic impact of a port can be divided into three related categories. The first is a *direct* impact, which includes the expenditures and employment generated by services (stevedoring, vessel supplies and repairs, and government services, among others), agency fees, on-shore crew, and capital spending by ports. Other direct port services – such as freight forwarding, ship agencies, customs brokers, and maritime insurance and banking – also contribute to the direct impact of a port on its region. Direct port activities have a considerable effect on other commercial and industrial sectors. The *indirect* impact of port operations includes economic activities of industries that base their location and operation at least partly on the port and the flow of commodities through it. The importance of the indirect economic impact on the port-city's economy is substantial. The third type of port economic impact is channelled through the economic multiplier of port activities, alternatively called 'secondary income' (Schenker, 1967, 135). This category normally includes the purchase of goods and services made possible because of the services and sales revenue generated by both direct and indirect port economic activities. Some fraction of the income generated by shipping and port services is used for purchasing goods and services from other sectors of the city's economy.

There have been numerous attempts to measure the economic impact of ports. Often, such studies were conducted because port authorities, as public entities, have had to justify their operation as well as promote a positive public image for development schemes. They have tried to show, therefore, that the port generates an impressive amount of its region's employment and income. The Port of New York–New Jersey once calculated that approximately 191,600 people in the port region are directly and indirectly employed in waterborne commerce, representing an annual payroll of $4.2 billion and generating $2.3 billion in business income and $0.4 billion in state and city sales taxes (The Port Authority of New York and New Jersey, 1985). A study for the Port of San Francisco concluded that some 44,450 persons in the San Francisco Bay Area in 1982 were being supported by the port industry, which led to the pumping of $2.1 billion into the Bay Area economy (Murphy, 1983). Impact studies have also been conducted for the Port of Baltimore (Hille and Suelflow, 1969), the Port of Seattle (Port of Seattle, 1976), and the Port of New Orleans (Viana & Associates, 1976), their conclusions sounding similar themes.

For port-city officials and for city and regional planners, it is important to understand the direct and indirect economic contributions of the port and to recognise their components in order to improve co-ordination between the physical and economic planning of the port sector on the one hand and the city and its region on the other.

Reduction in port labour

Modification of the urban-waterfront land-use structure that has accompanied the spatial and functional segregation of ports and traditional waterfronts has had its deficit side as well as its beneficial aspects. The reduction in port labour is one of the foremost economic setbacks deriving from technological changes and the relocation of port facilities (see Fig. 4.1).

The transfer of cargo between ocean carriers and land carriers is still, in the intermodal era, basic to the operation of a port. Moreover, with increasing volumes of containerised general cargo moving rapidly through a port, the transfer function is, in fact, magnified (Hayuth, 1985). The emphasis, however, is on the port's being a rapidly passed-through point, whereas formerly it served, as we have seen, as an abrupt break in the end-to-end transport haul. The result has been to reduce the importance of several traditional waterfront activities – such as warehousing – which has meant the loss of a very considerable number of jobs.

In order to accommodate the larger volume of cargo being transferred through ports, to improve the rate of loading and discharging of cargo from vessels and to speed up the in-port turn-around time of ships, ports went through a technological revolution which introduced gantry cranes and other sophisticated land-side equipment. The great increases accruing thereby to port productivity turned port operation from a labour-intensive venture to a capital-intensive industry. The amount of port manpower required in relation to the capital investment for a fixed output constitutes one of the major distinctions between containerisation and the conventional general cargo system. A container terminal requires only one-tenth of the man-hours per ton needed by a conventional terminal handling a similar amount of traffic.

In the process of adapting to containerisation, every port has experienced a massive reduction in manpower – a prime cause of the labour unrest and strikes erupting in many ports around the world in the 1970s. The port of Haifa, where a careful record of personnel has been conducted on a time-series basis, counted well over 3,000 employees in the early 1970s; by the mid-1980s, this workforce had shrunk to a little over 900 employees, despite increased traffic (Israel Ports Authority, 1986). Where the shift in emphasis from labour to capital has been coupled with the relocation of terminal facilities, the impact on port manpower has been even more drastic. Such is the case with the port of London, most of whose activities have been relocated downstream at Tilbury at the mouth of the Thames River.

The effects of the new shipping era on the cityport economy were not uniformly negative, though what may be termed the 'second stage' of the container revolution – intermodal transportation – has had a multi-dimensional effect on seaports. In order to carve out their own niche in this new transport concept, and to benefit from their strategic position in the total transport system, ports are acquiring new functions. Thus, some have started to offer extensive consolidation services to both shippers and shipping lines in cases where the cargo destination is a distant hinterland. Seattle is an example of a port that began offering such services and, in the process, also involved itself in freight forwarding – thus adding new jobs to its work complement.

Major ports have always served as distribution centres and as gateways between hinterlands and forelands. Intermodal transport has increased the direct involvement of ports in the physical distribution system, somewhat in compensation for the reduction in the labour force attendant on the diminishing conventional warehousing and storage functions. The port of Rotterdam (Chapter 7) provides a good example of this tendency.

Loss of business to inland terminals

Port activities along the traditional waterfront have suffered another economic setback from the relocation of selected port functions to inland depots. These facilities, variously called inland clearance depots (ICDs) or inland container terminals, have become a common phenomenon on most continents. The United States boasts a large inland terminal at Clearfield, Utah; England has an ICD at Birmingham. In South Africa, an inland container terminal is found near Johannesburg; in Asia one is situated at Nei Li, in the heart of Taiwan's northern industrial zone. These inland terminals normally provide several functions: warehousing, customs clearance, marshalling yards, repair facilities, transport agencies. Most of the jobs involved come at the expense of traditional waterfront areas (Hayuth, 1980).

The rationale behind the establishment of inland terminals lies in a combination of factors, some of which have been encountered previously: the lack of port back-up space, congested urban waterfronts, and the high cost of land and labour in the vicinity of seaports. Yet another reason for their interior location is the strategic situation of these terminals on long-distance trunk lines for intended container movements and their role as regional marketing centres.

Reduced seaman services

Traditional urban waterfronts to a great extent gained their unique character, atmosphere and reputation as a result of the services they provided to seamen. Until the beginning of the containerisation era, in the mid-1960s, a vessel used to remain in port for a week or more, allowing its crew to disembark for a reasonable amount of shore time. Today, seamen who sail on board a container vessel, a ro-ro ship or even an oil tanker are introduced to fewer ports than they used to be on a conventional, general-cargo vessel – and also to much shorter port-calls. The fast turn-around time characteristic of, and economically demanded from, the new ship ensures that only rarely will a container vessel remain in port for more than a day or two, and even then most of the crew must stay on board (Evans, 1969). Moreover, modern cargo vessels, no matter the type, are crewed with half or less of the number who sailed the older, conventional carriers.

As a consequence, the demand by seamen for such services as night clubs, bars and restaurants on the waterfront has greatly lessened. The virtual elimination of passenger ocean-liner services has further reduced the traditional entertainment function of the waterfront area. Many urban-waterfront renewal schemes have revitalized some of these services, but the business generated now comes more from the city than from the port.

The ecological dimension

The third component of the model presented in Figure 4.1 relates to ecological changes at the port–urban interface. The awakening of public interest in environmental issues and the growing pressure to improve the ecological structure of cities have been responsible for the initiation of many urban renewal programmes and for land-use changes along urban waterfronts (Wilson, 1977). When – prior to the mid-1960s – awareness by the public of various kinds of pollution caused by ports was scanty at best, the dominance of, and the priority consideration given to, port activities along urban waterfronts were rarely challenged. Neither did ports have to face up to any criticism of what they and the shipping lines did to those areas. In fact, this hands-off attitude lasted in many cases up to the 1980s.

In the end, though, it has been the growing public recognition, followed by that of the planning authorities, of the urban waterfront as a major asset for the urban community that has proved a strong catalyst for revitalising port–urban waterfront areas. Efforts have been made to integrate these areas – often among the most neglected and run-down sections of the port city – with other urban quarters and to develop them as a tourist attraction. On the other hand, this same community attitude could, and indeed has, become an obstacle for port growth and development (Pinder, 1981). Active citizen groups, particularly in the United States, are certainly responsible for putting pressure on port authorities to accelerate the process of vacating some of their traditional port sites in order to introduce waterfront renewal programmes (Manogue, 1980). During the early stages of the public's awareness of urban-waterfront problems, its lobbying was rather selective, focusing on air pollution, noise pollution, and hazardous cargo terminals. The public tended to differentiate between various port activities, bringing pressure to bear on those – such as storage areas – which could not firmly justify their location in the immediate vicinity of the waterline. At a later stage, different issues began to be addressed – such as improving the aesthetics of the waterfront or securing public access to the waterfront, which was denied in many ports.

The outcome of the public's attention is that ports are no longer given 'priority' status in the allocation of urban waterfronts. They must now compete for these lands with other commercial, recreational and residential users; and in this competition, ports do not always find themselves in an advantageous position. The cost of land along the waterline is increasing as the demand for it rises; and ports, as public authorities, often find it difficult to subscribe the required capital. In many cases the necessary land is not available at all. Secondly, obtaining a permit to expand port facilities along the waterfront may prove to be a long, tedious process. A port must often satisfy a series of requirements set down by planning and environmental authorities, among which may be the filing of both economic- and environmental-impact statements. In the United States, changes in the public's attitude toward waterfront lands are clearly manifest in the Coastal Zone Management Act of 1972. This Act requires any development programme along a shoreline to give full consideration to ecological, cultural, historic and aesthetic values, as well as to the need for economic development (Hershman *et al*, 1978).

Conclusion: restructuring the urban waterfront

An accelerated trend toward spatial segregation between ports and traditional urban waterfronts is recognisable in many port cities around the world. This phenomenon results from two parallel developments, one related to technological and logistical changes in maritime transportation and the other motivated by attitudinal changes on the part of the public toward the waterfront. Both factors, acting simultaneously and sequentially, are responsible for changing the characteristics and the landscape of traditional urban waterfronts. The unique atmosphere of an active coastal port and ocean waterfront devoted almost entirely to shipping and maritime trade is gradually fading (Hayuth, 1982).

The spatial separation between the port and the traditional waterfront has become obvious. Oil and bulk facilities have been relocated far from the traditional urban waterfront because of their need for extended landside space and deep harbours and their posing of environmental problems. Most modern container terminals have been constructed away from conventional ports. At their traditional sites, port activities – if left at all – consist of servicing shallow-draught vessels, passenger vessels (cruise ships and ferries), pleasure boats and fishing vessels. Many urban waterfront areas are occupied with port-related activities rather than active port operations. One may view the trend towards relocating port terminals as the latest stage in the decentralisation of industries from the central sections of the cities owing to the lack of space and to environmental pressures.

The functional segregation between cities and ports is a widespread phenomenon. Nevertheless, great variations exist among ports as to the extent and character of this trend. Obviously many direct port services have followed the terminals to the new sites. The short turn-around time of ships in ports has lessened the demand for traditional seamen's services at the waterfront, and therefore reduced the importance of the ties – and the distance – between ships and the urban waterfront. Furthermore, the development of advanced means of communications, such as telex, facsimile and direct computer-link between ship and shore, has even limited the need for personal interaction between a vessel's crew and the office ashore.

Despite the relocation of terminal facilities to new sites, no clear-cut trend yet exists among shipping-line headquarters, shipping agents, customs brokers, insurance companies and financial offices to follow terminals to the new locations. On the contrary, there is a tendency in many port cities for these functions to remain in the traditional waterfront area. Two examples will illustrate this situation. In Antwerp, some shipping-related offices have moved to the new port area. Many of these, however, are just branches, and most head offices remain by the old waterfront. Rotterdam, on the other hand, shows a much greater tendency for offices to follow the new port terminals.

Several factors account for the fairly strong ties of many port services to the traditional urban waterfront. Shipping-line headquarters and ship agents need to maintain close connections with related services, such as banking and insurance, which are normally more accessible in the downtown area. The slow development of decent restaurants, pubs and other meeting places in the new port zones also contributes to the desire of personnel to remain in a centrally located area. Customs agents are perforce closely tied to customs houses and these, like government agencies in general, are slow to relocate their offices from the traditional waterfront area.

Nevertheless, the urban waterfront is gradually changing its character as new land uses penetrate the area. The pitch-dark corners of the waterfront are being transformed into illuminated tourist and recreational facilities. The waterfront area is becoming more accessible and attractive to the public as maritime museums, aquariums, restaurants, waterfront parks and marinas take the place of abandoned storage facilities, obsolete aprons and rundown quays.

For city planners, development along the urban waterfront provides a unique opportunity to gain large tracts of vacant, centrally located land. Comprehensive planning that encompasses the entire urban waterfront should be the desired approach. In practice, however, this approach might be handicapped by several problems. Ports do not vacate the entire waterfront at once, and a gradual relocation of port facilities leaves the way open for sporadic development, at best. Multiple ownership of waterfront lands presents another constraint on a comprehensive approach. Even when the ownership issue has been settled, it is difficult to find one body that is willing and able to accept the challenge of reshaping the urban waterfront and reintegrating it with the city. But restructuring and revitalising its waterfront is often a necessity for the port city, and the opportunity is there, for the ultimate prosperity of the city's economy and the benefit of its citizens.

References

Ashar, A. (1984), 'Intermodalism: the case for on-terminal operations', *World Ports*, 46, 78–9.

Bird, J.H. (1963), *The major seaports of the United Kingdom* (London: Hutchinson).

Evans, A.A. (1969), *Technical and social changes in the world's ports* (New York: United Nations).

Hayuth, Y. (1980), 'Inland container terminal-function and rationale', *Journal of Maritime Policy and Management*, 10(2), 16–20.

—— (1982), 'The port–urban interface: an area in transition', *Area*, 14, 219–24.

—— (1985), 'The challenge of technological and functional changes', in *Ocean yearbook 5*, Borges, E.M. and Ginsburg, N. (eds) (Chicago: The University of Chicago Press), 79–101.

—— (1987), *Intermodality: concept and practice, structural changes in the ocean freight transport industry* (London: Lloyds of London Press).

Hershman, M., *et al* (1978), *Under new management: port growth and emerging coastal management programs* (Seattle: Washington Sea Grant Publication).

Hille, J.S. and Suelflow, E.J. (1969), *The economic impact of the port of Baltimore on Maryland* (University of Maryland, College Park, Maryland).

Hilling, D. and Hoyle, B.S. (1984), 'Spatial approaches to port development', in *Seaport systems and spatial change*, Hoyle, B.S. and Hilling, D. (eds) (Chichester: John Wiley & Sons), 1–20.

Israel Ports Authority (1986), *Statistical yearbook 1986/87* (Tel Aviv).

Manogue, H. (1980), 'Citizens groups: new and powerful participants in urban waterfront revitalisation', in *Urban waterfront lands* (Washington, DC: The National Research Council).

Murphy, M.M. (1983), 'Maritime industry is a $2.1 billion benefit to San Francisco Bay economy', *Ports and harbours*, 28(10), October 1983.

National Academy of Sciences (1980), *Urban waterfront lands*, (Washington, DC: Committee on urban waterfront lands).

Pinder, D. (1981), 'Community attitude as a limiting factor in port growth: the case of Rotterdam', in *Cityport industrialisation and regional development*, Hoyle, B.S. and Pinder, D.A. (eds), (Oxford: Pergamon Press), 181–99.

Port of Seattle (1976), *Impact – Seattle Harbor, Sea-Tac International Airport* (Seattle: Seattle Port Commission).

Schenker, E. (1967), *The port of Milwaukee* (Madison: The University of Wisconsin).

The Port Authority of New York and New Jersey (1985), *The economic impact of the port industry on the New York–New Jersey metropolitan region* (New York).

Viana & Associates (1976), *Economic impact: port of New Orleans*, (Port of New Orleans: Board of Commissioners).

Wilson, D. (1977), 'Planning for a changing urban waterfront: the case of Toronto' (Toronto: York University, Department of Geography, Discussion Paper 18).

Part II: Policy and practice

5 Policy convergence on the waterfront? A comparative assessment of North American revitalisation strategies
John Tunbridge

Introduction

The Commonwealth Conference in Vancouver (October 1987) was eloquent testimony to Canada's progress in a field not normally associated with such events: waterfront revitalisation. It was held primarily at Canada Place on the city's main waterfront, built in conjunction with Expo 86; and it doubtless promoted the global diffusion of waterfront development concepts, notwithstanding the more immediate concerns on the delegates' minds. North American observers, however, have become increasingly familiar with the potential of the waterfront since the United States Bicentennial (1976) which was marked by a tour of the Tall Ships and followed by periodic waterfront festivals.

North America is the essential birthplace of the contemporary waterfront revitalisation movement, which began in the USA in the 1960s and is now widespread across the continent. It extends far beyond the provision of simple waterfront parks and beyond traditional 'dockland'; some innovation is occurring on waterfronts which have never, or not recently, been ports. Most waterfront revitalisation involves an interrelated spectrum of issues, and this chapter complements others based on North American material by providing an overview of problems relating to policy formulation, and by drawing attention to certain underdeveloped themes, within a broad range of exemplification. The principal problems addressed are governmental conflict, social versus commercial objectives and conservation versus redevelopment approaches. Further themes include the role of conservation agents, and in particular the revitalisation of small city waterfronts, relative to their distinctive business, recreational and residential contexts. It must, however, be stressed that a chapter of this length cannot do full justice to the scale of the North American waterfront phenomenon, its internal diversity, or the range of perspectives and interpretations which it might engender.

The North American context

In no other continent have port activities been more fundamental to urban development than in North America. In this classic 'new world' context, water communication was indispensable to initial settlement and exploitation of the continental land mass; many urban centres developed around the initial focus of a river-, lake-, or seaport. However, the role of port facilities large and small for passenger movement, and for much freight movement, has been progressively displaced by rail, road and air transportation. In recent years, freight movement has experienced declines through market recession; and traditional port facilities for those goods which are still transported by water have been rendered obsolescent by larger-scale water terminals in new locations. Traditional shipbuilding and marine servicing industries have likewise declined. Consequently there is a wide-ranging potential for urban waterfront revitalisation: the withdrawal of port functions provides an exceptional opportunity to restore the historic links between the populace and the waterfront, to reclaim a heritage resource, and to exploit a prime reserve of inner-city redevelopment land. In absolute terms the issue is most prominent in the United States, but the waterfront plays a larger relative role in national life in Canada; much internal variation, however, exists within both countries, particularly in the local market for waterfront re-use, and national distinctions are not clear cut.

Factors which have prompted the general revitalisation of inner cities during the past twenty years include changing demography and house-prices favouring inner-city residence; growing heritage and quality-of-life awareness; growing urban tourism; and the energy crisis. A parallel and closely interdependent development has been the growth of a service-oriented inner-city economy, as traditional (typically port-related) heavy industries declined. Since few Canadian inner cities experienced the negative socio-economic conditions common in the United States (Goldberg and Mercer, 1986) it was relatively easy to regenerate interest in them. Paradoxically, inner cities in the USA have included the continental leaders, fuelled by more substantial 1960s federal urban-renewal funds than existed in Canada, but they have been less consistently successful in their renaissance. Waterfront revitalisation subsequently emerged as one of the mutually supportive strands of inner-city revitalisation, particularly related to the reclamation of railway lands (Progressive Architecture, 1988; Harrison, 1979). In some major cases, it has been stimulated by prior reclamation of original urban nodes adjacent to the waterfront – for example Gastow, in Vancouver, Lower Town in Québec and Pioneer Square in Seattle. In many cases, federal funding played a vital catalytic role in waterfront revitalisation (Cowey and Rigby, 1979).

The return to the waterfront cannot, however, be understood purely in terms of opportunity and latent demand. In the early 1970s, international concern for pollution of the natural environment prompted a substantial clean-up of waterways fouled by industrial and related effluents, which soon resulted in a changed perception of preferred built environments within the inner city. The most important North American case was the improvement in the Great Lakes water through efforts of the International Joint Commission. Waterfronts as blighted as those in Cleveland or Toledo thereby acquired potential for adaptive re-use, for a variety of functions for which water constituted an active or passive amenity. Related improvement also occurred in the atmosphere and general environment, through the gradual replacement of 'smokestack' industries by a service-oriented urban economy – which, in turn, constituted demand for such waterfront re-use. These changes made it worthwhile to consider removing, or mitigating the effects of, transportation barriers which had commonly developed between the waterfront and the adjacent inner city, such as freeways dating from the 1950s and 1960s. Portland, Oregon has demolished its Harbor Drive (*Architectural Record*, 1987) and Boston is planning to depress its elevated Fitzgerald Expressway below ground level. In this respect the concurrent drive to re-use railway land in inner cities has been very supportive – such as in Toronto, where its re-use for a domed stadium and other redevelopment could potentially re-link Harbourfront with the city centre (Land, 1987; see also Chapter 6).

Waterfront revitalisation has typically focused upon rehabilitation and redevelopment for a wide diversity of residential, recreational, and associated retail and service facilities. Recreational uses include marinas, museums, many commercial facilities variously related to the water amenity, and open space both wild and developed; retail and service uses are chiefly of the 'festival market' type, which is explicitly recreation-oriented. The leisure atmosphere is typically enhanced by periodic festivities and special events. Competing for space, particularly in the large centres, are various other components of the 'post-industrial' economy, perhaps including high-technology industries but more particularly service-oriented office uses; and public and institutional land uses may also be drawn to the waterfront amenity location. Ancillary to this mix of uses there is a renewed emphasis upon public water transportation – in the form of existing ferry services, water buses or taxis, pleasure boats and cruise-ship terminals – all of which tend to attract or reinforce commercial investment at their points of waterfront attachment. Water transportation is difficult to separate from the recreational appeal of ships, whether as spectacles, working vessels accepting visits, educational vessels, museum ships or in adaptive re-use; in some instances (eg Boston, Norfolk and Halifax) a naval presence enhances this appeal.

The spectrum of new waterfront land uses is closely comparable with that elsewhere in the western world; given the international enterprise and connectivity of leading participants, it would be unrealistic to expect otherwise. The revitalisation process has been particularly interactive between Canada and the USA, involving close interchange of ideas and leading entrepreneurs. Developments in Boston, for example, have been highly influential in Canada, while Canadian architects and development companies are active on waterfronts in the USA, such as Baltimore and New York. The waterfront profile in North America has become very prominent, involving a major architecture and planning literature (Merrens, 1980), organisations such as the Waterfront Center (Washington) and Centre for the Great Lakes (Toronto and Chicago), numerous conference activities and a support industry (Petrillo, 1987). In the USA, the resulting standardisation has now reached the point of reaction against 'Rousifying' (building festival markets like the Rouse Corporation's Faneuil Hall Marketplace in Boston and Harborplace in Baltimore) in favour of a quest for individuality. However, unless economic uncertainty puts the whole process on hold, the fashion-led investment momentum of the private market may continue to produce carbon copies of waterfront development.

Major examples

Nearly all the metropolitan ports of the USA and Canada are experiencing substantial waterfront revitalisation. Many river cities (ports or otherwise) – such as Ottawa, Winnipeg, Washington, Pittsburgh, Sacramento and San Antonio – are also participating strongly in waterfront activity; San Antonio is an exceptional case which dates from 1929 (Lomax, 1948). In the USA, the leading seaport revitalisations are globally prominent. In San Francisco, the tourist development of Fisherman's Wharf and the revitalisation of Ghiradelli Square (a former factory) date from the 1960s, being strategically placed near the waterfront terminus of the famous cable car. Seattle, New Orleans, Savannah, Baltimore and Philadelphia are all major examples of waterfront revitalisation. Some have multiple locations, notably Los Angeles and New York: The latter includes the South Street Seaport Museum and some major current projects (Doubilet, 1986). Boston, however, might claim pre-eminence, insofar as its waterfront revitalisation is both multi-faceted and intricately interwoven with probably the most successful inner-city revitalisation in the USA.

Boston is the oldest metropolis in the USA and was the first to experience economic decline, largely because of the increasing peripherality of its New England location. By the 1950s it found itself with the most urgent need for revitalisation – and also the greatest historic potential which might somehow be exploited to this end. Through remarkably astute manipulation of the many US federal urban assistance programmes, Boston has experienced over thirty years of continuous inner-city revitalisa-

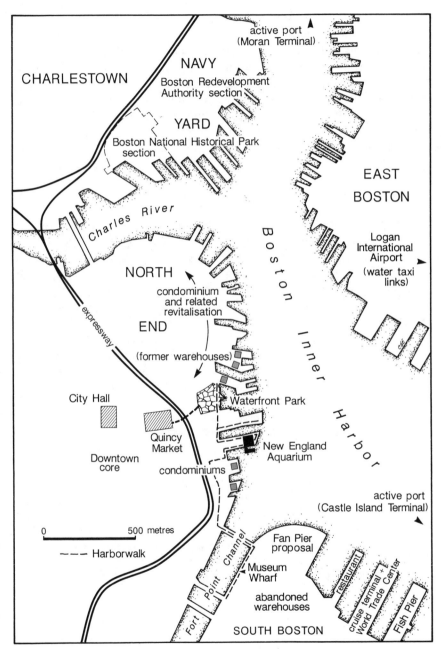

Figure 5.1 *Boston*

tion, notwithstanding the financial isolation from its affluent suburbs which afflicts all US (unlike Canadian) cities. From its inception, this revitalisation has been inseparable from the waterfront, initially on the historic downtown peninsula and subsequently radiating out to other sections of the intricate harbour (Fig. 5.1). From an initial emphasis on redevelopment, the city has moved to a sophisticated balance between redevelopment and rehabilitation. It has become a mecca for revitalisation planners, tourists and white-collar office activity, with the consequence that its waterfront now experiences enormous competitive pressures, and the city can largely dictate the terms of access to it. The 'gatekeeping' planning agency is the Boston Redevelopment Authority which negotiates with private developers to create diversified waterfront land use with a major housing component, in which it is now able to demand that a percentage of low-income accommodation be provided (BRA, 1984, 35).

Boston's renaissance began in the 1950s with the redevelopment of Scollay Square, then a run-down 'sailortown', for a new City Hall and government complex. Subsequent waterfront revitalisation focused upon the refurbishment of the old harbourside Quincy Market complex as Faneuil Hall Marketplace in the mid-1970s, and its linkage to the present (landfilled) waterfront by the Walkway to the Sea which terminates in a park on the site of demolished fishing sheds. The Marketplace, subsequently augmented by Marketplace Center built over the Walkway, was the prototype 'festival marketplace' – the first Rouse Corporation waterfront enterprise – and remains one of America's biggest tourist attractions (Fig. 5.2). The adjacent waterfront warehouses of the North End were contemporaneously refurbished into expensive condominium apartments, marinas and associated amenities.

In the 1980s, within a planning framework entitled 'Harborpark' (BRA, 1984), waterfront revitalisation has diffused north, south and recently east of the historic core. To the north, the North End has been steadily permeated, creating tension with the established Italian community there; and the former Charlestown Navy Yard has been divided between the BRA and a section of the Boston National Historical Park, integrating conservation and tourist attractions (notably the frigate *USS Constitution*) with what amounts to a new residential–commercial mini-city (Tunbridge, 1987). To the south, the peninsula waterfront has been redeveloped (Fig. 5.1). The Fort Point Channel area contains an extensive warehouse complex which is undergoing wide-ranging adaptive re-use as innovative museums, offices *et alia*. The formerly decaying piers of South Boston now contain a cruise terminal–world trade centre, various commercial elements including restaurants on and near the fishing pier, and the site of a contentious high-density 'mini-city' proposal known as Fan Pier. The East Boston waterfront remains largely dilapidated, but pressure from elsewhere is spilling over and there is incipient friction both with the local

Figure 5.2   *Quincy Market, Boston*

Figure 5.3   *Harborplace, Baltimore*

community and with Massport, the state-owned port authority which is now focused upon restricted inlying and peripheral terminals but has been jealously guarding its property in East Boston against further inroads of waterfront revitalisation.

In Canada, Vancouver merits particular comment as it has experienced the most extensive activity. Unlike other leading ports – notably Toronto, Québec and Halifax – in which revitalisation is essentially contiguous, in Vancouver it has occurred at a variety of locations, through different agencies and with quite distinct end products (Fig. 5.4), including locations in the metropolitan outskirts such as New Westminster and the Fraser River. Vancouver's natural setting is scenically unsurpassed and, unlike many ports, it always retained extensive waterfront areas devoted to recreational activity, notably around Stanley Park, an oasis of natural forest. Vancouver's natural amenity provided a catalyst in the 1970s for

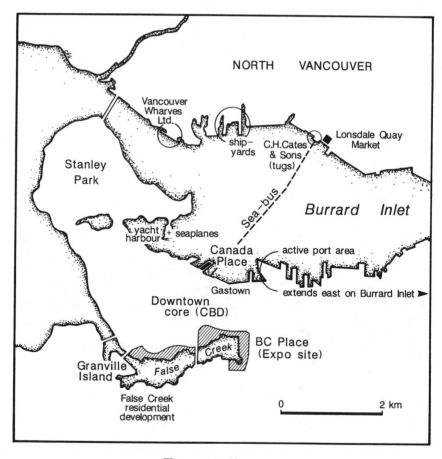

Figure 5.4 *Vancouver*

reclamation of the extensive waterfront areas experiencing industrial blight and port withdrawal – firstly False Creek and, secondly, areas on Burrard Inlet no longer required by the port of Vancouver.

False Creek has experienced several quite distinct phases and actors in its redevelopment, all of which required the clearance (or selective re-use) of a decayed industrial environment. In the early 1970s a 'people-oriented' city council presided over the mixed-income False Creek residential redevelopment. Through the 1970s the federal government was engaged in the revitalisation of Granville Island, in which old factories were adaptively re-used for market, retail and marine-associated functions, with great emphasis placed upon the retention of a nautically-related industrial heritage (Woodbridge, 1982). During the 1980s the railway yards on False Creek have been entirely redeveloped by BC Place, a British Columbia provincial corporation, initially for the Expo 86 World Fair. The subsequent dismantling of most of the World Fair's structures has left 64 hectares of prime development land, which has recently been open to bids from private developers for conversion into a mixed commercial–residential area (*Land*, 1986). The BC Place project is considered the largest urban-renewal scheme in North America, and an associated metropolitan rail transit system was constructed in time to serve Expo 86.

The federal government's chief contribution to Expo 86 was Canada Place, on Burrard Inlet, a major landmark in the revitalisation of the city centre waterfront. Apart from the convention centre, Canada Place contains a cruise-ship terminal, hotel, and world trade centre, with restaurants and shops (*et alia*) at the end of the pier, which provides outstanding harbour views; its construction displaced a former railway barrier to waterfront access. On the facing waterfront of North Vancouver, the BC Development Corporation has created the Lonsdale Quay Market mixed-use complex, one of several waterfront public markets in the region stimulated by the example of Granville Island (Cardew, 1987; Land, 1980a).

Vancouver does not represent a Canadian norm, but it does illustrate the scope and diversity of waterfront revitalisation possible within a single metropolis. It also points to the diverse and, at times, divergent public-sector involvement possible in a federal state. At the other extreme, in both Canada and the USA, are very many sub-metropolitan waterfront centres which have been slower to revitalise but which are now exerting a major collective impact on urban environmental quality across the continent. They range between 5,000 and 100,000 in population and include Canadian centres as mutually remote as Charlottetown, Prince Edward Island; Port Alberni, BC (Shack, 1986); and Yellowknife, Northwest Territories (Souchotte, 1987). In the USA they are innumerable, though there are also many more economically depressed small ports than in Canada. In the north-eastern industrial heartland, in particular, few have been so fortunate as Lowell, Massachusetts, which has been able to capitalise on its industrial canal heritage by becoming a national historical park.

Friction on the waterfront

It is axiomatic that urban development ensues from a process of conflict resolution, and waterfront development is a very explicit illustration of this. A central purpose of this chapter is to draw attention to three problem areas of North American waterfront revitalisation: conflicts between government agencies, social versus commercial objectives, and conservation versus redevelopment approaches. A universal problem is that of friction when past uses of land and water persist in juxtaposition to the newcomers. Although some juxtaposition is often favoured – and is becoming more accepted by newcomers – traditional uses may remain sufficiently active to raise concern about both competition and negative externalities. The port of Halifax, for example, is in fact expanding – and is concerned that its competitive position with other ports could become impaired as a result of waterfront competition with revitalising land uses, and by complaints from condominium owners about noise or other intrusion. Conflict may also occur over the use of water space or navigable channels, for example between recreational and fishing vessels (McCuaig *et al* 1981). The fishing industry – as both an amenity and a competitor for land and water space – has received significant comment in the US literature, in part because of local fishing decline (eg Petrillo, 1987; Harney 1979). Boston and Vancouver illustrate various land and water frictions which result from the persistence of an active port and its service facilities (such as tugs) at the head of a harbour otherwise largely revitalised (Schreiner, 1987); six other US cases of conflict are documented by Hershman (1979).

Governmental conflict potential

All three main government levels in the USA and Canada (federal, state or provincial, municipal) have an interest in waterfront activity, but their powers are constitutionally divided. In both countries conflicts arise – between governmental levels and between departments at the same level – through jurisdictional uncertainties and through divergent mandates and philosophy. On specific issues, the constitutional structures of Canada and the USA are very different, so that public mechanisms of waterfront (or any urban) development are nationally distinct. But the potential for conflict is similar and can be exemplified primarily by reference to the Canadian case, which provides a clear and well-documented illustration. The powers of the Canadian federal government are more circumscribed than in the USA, however, while those of the provinces and local governments (the latter vis-à-vis the private sector) are greater (Goldberg and Mercer, 1986).

In Canada, since trade and fisheries fall under federal jurisdiction, major port facilities are largely federally-controlled, but all land not owned or controlled by the federal government for the fulfilment of such specific functions falls under provincial jurisdiction, subject to such land-use control as the provinces have seen fit to delegate to municipalities (or to metropolitan regional governments). Thus latent tensions exist. The provinces have the dominant say over urban land use but cannot normally override the legal rights of other levels of government as owners, or with respect to their designated functions, so that in effect no level of government can unilaterally direct urban affairs. The latent tensions are compounded on the waterfront, since although the federal government has jurisdiction below low-water mark and over public harbours, both are subject to definitional problems (Le Hénaff, 1986, 11), broadly comparable to those in the USA (Carpenter, 1974). Definitions aside, there are residual legal uncertainties as to the ability of provincial and municipal governments to exercise their normal planning controls over federally owned land; this is subject to considerable jurisprudence (Ward, 1986). Fortunately, the fact of divided powers, and the need to compromise and accommodate, is well understood in everyday Canadian public life, so that latent tensions do not engender conflict as frequently as might be expected; and there are many examples of bi- or tri-level co-operation in the resolution of urban problems, now including waterfront development issues. For example, Halifax's Waterfront Development Corporation was initially a federal–provincial creation, and in Vancouver, the re-use of Expo 86's geodesic dome as a science centre is by tri-level agreement.

Development options may appeal differently to the several governments, however, depending on their commitments, resources and political hues, and conflicts do indeed occur. They are most apparent in the largest or politically highest-profile cities and may involve governments either directly, or indirectly – as in the case of contentious policy emanating from Crown Corporations or task forces with specific waterfront mandates. For example, the City of Vancouver and the Province of British Columbia were initially at loggerheads over BC Place's 'megaproject' redevelopment approach to the Expo 86 site. In contrast to the city's south shore False Creek project, its mandate was profitability rather than livability and it was largely immune from city planning control. In Montreal, conversely, waterfront revitalisation has been retarded by the failure of the federally created steering committee to consider city concerns, thereby engendering strong local opposition to its proposals (London, 1982). In the case of Québec City, implicit tension underlies the documented tri-level approval of the federal government's revitalisation of the old port (*Land*, 1980b), which was undertaken as a complement to provincial restoration in adjacent

Lower Town. Designed specifically to be in time for the 400th anniversary in 1984 of Jacques Cartier's historic landing it provided the federal government with a windfall opportunity conspicuously to advertise this major cultural and economic service to the Province of Quebec, the Parti Québécois government of which had systematically denied the relevance of the federal government.

To compound the jurisdictional problem, government departments at all three levels in both countries have longer-established areas of responsibility which intersect, but do not comprehend, the package of issues comprised in waterfront revitalisation, so that tracing the patterns of government intervention is a labyrinthine exercise. At the Canadian federal level, the following are the departments with the clearest mandate for waterfront involvement: Transport (Harbours and Ports, and other divisions), Fisheries and Oceans (Small Craft Harbours), Environment (Parks Canada, the national parks organisation), Public Works, Indian and Northern Affairs, and CN Marine (the ferry derivative of Canadian National Railways). Federal government intervention and involvement in waterfront redevelopment have been researched by the Lands Directorate of Environment Canada, which has been given the mandate of clarifying overall federal impacts and reducing jurisdictional confusion in different spheres of land use (Le Hénaff, 1986). The federal ministry which might best have co-ordinated waterfront revitalisation, the Ministry of State for Urban Affairs, was terminated in face of costs and provincial jurisdictional jealousies. During its existence in the 1970s, however, it pioneered federal–municipal joint planning (with Vancouver) and national documentation on waterfront revitalisation (Merrens, 1980, 16, 83). Other departments may also be tangentially involved – for example, Regional Industrial Expansion, which has an agreement with Ontario for tourist development. The literature on federal waterfront involvement reveals considerable interdepartmental collaboration, commonly resulting in the creation of an autonomous body such as a Crown Corporation to manage the federal interest in specific sites – for example, the Harbourfront Corporation in Toronto and the Canada Lands Company (Vieux Port de Québec) Inc. in Québec (Allaby, 1984). Notwithstanding collaboration and agreements, however, it is acknowledged that considerable problems remain with respect both to ownership vis-à-vis the provinces and to jurisdiction between federal departments. These are potentially exacerbated by departmental rivalries, budgetary constraints and the future uncertainties induced by a cost-cutting Conservative government (Le Hénaff, 1986).

At the provincial level, the number of concerned ministries is similarly large. In the case of Ontario, the following play a major role, either promotionally or reactively: Municipal Affairs, Natural Resources, Environment, Tourism and Recreation, and Northern Development and Mines.

Tourism and Recreation is a significant promoter of waterfront development through its facilitation of marina and related projects. Fortunately, the Ministry of Municipal Affairs has assumed a certain co-ordinating role with respect to provincial (and the most relevant federal) ministries in a publication promoting waterfront development (Ministry of Municipal Affairs, 1987).

Co-ordination of effort within – and particularly between – jurisdictions remains imperfect, and there is never likely to be a master plan for Canadian (or US) urban waterfront revitalisation. There is, however, some likelihood of policy packages developing at the instigation of leading provincial ministries, specific to the legal framework of each province but mutually influential between them, which will perpetuate the subtle regional distinctiveness which is a hallmark of Canadian urban development. Such policy packages are likely, however, to involve a public–private mix of investment, since the large-scale government funding which has (however disjointedly) fuelled much existing waterfront development has now ended, in Canada as in the USA.

In the USA, the federal Coastal Zone Management Act (1972) provided a national background for waterfront improvement; however, compliance by the states to its terms was left voluntary and its application is accordingly uneven and incomplete. The relevant US federal government agencies include the National Research Council (NRC, 1980); Maritime Administration; the Department of the Interior, notably through its Heritage Conservation and Recreation Service (Department of the Interior (US), 1979), Office of Water Resources Research, and through the activities of the National Parks Service; and the Office of Coastal Zone Management (US Department of Commerce, 1980; Cowey, 1979). The various federal departments, such as Housing and Urban Development, which have heavily subsidised urban development, have thereby become major waterfront players to a greater extent than their relatively low-profile Canadian counterparts. US federal waterfront resources are reviewed by Harney (1979).

At the state level, interactivity concerning legal and practical aspects was illustrated in the Western States Land Commissioners Association conference in Seattle, July 1987. Port authorities are usually state-run, and their policies are highly influential in the amount of land freed for waterfront revitalisation. Some states actively promote this through environmental management and specifically coastal agencies; the California State Coastal Conservancy, for example, was created to support small-city local government waterfront initiatives, with planning assistance, seed funding and co-ordination of the various federal, state and community financial assistance available for environmental emergency work, wildlife and other waterfront-related improvements (Petrillo, 1987). Local government may find itself in conflict with unco-operative private owners in its efforts to formulate a coherent overall master plan for the waterfront. The role of cities vis-à-vis state and national coastal management programmes is discussed by Warren (1979).

Social versus commercial motivation

Conflict potential also exists between socially and commercially motivated concepts of the optimum re-use of waterfront space, since 'the essential interest of the developer is to capture the complete value of the amenity' (Petrillo, 1987, 201). While the profit motive is primarily associated with the development industry, governments have become increasingly cost-conscious and thus more prone to accept profit-motivated proposals, sometimes to the detriment of their relations with other levels of government, as noted above. The social conflict is most visible in the largest cities, where space pressures are greatest and the release of waterfront land has particularly proved to be a bonanza both to the general public and to developers. Social confrontation in the largest cities also generates the highest political profile; thus in 1987 the alleged overdevelopment of Toronto's Harbourfront for commercial ends became a national political issue. Growing pressure of high-income condominium development is the crux of the problem in Toronto, as it is in Boston and Halifax. Public access (physical and visual), recreational open space and lower-income housing are typically compromised by such development unless governmental action is taken to safeguard them. Concern for job creation, discussed elsewhere in this volume in a British context, is present in Canada and the USA (BRA, 1984) but is generally less prominent. These concerns were largely instrumental in stalling and later moderating Montreal's development proposals, which had initially focused on high-density luxury accommodation at the expense of all other potential elements (London, 1982). In the light of Ley's observation that waterfront land is one of the few viable options for rehousing the displacees of gentrification, the lower-income housing issue is a matter of particular urgency (Ley, 1986/7). The severity of the problem is, however, dependent on the overall success of inner-city revitalisation, and it is accordingly likely that Canadian cities have, in general, a somewhat greater conflict to reconcile than those of the USA. It should be noted, however, that the highest-density waterfront revitalisation is occurring in Manhattan and here (in Battery Park City, for example) a major public concern is that of design, relative to adjacent skyscrapers (Wiseman, 1987).

   Harbourfront in Toronto was conceived originally as a recreation-oriented restoration of the city's inner harbour (Allaby, 1984). The federal Harbourfront Corporation was subsequently established to undertake the revitalisation, but its ultimate mandate involved the attainment of profitability by 1987; and partly in order to achieve this it has planned for a concentration of high-rise condominiums which is now regarded as an excessive encroachment on public and low-income provision. The federal government froze further development in February 1987, pending a review of Harbourfront's policy; this move is, however, fraught with legal risks from developers to whose plans prior approval had been given. Following much tension, highest-level collaboration between all three relevant governments produced a revised plan; its effect on open space and densities remains to be seen.

Such social–commercial conflicts are not a simple questiôn of available space. Market imperatives dictate that residential condominiums will tend to be high-density, and where this entails high-rise development both the overall aesthetics and the obstruction of views are likely to give grounds for public objection. Furthermore, provision of waterfront access (actual and perceived) to the public may be resisted by condominium developers because of the security problem it creates for accompanying berthing facilities. The problems are recognised as having a wide potential application and are discussed in Ontario's waterfront guidelines; examples of significant conflict in smaller communities include Kingston and Brockville, on the Ontario shore of the St Lawrence (Ministry of Municipal Affairs, 1987). Similarly, Oceanside in California has experienced conflict over density, height, views, access, traffic and parking in connection with condominium and other commercial development, a conflict characteristically resolved in part by the local political process (Petrillo, 1987). The more the smaller centres succeed in regenerating interest in their waterfronts, the more potential for such conflict will arise.

The degree to which government-created waterfront agencies are promoting social over commercial ends varies; not all have leaned in the direction of profit in recent time. The California State Coastal Conservancy, for example, has identified a variety of methods of assuring land availability to meet social objectives in small centres, including direct purchase, easements, land trades and in-lieu payments by developers (Petrillo, 1987). The Waterfront Development Corporation in Halifax (formerly part-federal, now provincial) maintains strict standards of social responsibility. Criticisms of developers confronted with its regulations include the stifling of creativity and the costs imposed by delays in the various review processes. Boston, however, indicates that it is possible to assert very significant social responsibility in a successful major revitalisation environment, such that waterfront developers are willing to accept not only a proportion of low-income provision in their projects, but also linkage payments designed to channel benefits to less-favoured outlying neighbourhoods.

Conservation versus redevelopment

Conflict potential also exists between conservation/adaptive re-use of historic structures and higher-intensity redevelopment. Conflict may arise through direct redevelopment pressure or the indirect stress of incompatible juxtaposition. This may form an extension of social–commercial tension, in that conservation of heritage may reflect popular sentiment, linked with concern for water access, open space etc; this is exemplified by Halifax, which has strong waterfront heritage controls. In a generation, following the 1966 Historic Preservation Act in the USA and the 1967 Centennial celebrations in Canada, North American public attitudes have moved from indifference to interest in most waterfront conservation; many people now appreciate the adaptive re-use of warehouses, docks, and historic ships or their replicas.

In some cases, however, conservation may still represent a minority viewpoint without general public support. Relatively few may fight for grain silos, a distinctive feature of Great Lakes–Midwestern waterfronts such as Buffalo and Minneapolis, which suffer from debatable aesthetic merit and the difficulty of adaptively re-using tall, massive structures without windows. Recent press comment has in any case questioned the commercial adaptive re-use of these structures, which are considered important influences on the rise of architectural modernism. Their best protection may be the cost of demolition but, despite this, silos on the Montreal and Toronto waterfronts have already been demolished, and more are threatened in Toronto (Kalman, 1984). The Ontario Heritage Foundation has funded the quest for sensitive re-use of the Toronto silos, but Harbourfront, as a Crown Corporation, is not bound by heritage regulations applicable to other federal properties and may not be greatly pressured by public opinion (Heritage Canada, 1987).

A classic case of conflict which was finally resolved in favour of conservation is that of Historic Properties on the Halifax waterfront. In the 1960s Halifax City Council planned a redevelopment of early waterfront warehouses in favour of a new highway, reflecting the vulnerability of decrepit waterfronts to public urban renewal at that time. A crusade by a handful of conservationists heightened public awareness of the historic value of the warehouses (a base for privateers during the early conflicts with the USA). This ultimately led to a reversal of the City's plan and, in 1971, a co-operative scheme to rehabilitate the warehouses between a private developer and Parks Canada, which took office space in one building (McDougall, 1984). The result, Historic Properties, is one of the most successful waterfront revitalisation projects in Canada, containing many tourist-oriented shops, pubs and restaurants; providing mooring space for the nationally famous schooner *Bluenose II*; and helping to catalyse other adjacent conservation activity, notably the provincial Maritime Museum of the Atlantic, several museum ships including the last

Second World War corvette, and the Brewery retail/office rehabilitation (McDougall, 1984). This environment, among other things, augments the nearby naval base in projecting the naval heritage of Halifax. Parks Canada, as owner of the historic Citadel overlooking the city centre, has an overall interest in the waterfront and its redevelopment.

Other examples of heritage–redevelopment conflicts have arisen in Montreal and in Kingston, Ontario. In Montreal, local reaction against the redevelopment proposals resulted partly from concern over loss of the port heritage and blocking adjacent Old Montreal from the waterfront (London, 1982). In Kingston, proposals for a waterfront shopping mall and apartments have been opposed because they threaten the historic skyline and limestone character along the waterfront (Hodge, 1980), but some such development has proceeded. The revitalisation of the former Charlestown Navy Yard in Boston has incurred tension over the selective conservation required by the Department of the Interior when the federal government sold most of the property to the Boston Redevelopment Authority. Some buildings proved difficult to re-use adaptively (such as the long, narrow Ropewalk) or were regarded by developers as economically suboptimal (Tunbridge, 1987).

The national parks organisation has locally been of great importance to waterfront conservation in both US and Canadian centres, as in Québec and the National Historical Parks in Boston (including part of the Navy Yard) and Lowell, Mass.; it is therefore an institutional factor to be reckoned with. A special case of Parks Canada's involvement is Heritage Canals, notably Rideau in Ottawa and Chambly in the St Jean area, Québec (Lands Directorate, 1985). Both governmental conservation agencies and the voluntary conservation sector, nationally led by the US National Trust for Historic Preservation and the Heritage Canada Foundation, have been instrumental in moulding public attitudes and now function as major players in waterfront-conservation issues.

In general, the participants in waterfront revitalisation have learnt that conservation and adaptive re-use of heritage structures can often be blended compatibly into larger redevelopment environments; this provides, after all, the continuity of local identity and sense of place. In the USA, major tax incentives aided conservation in the early 1980s. Developers have in any case found it highly profitable to show heritage sensitivity in attracting the crucial tourist and leisure markets to the waterfront. A notable example of blending old and new is Market Square, Saint John, New Brunswick, the location of the World Chess Festival in 1988; this is a festival market retail and convention complex which integrates existing waterfront warehouses into its structure. Market Square overlooks the new Loyalist Plaza, which commemorates the landing of United Empire Loyalist settlers in 1784; it also interrelates with a new hotel, condominiums, library and city hall (Lindgren, 1984). Some notable adaptive rehabilitations of individual historic structures also occur on waterfronts; Queens Quay Terminal on Toronto's Harbourfront is a massive warehouse revitalised for shops, offices and condominiums. Extensive quayside warehouse re-use was involved in the distinctive revitalisation of Factors' Walk, Savannah, Georgia (Carpenter, 1977). More generally, the revitalisation of industrial and warehouse structures by the private sector on or near waterfronts is now well advanced: Boston, Charlestown and Montreal provide outstanding examples.

It is apparent that the conservation–redevelopment issue is interactive with the other two problem areas highlighted in this chapter. It is in the speculative environment of the largest cities that all three are most prominent. In this environment, historic structures must contend not only with competitive redevelopment but also with the tendency for North American conservation areas to be threatened by intensification pressures consequent upon their own success as 'people places'. Adaptive re-use notwithstanding, the conservation of heritage environments cannot be taken for granted.

Small communities

Waterfront revitalisation in small ports is important in the USA but is a more fundamental part of the Canadian national perspective, and is particularly well exemplified in Ontario. Few parts of Canada have been historically more water-dependent than Ontario, and probably none is so comparatively dependent upon contemporary waterborne tourist activity. The provision of transient docking facilities in most lake and river towns is a direct incentive for revitalisation of the waterfront, which constitutes both the point of entry of such tourists and commonly the part of town most appealing to heritage-sensitive contemporary tourism.

Furthermore the waterfront is usually adjacent to the main shopping district and its revitalisation has consequently become closely linked with 'Main Street' revitalisation, which has become a high-profile North American concern during the 1980s. US illustrations of this link are Wilmington, North Carolina and Burlington, Vermont (*Progressive Architecture*, 1988). Most Canadian provinces, and notably Ontario, have developed assistance schemes to boost the sagging economies of small-town centres, most immediately the result of competition created by planned shopping centres to established 'Main Street' business. Because of the perceived threat to the physical heritage of small communities, Heritage Canada created its own 'Main Street' assistance programme, following the example of the US National Trust. This encourages small communities to utilise their innate resources and provincial assistance so as to capitalise most effectively upon the heritage resource, emphasising physical rehabilitation, economic promotion and social involvement (Holdsworth, 1985). In Canada particularly, many of the beneficiaries are waterfront communities, and a boost to 'Main Street' activity is generating a positive spinoff to waterfront revitalisation (or vice versa); examples are St Jean, Québec and Perth, Prescott and Sarnia, Ontario. In all of the port examples discussed below, some kind of 'Main Street' revitalisation is a closely associated phenomenon and mutual stimulus.

In consequence, the range of government departments and programmes – and quasi-public interests – indirectly involved in small-town waterfront activity is even greater than indicated above; in particular, there are high-profile conservation bodies which include the Ontario Heritage Foundation, a government-sponsored organisation (Ministry of Citizenship and Culture, 1987). However, the critical government participants in Ontario invariably include federal government departments, the Small Craft Harbours branch of Fisheries and Oceans and/or the Ports and Harbours branch of Transport, since there are 381 federal harbours in the province which cover practically every conceivable location of waterfront

Figure 5.5 *Kingston and southern Ontario*

revitalisation (Department of Fisheries & Oceans, 1987; Le Hénaff, 1986); and by definition all relevant Ontario ministries are involved (Ministry of Municipal Affairs, 1987).

Among the many communities around the Great Lakes and along the St Lawrence and Ottawa Rivers, the majority in both Ontario and the USA are experiencing some degree of revitalisation, varying with market conditions and civic–commercial enterprise. Some ports, such as Owen Sound, are at a comparatively early stage; others are well advanced, such as Midland, where the waterfront was used as a film set in 1987 (Ministry of Municipal Affairs, 1987, 76). On Lake Ontario and the St Lawrence, Port Dalhousie (port for St Catherines), Kingston, Brockville, and Prescott are all examples of substantial revitalisation (Fig. 5.4). The Fisheries and Oceans Department is particularly active in small craft harbour development in Ontario, for example in Pembroke and Deep River, on the Ottawa River west of Ottawa. In the case of Pembroke this investment, matched by municipal development of shore facilities, has catalysed private recreational and condominium development in what was formerly a run-down lumbering environment. The cases of Collingwood and Kingston, however, merit particular attention.

Collingwood (population 12,000) has two distinctive attributes permitting an unusual scale of waterfront revitalisation: a shipyard which closed in 1986 and a year-round recreational industry, focused upon marinas on Georgian Bay (Lake Huron) and a nearby ski hill. On the strength of its established recreational status, a 'Shipyards' revitalisation scheme has been proposed by the shipyard owner. This will selectively retain attractive buildings of the closed shipyard and specifically its two docks, into one of which a ship will be inserted and adapted for museum, retail and other uses, thus re-establishing a familiar skyline at the end of the revitalising 'Main Street'. Across the other dock a hotel will be constructed, with an adjacent office–retail plaza extending the main shopping street, and extensive residential development. The scale of the facility and its revitalisation is worthy of a larger port. There are naturally concerns about continuing market buoyancy in a small recreational community, but by late 1987 it had received municipal planning approval and was seeking financial assistance from the Canada–Ontario Tourism Development programme, already extensively used in the area.

Kingston is a larger (population 53,000) and extremely historic community which illustrates waterfront revitalisation in an environment with major recreational and residential appeal. It was one of the principal Loyalist settlements following the American Revolution and was a contender for the national capital during the nineteenth century, when its relative importance was much greater. Having failed to industrialise, it has retained its early character and a generally high environmental quality. For these reasons – together with its accessibility and location at the junction of the Rideau Canal, the St Lawrence and Lake Ontario – it is a well-established

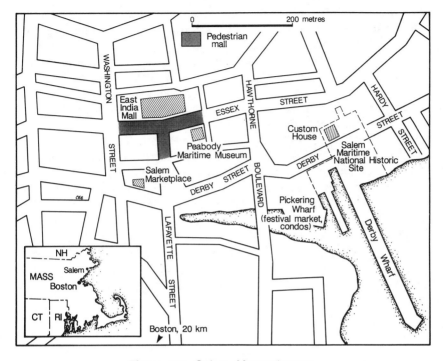

Figure 5.6 *Salem, Massachusetts*

recreational and élite residential centre. Kingston's amenities are accessible to and marketed in Toronto, Montreal, Ottawa and New York State;
they are greatly enhanced by Parks Canada's local waterfront attractions
(Rideau Canal, Martello towers, Old Fort Henry, Thousand Islands
National Park) and the provincial St Lawrence Parks Commission's shoreline improvements. Kingston's status as a lake port declined with the
opening of the St Lawrence Seaway in the 1950s, so that it had an early
opportunity to develop an attractive waterfront by accentuating its limestone heritage buildings. To this end a waterfront park was created in front
of its old city hall as a centennial project in 1967, displacing railway tracks.
The waterfront's potential has since, however, generated continuing conflicts over large-scale redevelopment; and the traditionally poorer northern
side of the city is now experiencing gentrification partly linked to condominium development on recently vacated port land. Kingston has
developed a waterfront access path, attractively signposted, which links
diverse activity areas (Fig. 5.5) but the overall degree of success is contentious and this indicates the extent to which even a small-city waterfront
with high amenity and accessibility can succumb to market pressures,
despite the presence of powerful conservation forces.

Ontario has a continental prominence in small-city waterfront revitalisation, partly by virtue of US tourist business but it is also an active

concern in the USA itself, as the Californian case cited above. Wilmington, North Carolina, and Portland, Maine, are two of many medium-sized US port cities undergoing revitalisation. The example of Salem, Massachusetts (Fig. 5.6) merits brief elaboration because it illustrates the 'Main Street' link, the role of the National Park Service and also the universal reality that small-port revitalisation may now involve outlying parts of a metropolitan area, with its associated market pressures. Salem is a seventeenth-century port which was at the forefront of the oriental clipper trade but has now been effectively absorbed into metropolitan Boston. The chief catalyst for its waterfront revitalisation is the conserved clipper wharves which form the focus of the Salem Maritime National Historic Site. Contemporary commercial redevelopment has emerged nearby – notably the Pickering Wharf retail and condominium complex – and has been linked to Essex Street, the revitalised main street, by signposting. Unfortunately Essex Street is sufficiently distant to make walking inconvenient, and it has lost trade to Pickering Wharf rather than becoming integrated with it. Since this main-street revitalisation is one of the most sensitive in North America, and includes within it Salem's maritime museum, this is particularly regrettable.

Conclusion

Overall, waterfront revitalisation is comparable and closely interrelated in the USA and Canada, jurisdictional differences notwithstanding; and it is mutually influential with that elsewhere in the world. However, size disparity implies that no simple and predictable pattern of waterfront revitalisation exists in North America. Local circumstances vary considerably with respect to physical, political and economic environments; it is not surprising that both national capitals are more prominent examples than are heavy-industry centres in either country. In absolute terms, the USA leads not only Canada but the world in the extent of its waterfront revitalisation; on the other hand, it still contains considerable waterfront dereliction (Petrillo, 1987). Canada's urban base, while much smaller, is more consistently water-related and more consistently revitalising; considering also the particularly high profile of the waterfront in its tourist economy, Canada may well enjoy a global leadership in the relative prominence of its waterfront revitalisation.

While waterfront revitalisation is particularly extensive in North America and displays many positive attributes, there is an emerging conflict between profit-oriented development and interrelated concerns for social equity and heritage conservation. A background conflict, over the viability of traditional port-related activities, involves jobs and port character and may therefore be interwoven with these concerns. The position of government in this context depends upon which of its many heads is speaking; and therein lies one of the three problems which this chapter has particularly addressed.

One, potentially international, dimension deserves closer study. Water pollution, not to speak of hazardous wastes, may be increasing again through dumping or leakage of the refuse of revitalisation. Condominium development on Boston Harbour, for example, is adding significantly to a major environmental problem in the form of sewage load. This is publicised in the waterfront Aquarium, and is now the subject of a court-ordered cleanup estimated to cost the Boston metropolitan community $6 billion. There is media discussion of the same problem with respect to Halifax, and (in late 1988) of the storage or past dumping of dangerous chemicals on waterfronts elsewhere in Canada. Beyond the environmental facts is the question whether, and when, popular perception will catch up, with interesting consequences for the market evaluation which rests upon it. In sharing patterns of waterfront development throughout the western world, it behoves us to ensure that we do not transmit environmental regression from one location to another. This point is a salutary reminder that waterfront revitalisation concerns not only inner cities, and usually port activity, but also the wider environment within which they are set.

Acknowledgements

The author is greatly indebted to many individuals for their willing assistance, including Chris Earl for cartography and Marie Raymond for typing. Sources not otherwise acknowledged include the *New York Times*; *The Globe and Mail*, *The Financial Post*, and *MacLean's* (Toronto); L. Brophy (Boston Redevelopment Authority); S. Kennedy (Ontario Ministry of Municipal Affairs, Ottawa); P. Bircham (Lands Directorate, Environment Canada, Ottawa); A. Besse (Solicitor for Shipyards, Collingwood); J. Sinclair and S. Mackenzie (Geography, Carleton University); D. Ley (Geography, University of British Columbia); W. Stanley (Geography, University of South Carolina); and participants in the conference *A future for our rivers* (Ottawa, National Capital Commission, June 1987), in particular A. Breen and R. Rigby (The Waterfront Centre, Washington, DC) and M. Webb (Centre for the Great Lakes Foundation, Toronto and Chicago).

References

Allaby, I. (1984), 'The Harbourfront lands: revitalizing Toronto's waterfront', *Habitat*, 27(2), 2–7.
Architectural Record (1987), 'River Place Athletic Club, Portland, Oregon', *Architectural Record*, August, 100–5.

Boston Redevelopment Authority (1984), *Harborpark: a framework for planning discussion* (Boston: BRA).

Canadian Heritage (1988), 'How many grain elevators are left in Toronto?' *Canadian Heritage*, October–November, 12.

Cardew, P. (1987), 'Lonsdale Quay Market, North Vancouver', *Canadian Architect*, July, 20–9.

Carpenter, E.K. (1974), 'San Francisco Bay', *Design and Environment*, 5(4), 16–17.

—— (1977), 'Savannah waterfront', *Urban Design*, 8(4), 40–1.

Cowey, A. (1979), 'Urban waterfronts: the forgotten Z in CZM', *National Oceanic and Atmospheric Administration Magazine*, January, 10–13.

—— and Rigby, R. (1979), 'On the waterfront', *Planning*, 45(1), November, 10–13.

Department of Commerce, National Oceanic and Atmospheric Administration, Office of Coastal Zone Management (1980), *Improving your waterfront: a practical guide* (Washington DC: US Government Printing Office).

Department of Fisheries and Oceans (Canada) (1987), *Guide to federal harbours in Ontario* (Burlington: Small Craft Harbours Branch).

Department of the Interior (US), Heritage Conservation and Recreation Service, Water Resources Section (1979), *Urban waterfront revitalization: the role of recreation and heritage*, Volume 1: *Key factors, needs and goals* (Washington DC: US Government Printing Office).

Doubilet S. (1986), 'P/A profile: Cooper, Eckstut Assoc.', *Progressive Architecture*, July, 98–105.

Goldberg, M.A. and Mercer, J. (1986), *The myth of the North American city* (Vancouver: University of British Columbia Press).

Harney, A.L. (ed.) (1979), *Reviving the urban waterfront* (Washington, DC: Partners for Livable Places/National Endowment for the Arts/office of Coastal Zone Management).

Harrison, P. (1979), 'Railway relocation and port dispersion in Canada', in *The management of publicly-owned land in urban areas*, (Paris: Organisation for Economic Cooperation and Development).

Hershman, M.J. *et al* (1979), *Under new management: port growth and emerging coastal management programs* (Seattle: University of Washington Press).

Hodge, G. (1980), 'On the waterfront: new construction threatens Kingston's lakeside', *Canadian Heritage*, August, 6–8.

Holdsworth, D. (ed.) (1985), *Reviving Main Street* (Toronto: University of Toronto Press/Heritage Canada Foundation).

Kalman, H. (1984), 'This elevator is coming down', *Canadian Heritage*, February–March, 18–24.

Land (1980a), 'Plans completed for Lonsdale Quay', *Land*, (Environment Canada) 1(1), 3.

—— (1980b), 'Window on the St Lawrence', *Land*, 1(2), 4.

—— (1986), 'Vancouver landscape changes under Expo 86', *Land*, 7(1), 10.

—— (1987), 'Facelift for Toronto's railway lands', *Land*, 8(1), 1–2.

Lands Directorate (1985), *Canada's federal lands* (Ottawa: Environment Canada).

Le Hénaff, A. (1986), *Administration and management of federal marine facilities and lands in Canada* (Ottawa: Environment Canada, Lands Directorate, Working Paper No. 49).

Ley, D. (1986/7), 'Gentrification: a ten-year overview', *City Magazine*, 9(1), 12–19.

Lindgren, E. (1984), 'Mixed use: rebuilding a waterfront', *Canadian Architect*, June, 20–9.

Lomax, L. (1948), *San Antonio's River* (Texas: San Antonio, The Naylor Company).

London, M. (1982), 'On the waterfront: the fight for Montreal's Vieux-Port', *Canadian Heritage*, December, 20–3.

McCuaig, J.D. *et al* (1981), *The land-use impacts of small-craft harbours: a preliminary investigation* (Ottawa: Environment Canada, Lands Directorate, Working Paper No. 11).

McDougall, T. (1984), 'How John Fiske helped save the waterfront', *Canadian Heritage*, August–September, 37–9.

Merrens, R. (1980), *Urban waterfront redevelopment in North America: an annotated bibliography* (Toronto: University of Toronto/York University, Joint Program in Transportation, Research Report No. 66).

Ministry of Citizenship and Culture (Ontario) (1987), *Heritage: giving our past a future* (Toronto: MCC).

Ministry of Municipal Affairs (Ontario) (1987), *Urban waterfronts: planning and development* (Toronto: Community Improvements Series Volume 4).

National Research Council (US), Committee on Urban Waterfront Lands (1980), *Urban waterfront lands* (Washington DC: National Academy of Sciences).

Petrillo, J. (1987), 'Small city waterfront restoration', *Coastal Management*, 15, 197–212.

Progressive Architecture (1988), 'Citations' (including Burlington, Vermont waterfront/main street and Mission bay, San Francisco waterfront/railyards revitalisation), *Progressive Architecture*, January, 128–36.

Schreiner, J. (1987), 'The Port of Vancouver', *Canadian Geographic*, August/September, 10–20.

Shack, J. (1986), 'Cultivating a place-story', *Canadian Architect*, October, 20–7.

Souchotte, S. (1987), 'Thinking North', *Canadian Heritage*, February–March, 20–7.

Tunbridge, J.E. (1987), 'Conserving the naval heritage: its role in the revitalisation of North American urban waterfronts', in *Urban conservation: international contrasts* (Portsmouth Polytechnic, Department of Geography, Occasional Paper No. 7, 14–24).

Ward, E.N. (1986), *Heritage conservation – the built environment* (Ottawa: Environment Canada, Lands Directorate, Working Paper No. 44).

Warren, R. (1979), 'The role of cities in managing the urban coast', *Coastal Zone Management Journal*, 6(2–3), 125–33.

Wiseman, C. (1987), 'A vision with a message: Battery Park City, New York City', *Architectural Record*, March, 112–21.

Woodbridge, S. (1982), 'Granville Island, Vancouver: new goods in old tins', *Progressive Architecture*, November, 102–9.

6 Redevelopment on the North American water-frontier: the case of Toronto

Gene Desfor, Michael Goldrick and Roy Merrens

Introduction

In the 1950s, throughout North America, traditionally important uses of waterfront land for industrial, warehousing and transportation purposes were declining. The scene at the water's edge was increasingly characterised by disused sites and obvious signs of abandonment. Although a handful of urban waterfronts was beginning to receive a little attention, there was no substantial impetus for redevelopment from politicians, planners, developers, or citizenry. During the 1960s, however, waterfront redevelopments got underway in a number of places in the United States, beginning with Boston. In Canada, where decay and disuse had been less prevalent, new initiatives were also evident in at least a few of cityports in the 1960s. Subsequently, during the 1970s, waterfront redevelopment projects and highly visible achievements became more widespread, in both Canada and the United States.

By the mid-1980s, some degree of redevelopment was ubiquitous on North American urban waterfronts, and the process was well-advanced in many of them. The popular media were full of news reports and feature stories about waterfront redevelopments in particular places, generally hailing them as renewal, revitalisation, revival, or rejuvenation. Buffalo sought to emulate Baltimore's waterfront, just as boosters of Liverpool's waterfront had identified Boston as the model for Merseyside. Annual waterfront festivals were being celebrated in many places. The allegedly arresting sights and sounds of the new waterfront era were being proclaimed in tourist brochures. And waterfront maps and guides were being prepared and distributed to help citizenry and tourists alike discover the much-touted delights of the new-found land at the water's edge.

In the 1980s, too, some voices began to raise questions about the course of contemporary waterfront redevelopment. 'Tugs, Barges Battling Quiche and Fern Bars' was how a headline writer in the *Wall Street Journal* put it in 1985. The sameness of what was being created on urban waterfronts was deplored by some, as they drew attention to the replication of key components of the new scene on waterfront after waterfront. Questions were articulated about other features of waterfront redevelopment: over-development, inhibited public access, and the disappearance of the 'working waterfront' began to be perceived as problems warranting attention and remedial policies.

The course of this contemporary phase of waterfront redevelopment over two or three decades has been accompanied by the appearance of a diverse literature pertaining to this or that aspect of the process (Merrens, 1980). Planners, developers, engineers, politicians, consultants, architects and others have commented upon various aspects of waterfront redevelopment in general, or have scrutinized its results in particular places, or have proposed specific waterfront redevelopment plans and projects. And there is probably no waterfront town or city in North America that cannot point to some documentary evidence of its achievements in, or at least its hopes for, encouraging redevelopment along its waterfront. The amount and the diversity of the literature is scarcely surprising and simply reflects both the ubiquity of the phenomenon and the fact that it has been with us, in its latest form, for over a quarter of a century.

What is remarkable, however, is the paucity of scholarly work in this bulky literature on urban waterfront redevelopment in North America. Few scholars have paid much attention to what has been happening on urban waterfronts. The Waterfront Center in Washington, DC, has been mounting an annual waterfront conference every year since 1983. These forums to review waterfront issues have been remarkably successful, as is apparent from their published legacy of volumes of edited proceedings (see, for example, Breen and Rigby, 1986). But these occasions are not designed by or for scholars, and few have participated in them. And, to date, nothing has been organised – either in the United States or in Canada – comparable to the assembly of scholars in England at the seminar on Waterfront Development and the Cityport Economy held at the University of Southampton in November, 1987.

The few scholarly studies of North American waterfronts that have been published are, for the most part, restricted in scope in two important ways: first, because they are a-historical, paying little or no attention to the longevity and constancy of urban waterfront redevelopment, and showing little or no concern either with the roots of the current phase of redevelopment or with its relationship to antecedent waves of redevelopment; secondly, because they are spatially blinkered, confining themselves by and large to the spatial limits of the waterfront, and ignoring critical relationships between waterfronts and their urban settings. It is perhaps because of these restrictions that they have been more descriptive than analytical, and have usually not gone much beyond explaining the current phase in terms of pollution clean-up efforts that are seemingly creating healthier water on urban waterfronts, thereby attracting redevelopment.

The analysis of waterfront redevelopment presented in this chapter represents something of a departure from other North American studies.

The assumption in this study is that current urban waterfront redevelopment in North America can only be understood as a function of structural economic change. The analysis is approached in terms of two key variables: the temporal and the spatial. One particular North American cityport is examined in terms of these two larger perspectives.

The *temporal* dimension of waterfront redevelopment is the more difficult of the two perspectives to present, because the current phase represents only the most recent manifestation of a constant and long-continued process of waterfront change. The presentation here, while not an historical study, will try to treat the current phase of redevelopment dynamically. This will be done in two ways: first, in summary fashion, by presenting the current phase in the context of previous waves of redevelopment; and secondly, by reviewing in more detail the progress of the current phase over the past quarter-century it has been underway.

An appropriate *spatial* perspective requires that the urban waterfront be viewed as an integral part of the entire urban region which surrounds it. Current waterfront redevelopment cannot be understood in isolation from the city. Rather, it can best be comprehended as a function of structural economic changes and processes at work in the larger metropolitan area of which it is a part.

The term 'water-frontier' is used in the title of this chapter quite deliberately. The word 'frontier' usually evokes an image of North America's preoccupation with spatial expansion and social displacement: the frontier mythology has for long centred around the notion that rugged, self-sufficient pioneers played the major role in the development of wilderness regions. This is not the meaning intended here. There is a quite different interpretation of the contemporary urban frontier, one which regards it as a spatial economy in which expansion and displacement are generated less by pioneering individuals than by financial institutions, land-development companies (often railways), and the state and its agencies. It is this alternative and less traditional view of development on frontiers that is being evoked here. More specifically, the analysis in this chapter can be placed in the context of the current debate on gentrification, the frontier, and the restructuring of urban space, a debate recently joined by Smith and Williams in their edited collection of studies on *Gentrification of the city* (1986).

The water-frontier analysed in this chapter is that of Toronto. It is impossible yet to be entirely certain that the most recent phase of redevelopment in Toronto, which has now been going on for almost three decades, is typical of the experience of most North American cities. Toronto's changing waterfront does seem to display redevelopment qualities found elsewhere in North America, but firm conclusions about its validity as a model will have to await similar analyses of the pattern of redevelopment in other places. Meanwhile, however, Toronto represents a particularly appropriate case study because its port and waterfront have recently been subjected to more scrutiny than that of virtually any other North American city. In the past decade or so, over a dozen studies of facets of the development of Toronto's port and waterfront have appeared, embracing topics ranging from the major redevelopment scheme launched in 1912 (O'Mara, 1976) to the causes and consequences of the decline of port industry in more recent decades (Norcliffe, 1981). The findings of some of these studies will be drawn upon here.[1]

The changing city and waterfront redevelopment

Toronto was formally established as a town in 1793, when the name 'York' was bestowed by John Graves Simcoe, the first Lieutenant-Governor of Upper Canada, upon a promontory-sheltered harbour on the north shore of Lake Ontario. Earlier, the location had been the site of a small trading post, sometimes known as Fort Toronto. Simcoe wanted the new imperial base to be both an effective military garrison and a thriving commercial centre. Its initial growth, however, derived mainly from its role as the seat of government of Upper Canada, comprising a small urban community of soldiers and government officials, their families, and those who served and supplied their needs. Not until the second quarter of the nineteenth century did it really emerge as an important commercial port town. In short, its early history illustrates a typical component of the pattern of urbanisation in North America, with imperial footholds becoming commercial towns prospering with the spread of hinterland settlement (Careless, 1984, 19–41).

During the first half of the nineteenth century, the waterfront of Toronto reflected its role as an emerging commercial port town. Wharves, slips, and piers were built to accommodate increasing numbers of vessels, carrying cargoes destined either for the local market or for transhipment. Water lots were granted to private individuals, who used them for residential or commercial purposes, although some efforts were made to preserve public access and use of the waterfront, and an esplanade was proposed to serve as a carriage drive and public walk.

During the latter half of the nineteenth century, Toronto's waterfront experienced its first major wave of redevelopment. The waterfront changes were partly a result of global forces, such as the growth of industry and the emergence of new shipping patterns and transportation technology, and partly a result of events particular to Canada and Toronto. Two conspicuous components of change in this new phase of waterfront redevelopment were industry and railways.

The industrial presence reflected the fact that the last three decades of the nineteenth century were the beginning of the industrial era for many Canadian cities. During this period, Toronto experienced extraordinary growth in industrial activity: between 1871 and 1891, the number of manufacturing enterprises rose from 530 to 2,401, an average increase of more than 22 per cent per year (Careless, 1984, 109). A notable increase was also apparent in relative terms: Toronto's share of the industrial workforce in Southern Ontario grew from 10 per cent in 1871, to 25 per cent in 1891, and 34 per cent in 1901 (Spelt, 1973, 58).

The second and more conspicuous element in the new waterfront landscape in the latter half of the nineteenth century was the railways. Their appearance on the waterfront was testimony to Toronto's challenge to Montreal's control of the old commercial order. Essential to this challenge was the development of a system of railway transportation to undermine the port of Montreal's monopoly in shipping interior staples across the Atlantic to Great Britain. Railways were means for establishing radically different patterns of trade. Toronto's bid to establish a new trading order rested on the construction of a railway network designed to funnel raw materials into the city, to open up new market areas, and to concentrate distribution services, business, and financial power in Toronto.

Major elements in the new railway network were the tracks and terminals built in Toronto itself, particularly those located on the southern edge of the city between the core of the historic urban area and the shore of Lake Ontario. Along this strip, the railway companies inserted their presence, either by acquiring existing land or by filling in the edge of the lake to create and then occupy new land. The imprint of the railways was the dominant motif of the waterfront redevelopment era of the latter half of the nineteenth century. Because of this invasion, and the subsequent ancillary growth of industry and warehousing close by the tracks and terminals, the waterfront's potential as a public amenity was effectively destroyed.

During the first two decades of the twentieth century, a variety of factors initiated another new era of large-scale waterfront redevelopment (O'Mara, 1976; Desfor, 1988). Late in the nineteenth century and early in the twentieth, Toronto's position as a financial and commercial centre had strengthened. At this time the most effective organisation in the city's business community was the Toronto Board of Trade. Seeking ways to erode the primacy of Montreal and to enlarge Toronto's role, the Board promoted all developments that would expand Toronto's trading hinterland and tighten control over its area (Stanford, 1974, 74–78, 102–103). The Board was particularly concerned with transportation improvements, and was the major force behind a new approach to Toronto's port and waterfront (Schaeffer, 1981).

The new approach was enshrined in the Canadian government's legislation establishing the Toronto Harbour Commission in 1911 as a local agency within the national framework for port and harbour administration. Ownership and control of the entire waterfront was concentrated in the hands of this new commission, which was empowered to develop it, not merely as a harbour, but also for industrial and commercial uses. The

Commission was to be much more than the harbour-minding authority signified by its name. With broad powers to control land, with extensive land holdings *ab initio*, and with the opportunity of creating a land bank through the mechanism of landfill, the Commission quickly began to function as a land-development agency (Merrens, 1988).

In 1912, acting on the basis of a consensus which had emerged over the previous thirty years or so among various interest groups, the Harbour Commissioners published a comprehensive Waterfront Development Plan (Toronto Harbour Commissioners, 1912). The Plan represented a large-scale refashioning of the waterfront along its entire length for port, industrial, transportation, and recreation purposes. A key part of the scheme was systematic lake-filling all along the water's edge. The net effect of the 1912 Plan – and related agreements made between the Commission and the city council – was the creation of a new waterfront, located south of the previous one, much of which had been taken over by the railways by the end of the nineteenth century.

The Harbour Commission and various civic organisations promoted the location of industry on the waterfront, and especially on the 400 hectares of reclaimed marsh in the eastern section of the waterfront (see Fig. 6.1, which shows waterfront industry existing in 1915, in the foreground, and marshland being reclaimed for new industrial sites, in the background). Here, as elsewhere in the city, the First World War stimulated the growth

Figure 6.1 *The eastern end of Toronto's waterfront in 1915: industrial land use and reclamation for industrial development*

of manufacturing. By 1929, the Commission had created about 182 hectares for industrial sites and had leased or sold 52 hectares to 28 firms, amounting to 29 per cent of this available land (Langton, c. 1928). While the Commission's industrial lands were probably not fully utilised, they were nevertheless the site of significant industrial activity. Grain elevators, ship builders, coal processors and storage, ice companies, metal fabricators, sewage treatment, fishing companies, construction companies, oil tank storage and gas companies all were located on the waterfront.

By the end of the 1940s, the major goals of the 1912 Waterfront Plan had been largely achieved. By then, the wave of waterfront redevelopment for industrial purposes had spent its force, although widespread redevelopment of the waterfront for new purposes would not begin for at least another decade (Fig. 6.2 testifies to the lingering importance of the presence of industrial and transportation uses as late as 1955). The origins of this most recent and ongoing era of waterfront redevelopment can be discerned in changes that were becoming evident in the city as a whole, and especially in the central area of the city.

Figure 6.2 *Toronto's central waterfront, including Railway Lands, in 1955*

After the Second World War, the Toronto region attracted substantial growth in terms of population and economic activity (City of Toronto, 1974). By the 1950s, two facets of this growth were becoming increasingly evident. One was the rapid suburbanisation of population and employment. Suburbs were not new, but the rate and extent of suburbanisation were unprecedented, characterised by the rapid transformation of farmland into housing estates, schools, industrial parks and shopping centres. A second feature of the 1950s growth era was the declining importance, within the central city, of industry and associated rail and water transportation.

Both tendencies seemed to challenge the traditional dominance of the city of Toronto in the metropolitan region. City politicians were alarmed, fearing a decline of their central city such as was occuring in many urban areas in the United States in the late 1950s and 1960s. To counter what was perceived to be a serious threat, a new Official Plan was prepared in the mid-1960s and formally adopted in 1969. The Plan was essentially an aggressive effort to promote more commercial development in the central city, along with residential accommodation for the anticipated middle- and upper-middle-class commercial labour force.

The centralisation strategies adopted as a result of the Plan had unanticipated political consequences. The intrusion of high-rise apartments into low-density neighbourhoods, the loss of family housing, the encroachment of giant commercial and institutional buildings on residential areas, and the threatened or actual destruction of middle-class neighbourhoods by superhighways were among the new developments that led to a voter revolt. In a civic election late in 1972, most of the pro-development old-guard Toronto aldermen were replaced by a reform-minded group.

The new council had a clear mandate to reorient policy for the downtown area. The aims it adopted were: the stopping of extensive redevelopment of established downtown residential neighbourhoods; the encouragement of the construction of housing in mixed-use buildings in the Central Area; the preservation of the industrial zones on two sides of the Central Area; and the support of expansion of commercial activity – but only to the extent that it was compatible with the transportation system's capacity (Fig. 6.3). While the 1969 Official Plan had been designed to expand the Central Area as a place for employment activities and to separate residential areas, the new reform council's policies were aimed at limiting growth in the Central Area and diversifying its land uses.

The reform-minded council was responsible for developing a new Official Plan for the Central Area[2] (City of Toronto, 1978). According to this new plan (eventually adopted in 1978), Toronto's expected economic growth, particularly in terms of commercial activity, was to be accommodated by further intensification within the core area and by adopting deconcentration strategies which would redirect excess growth to regional sub-centres. The Plan recognised that there would be strong pressure from an expanding economy to make room for new commercial, institutional, and residential activity. By intensifying land use within the existing Central Area, some of the demand created by the expanding economic activity could be satisfied. Other development, requiring transportation facilities in

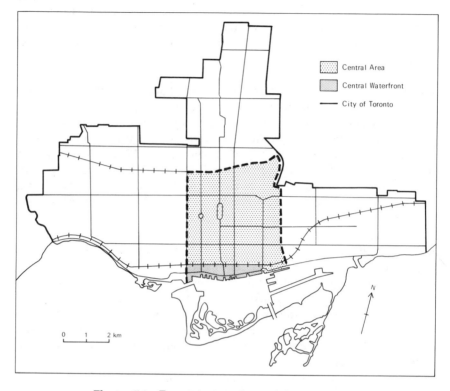

Figure 6.3   *Toronto's waterfront and central area*

excess of the system's capacity, would be directed to the regional sub-centres. In this way the reform council intended to seal off residential neighbourhoods surrounding the Central Area so as to protect them from intensification and also to protect adjoining industrial areas from commercial encroachment and institutional expansion.

The new Official Plan had the effect of opening development possibilities on that side of the Central Area which had no neighbourhoods or organised interest groups. This was the southern side, which is, of course, the waterfront. At least initially, the Plan largely ignored the redevelopment potential of this vast tract. With minor modifications, the existing industrial designation of the waterfront lands was simply reaffirmed. But far-reaching structural change was gathering momentum in the city and would soon alter these land uses.

Changes in the economic structure of the Toronto region reflect the continuation of a long-term trend toward concentration in the Central Area of high-order, information-based services. By 1981, trade, finance, insurance, real estate, and community, business and personal services employed two-thirds of the Toronto Census Metropolitan Area labour force (City of Toronto, 1986). Massive relocation of corporate headquarters to the central city area has centralised many of the functions that control corporate operations throughout the country (Goddard, 1985). Thus, for example, more than 39 per cent of the top 500 Canadian companies and over half of the largest financial institutions have head offices in the Toronto area (*Toronto Star*, 21 November 1987); of domestic corporations that relocated somewhere in Canada between 1970 and 1982, Toronto was the preferred destination for more of them than for all other cities combined (Semple and Green, 1983); and in terms of non-American multinationals, Toronto is the fifth most important corporate headquarters city in the world (*Toronto Star*, 9 September 1986). To illustrate the point in a slightly different way, 48 per rent of the total Canadian computer capacity was located in Toronto in 1983. The next largest concentration was in Ottawa, with slightly less than 12 per cent (Hepworth, 1986).

The occupational structure has also shifted dramatically toward clerical, managerial, scientific, technical, and service categories. Between 1971 and 1981, managerial and administrative employment grew by 158 per cent; and the number of scientific and technical workers increased by 75 per cent in the same period. The two occupational groups together accounted for about one-third of the growth in the employed labour force (City of Toronto, 1987, 9). The changes in both industrial and occupational structure highlight the growth of services in the economy of Toronto. About 55 per cent of service-sector jobs entail the production, processing, and distribution of information. This has led to the characterisation of the Toronto region as an 'information-based service economy' (*ibid.*, 10).

The shift from traditional to information- and service-based industries has produced an affluent white-collar labour force. Preliminary research suggests that a significant proportion of these workers prefer a downtown residential location. This is not surprising. Because of the constraints of the 1978 Plan, with its bias against redevelopment and intensification of established residential neighbourhoods adjacent to the Central Area, the growing demand for inner-city housing was satisfied in alternative ways. First, extensive gentrification occurred in neighbourhoods adjacent to the Central Area, with considerable working-class family housing being renovated for upper-middle-class families and childless households. From 1976 to 1985, almost 17,000 housing units were converted from multiple unit to single occupancy use, while a further 8,000 units were lost through the deintensification of multiple unit properties to contain fewer, larger and, probably, more expensive units (City of Toronto, 1986, 78). Secondly, the supply of downtown housing is also being partially satisfied by the construction of expensive condominiums within the Central Area. The 1978 Plan contemplated the development of 20,000 units of this character by 1986, and the target was actually exceeded by over 10,300 units in the period, with 57 per cent of them clustered in the core of the Central Area (*ibid.*, 75–77). Thirdly, new Central-Area housing was being located on the waterfront. The essentially unsealed, southern side of the Central Area represented a wide-open frontier, providing developers with a golden opportunity to build for the emerging high-income housing market.

Institutions mediating waterfront redevelopment

The impact of the southward-moving market forces was mediated by several major institutions. Three of them in particular controlled most of the land along the central waterfront. Two of these institutions, the Toronto Harbour Commission and the national railways, were facing the decline side of the current round of structural change – the obsolescence of the port, railways, and industry on the waterfront. The third, the Harbour-front Corporation, was created by the government of Canada in 1972 with the express purpose of protecting the waterfront from commercial exploit-ation. (Figure 6.4 shows the location of the lands controlled by Harbour-front and by the railways; much of the rest of the waterfront north and east of the Inner Harbour is, or once was, controlled by the Toronto Harbour Commission.)

The Toronto Harbour Commission is responsible for port operations and land development. Since it was established in 1911, the lease or sale of its waterfront lands primarily for industrial purposes has been the tradi-

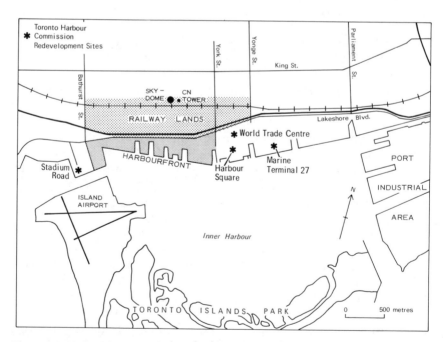

Figure 6.4 *Redevelopment on Toronto's waterfront: Harbourfront Railway Lands and Harbour Commission sites*

tional foundation of the Commission's financial and institutional independence (O'Mara, 1984). As has been suggested, it was the transformation of waterfront lands and waterlots for industrial uses that characterised the wave of redevelopment immediately prior to the current one.

Serious difficulties faced the Harbour Commission's port and development operations in the mid-1960s and early 1970s. The Commission's operating revenue did not cover expenses, and a debt began to accumulate. In the early 1970s the debt had reached $10 million, and increased steadily until 1984, when it peaked at about $33 million. The debt originated from a number of the Commission's capital-investment decisions (Toronto Harbour Commissioners, 1984), and it was enlarged by declining shipping revenue and mounting interest charges. The Commission had invested heavily in new port facilities for the opening of the St Lawrence Seaway in 1959, but the increase in shipping due to the Seaway's opening was not to last long. Port tonnage more than halved between 1969 and 1974, despite the Commission's long-range capital development programme in the late 1960s. Furthermore, industry migrated to new locations or simply closed down, reducing the value of the Commission's industrial lands. By the mid-1960s, these difficulties led the Commission to revise its development strategy. Instead of industrial uses in the central waterfront, it now began to promote residential and commercial development on its lands lying closest to the downtown area (Toronto Harbour Commissioners, 1968).

The Commission's first major effort in this new redevelopment strategy was the sale of a prime waterfront site that became available when a steamship line moved to another city. The sale involved a three-party agreement between the Commission, the city, and a private developer. After considerable negotiations the Harbour Commission completed the redevelopment agreement in 1964. Since then a hotel and a number of residential towers, called Harbour Square, have been built on the site (Fig. 6.4). Commercial high-rises, as well as more residential towers, are currently being built or are in the final planning stages. Together these buildings constitute a conspicuous wall along the very core of the central waterfront.

During the 1970s, the Harbour Commission's position on redevelopment shifted drastically, but only temporarily. For much of the decade, the Commission played no major role in redeveloping the waterfront, mainly because a reform-oriented majority of Commissioners placed a freeze on land sales for several years. By the 1980s, however, with new pro-development Commissioners dominating its Board once again, the Commission returned to the business of central waterfront development. It launched several major projects (Toronto Harbour Commissioners, 1986; World Trade Centre Toronto, 1987). The most dramatic has been the World Trade Centre, on which construction is about to begin. First announced in 1984, the scheme was approved by the city council in

December 1986. It occupies three hectares and comprises three 26-storey office towers, two residential towers with luxury condominiums of 25 and 32 storeys, and several low-rise connecting buildings. The Harbour Commission's other current redevelopment projects are located on the eastern and western ends of the central waterfront (Fig. 6.4).

The second institution that mediated the southward-moving market for development was Harbourfront. This public agency was established in October 1972, when the government of Canada set aside 35 hectares of prime central waterfront land as an urban park (Fig. 6.4). The government had quietly started the process of acquiring the land from the Harbour Commission and from private owners. The new agency, Harbourfront, was charged with administering these waterfront lands as an urban park. Not surprisingly, some viewed the 'gift' of the proposed park as a pre-election ploy, especially since the governing Liberal Party was losing support in the Toronto area and a general election was just a few weeks away (Toronto *Globe and Mail*, 17 and 18 October 1972; *Toronto Star*, 17 and 18 October 1972).

For its part, the government emphasised a somewhat different motive for setting aside the 35 hectares as a park, insisting that it was moving to avert a new threat to the waterfront. This was symbolised by the beginnings of construction on the first buildings of the towering high-rise redevelopment project, Harbour Square, just to the east of the newly announced park (Fig. 6.5). The government insisted that Harbour Square represented the kind of high-rise development that could soon be replicated elsewhere along the central waterfront. The government's avowed and much-publicised intention was to save the waterfront for the citizens of Toronto by forestalling the construction of a 'ceramic curtain' or wall of high-rise structures along the shoreline (*Toronto Star*, 17 October 1972).

The first five or six years of redevelopment efforts at Harbourfront were marked by indecision and an apparent lack of direction. While the initial objective of the government of Canada was to develop the site as an urban park, Harbourfront had difficulty in realising this mandate. After a number of years of strained relations between politicians and planners representing different levels of government, some largely unsuccessful public participation planning programmes, various fruitless attempts to produce a consensus on the objective of development, and reorganisations of Harbourfront itself, the institution was transformed into a Crown Corporation to enable it to operate more effectively as a developer. In 1978, the new Harbourfront Corporation brought forward a generalised plan favouring a mix of land uses with commercial and residential development set among a variety of recreational facilities. The acceptance of Harbourfront's 1978 strategy marks an about-face from an initial concept of developing an urban park, to a notion of extending the 'urban fabric' to the waterfront (Harbourfront Corporation, 1978).

Harbourfront's 1978 proposed *Development Framework* was based on

Figure 6.5 *Redevelopment at Harbour Square, in the core of Toronto's central waterfront, in 1973*

the Corporation being able to achieve financial self-sufficiency. By 1978, it was clear that enormous expense was required to realise the new plan's objectives. Clearance of the site's industrial buildings and the reconstruction of the wharves were expected to be costly. More expensive, though, was the provision of roads, piped services, and other infrastructure to support the development contemplated in the mixed-use plan. Furthermore, Harbourfront had created and was expected to maintain its extensive but expensive arts and recreational programmes, which by then enjoyed considerable public support. In 1986, for example, $11 million were required to fund programmes embracing 4,000 public events (*Toronto Star*, 24 September 1987). The magnitude of these costs and the unattractive prospect that a continuing subsidy for capital and operating expenses might precipitate a loss of enthusiasm on the part of the government led Harbourfront staff to suggest that a new strategy aimed at financial self-sufficiency would be appropriate.

The new strategy for development, as well as the detailed plans for its implementation, were all in place by the end of 1980. According to 1984 plans, almost 65,000 square metres of residential, retail, and office space development were contemplated. Of this total, just about 60 per cent was for residential uses (Harbourfront Corporation, 1984). Harbourfront's plans had been approved by the government and by the city council in a special agreement that provided for the lease of sites to private developers at prices which would repay the site preparation, infrastructure and programming costs. The economics of the situation ensured that in order to generate the required revenue, development would take the form of high-density residential schemes, luxury condominium projects, and expensive commercial and retail space. The current price range for a two-bedroom unit at Queen's Quay Terminal, the first major building completed in Harbourfront and the one which contains the most expensive condominiums, begins at $400,000 and goes to well above $1,000,000. By the late 1980s, residential accommodation had become a prominent use of land along the shoreline (see Fig. 6.6).

By 1986, the rapid rate and increasing amount of new development at Harbourfront was beginning to generate public controversy. While the chairperson of Harbourfront insisted that there was still 'too much green' at the site (*Toronto Star*, 3 July 1986), critics deplored what they perceived to be a 'quayside concrete curtain' (*Globe and Mail*, 15 November 1986). In 1987, while a moratorium was briefly imposed on new construction at a few project sites, several governmental reviews of the development plans were conducted. While the results of the re-assessments are not yet entirely clear, it seems as though the only major change may come from pressure

Figure 6.6 *New marina, residential and office construction at Toronto's Harbourfront in 1986*

on Harbourfront by the city's Parks Commissioner to provide a few more hectares of on-site park space.

The third mediating institutional group comprised Canada's two giant national railway systems, anadian National and Canadian Pacific. Between them they controlled about eighty hectares of rail yards lying between the Central Area and Harbourfront (the area is now known as the Railway Lands – see Figures 6.2 and 6.4), a tract that represents the real-estate legacy of the nineteenth-century invasion of the waterfront by a large number of smaller railway companies. The railways were interested in converting these lands to commercial and residential uses because their value for rail purposes had declined sharply. The conversion would enable the owners to capitalise on the development potential of the strategically located site by capturing a share of the growing demand for office and residential space in the Central Area. While the objectives of the proponents were clear, the scale, timing, and character of the scheme made its realisation problematic. The strategies adopted by the principal actors had a substantial effect upon the redevelopment of this massive tract of waterfront land.

In 1968, the railway companies brought forward a grandiose redevelopment scheme, known as Metro Centre. This was to replace, gradually, their marshalling yards with commercial and residential development. Its main components included a multi-mode transportation terminal, a commercial precinct to accommodate 60,000 workers, an area devoted to communications industries, and a vast residential community encompassing about three-fifths of the site (City of Toronto, 1983). The scheme moved through the approval process, beginning with endorsement by the pro-development city council in 1971, but it ran into some problems. One was a rapid rise in interest rates which discouraged development; another was a less-than-enthusiastic response from the reform-minded council. The majority of the reform aldermen recognised in Metro Centre the kind of extravagant growth that it had been elected to curtail. For these reasons the scheme was delayed and finally abandoned in 1975.

In the early 1980s the railways, in conjunction with city planners, came forward with a new proposal for the Railway Lands. At $2 billion it was the largest redevelopment scheme in North America at the time. With the Central Area Plan having been approved only two years earlier, it might be supposed that a proposal of this magnitude would have been dismissed immediately. But it was not, for several reasons. First, less reform-minded individuals had gradually returned to the city council. In part, this reflected the complacency of activists who in 1972 had ousted the earlier pro-development council (Goldrick, 1978). The activists believed their neighbourhoods had won the protection of the 1978 Central Area Plan and their interest in civic politics waned. Furthermore, the Railway Lands proposal did not have a resident population to mobilise against the scheme.

As the new proposal took shape, however, its possible consequences for inner-city residential neighbourhoods gradually became apparent.

Both the railways and city planners maintained that the scheme 'followed on the goals and objectives adopted in the 1978 [Central Area] Plan' (City of Toronto, 1985a). Public debate soon revealed discrepancies and what came to be viewed by critics as major deficiencies. The Plan made provision for the construction of about 1.4 million square metres of commercial space. This was equivalent to about one-half of all similar existing space in the financial core of the Central Area. It was also twice the space specified for the site in the 1978 Central Area Plan. Not only did this appear to undermine the Plan's deconcentration policies, but it also appeared to invite demands for the construction of more transportation corridors through the inner residential neighbourhoods to connect the Central Area and suburbs. Furthermore, the scheme appeared to skimp on housing. To critics, there was too little of it, it was too expensive, and it was planned at excessive densities. Even the city's Planning Commissioner reinforced this impression when he was reported to have stated that, 'The good news is that there's housing downtown. The bad news is that no one can afford it' (Toronto *Globe and Mail*, 5 May 1984).

These criticisms greatly concerned the proponents, who had no wish to see their second attempt founder as the first had done. For this reason they developed a special interest in a much-publicised and popular amenity which had been proposed for the emerging 'bourgeois playground' of central Toronto. To complement new opera and concert halls, theatres, elaborate public buildings, Harbourfront, a convention centre, and the like, a giant 55,000-seat sports stadium had been proposed. The cost of the facility, currently under construction, was recently estimated to be about $383 million (*Toronto Star*, 28 October 1987). Financing and locational problems threatened the Skydome, as it has become known, at about the same time as opposition appeared to be mounting against the Railway Lands scheme. In an unexpected and bold move, one of the proponents, Canadian National, proposed not only to provide a site for the stadium (see Fig. 6.4) at no charge but also to spend $25 to $30 million for ancillary roads and other infrastructure associated with the building.

The proposal served the interests of both the Skydome proponents and the railways. For the former, it seemed to assure the financial feasibility of the Skydome. From the standpoint of the developers, the offer achieved two objectives. First, it promised to impart activity and identity to a relatively isolated and hard-to-market site on the Railway Lands. It would achieve this because it was designed as an urban stadium; that is, a mixed-use structure housing a variety of traffic-generating uses such as a hotel, trade show facilities, and retail and commercial space. Second, and more important, at least in the short term, the offer of free land locked together the stadium financing and approval of the overall site plan. Canadian National stipulated that its offer was contingent upon expeditious passage through the planning approval process of the entire 80-hectare Railway Lands scheme. Critics of the scheme were faced down by its proponents, who, with a steady eye on the substantial public approval for it, frequently threatened to withdraw their support for the stadium and scuttle the entire project if the overall plan were modified (Toronto *Globe and Mail*, 22 July 1986; 29 August 1986).

The strategy was successful. Undoubtedly, a favourable political climate in the city council, and a public uninterested in the Railway Lands proposal as a whole, increased the odds of the proposal gaining planning approval. Community activists challenged the overall plan, but they were not able to mobilise strong public opposition to it, even after tactically supporting the construction of the Skydome. Furthermore, the massive allocation of commercial space to the scheme was not obviously threatening deconcentration policies: in the economic boom of the mid-1980s, regional sub-centres were thriving with plenty of developments to house 'back-office' and other functions (City of Toronto, 1986). Consequently, the councils of municipalities in which sub-centres were located could not be mobilised to provide the opposition to the Railway Lands scheme that might have been expected by its critics. At the conclusion of the protracted planning approval process, the solicitor for Canadian National could say, 'We're pleased with the decision in its entirety' (*Toronto Star*, 12 September 1986).

The introduction of the Skydome to strengthen the bargaining hand of the proponents had important consequences for the composition of the final development package. Its accommodation on the site did not lead to a compensatory reduction of displaced land uses. Rather, development was simply compressed on other parts of the site, increasing overall densities.

Conclusion

The foregoing analysis of waterfront development in Toronto leads to three conclusions.[3] The first has to do with the historical nature of the process of waterfront development. Current changes on the Toronto waterfront have been remarkable even in the accelerated timescale of contemporary urban restructuring. The rapidity of the process has led many to describe it as 'unprecedented' and 'unique'. But from even a cursory review of the waterfront's earlier history, it is clear that the present wave of change, while certainly dramatic, is simply another phase in a long series of adaptations. In little more than a quarter of a century, the waterfront – formerly characterised by predominantly industrial and transport land uses – has become a place primarily accommodating services and residences. In the case of Toronto, the transformation has been magnified and accelerated by a simultaneous and serendipitous conjuncture of several major development forces: most notably the revenue needs of major waterfront landowners, service industry expansion, and neighbourhood protectionism.

The second conclusion is that the evolution of waterfront lands is best understood as part of the broader political economy of the city. In the case under review, a waterfront industrial zone lay under-utilised until its revalorisation occurred. A variety of political and economic factors was responsible. Most fundamentally, the process of structural economic change resulted in Toronto's economy becoming dominated by information processing and service provision. When the spatial consequences of this transformation threatened to engulf residential enclaves of the powerful middle class, new exclusionary regulations were adopted by the local government. These tended to generate demand for new commercial space in the open water-frontier, rapidly inflating land rents to the point at which the construction of high-density, luxury space was economically feasible. Contemporary massive new development on many of the world's water-frontiers is one physical expression of the economic restructuring of capital. Along with such phenomena as gentrification and the discovery in North American suburbia of so-called urban villages (Leinberger and Lockwood, 1986), redevelopment of water-frontiers offers capital a new opportunity for accumulation and also serves to redifferentiate geographical space according to the economic and social needs of the corporate city (Smith, 1986, 15–20).

A profound process of transformation is thus altering the water-frontier's space economy. Change on this frontier involves the establishment of new relationships between a peripheral area with a set of declining activities and a central area with expanding economic forces. One of the development agencies viewed this process as merely extending the urban fabric to the water's edge. Another development company proclaimed that its intention on the waterfront was to redevelop Toronto's 'last frontier'. To us, the frontier analogy seems appropriate because it draws attention to the external forces involved, to the fact that what is happening along the urban waterfront is a reflection of changes in the city itself and, more importantly, of the changing political economy in which the city is located.

The third conclusion is that the details of the market-driven redevelopment of the waterfront, such as its pace, extent, and composition, are mediated by the particularities of the local political system, and the corporate interests of local proprietary institutions. The three institutions investigated in this study exemplify the point.

First, the Toronto Harbour Commission habitually promoted waterfront development as a central strategy in its struggle for financial solvency and institutional independence. Second, while Harbourfront was fumbling for a direction in its early days, it inaugurated a popular but expensive artistic and recreational programme. The programme gave Harbourfront the identity and public support which it needed to justify its existence and to win recognition as an independent political actor. But the cost of maintaining the programme was exorbitant, and Habourfront plunged heavily into a development programme that all but eliminated any chance of achieving the original park and community uses intended for the site. Third, and somewhat different is the case of the Railway Lands. Here, redevelopment was not primarily a vehicle for achieving non-monetary goals. Rather, the railways, public and private alike, simply wanted to maximise the return on their assets. But a variety of factors mediated the pace of planning approvals and the composition of the final development package. The absence of a local residential community, the reappearance of a pro-development council in Toronto, and the shrewd use of the Skydome as a bargaining chip had the effect of expediting planning approval, substantially increasing utilisation of the overall site, vastly increasing housing densities, intensifying commercial development, and increasing pressure for the addition of new transportation facilities. Taken together, the three examples of mediating institutions demonstrate that while waterfront redevelopment is a consequence of deep-seated changes in the space economy of the city, the detailed form and timing of the process is governed by more pragmatic contingencies.

The aim of this chapter has been to explain waterfront redevelopment in one particular North American cityport. The extent to which the case of Toronto is typical must await similar analyses of other cities. But at this time it seems reasonable to speculate that the spatial consequences of economic restructuring to which attention has been drawn in this chapter have far from run their course. Currently, major changes are occurring in the composition of service-based economies such as Toronto. Over time, these changes are likely to have considerable impact on investment opportunities and occupational patterns, which in turn will inevitably affect the function of waterfronts in relation to the overall space economies of cityports.

Notes

1   We gratefully acknowledge the help we have received from Janet Thompson (who corrected and processed draft versions of the manuscript), Annemarie Gallaugher (who edited the manuscript), and Carolyn Gondor and Carol Randall (who drew the maps). Figures 6.1, 6.2 and 6.5 were provided through the courtesy of the Toronto Harbour Commission and Figure 6.6 by Harbourfront Corporation.

2   The Official Plan for the Central Area, adopted in 1978, was technically an amendment to the existing City of Toronto Official Plan of 1969. For purposes of convenience, we use the phrase Central Area Plan as though it were a discrete plan, which it is not.

3   The City's waterfront planning efforts have been virtually ignored in this analysis because we have focused upon them in a separate study. In this companion piece, published in a special issue of *Geoforum* devoted to urban

waterfront issues, the emphasis is placed upon the relationship, or lack of it, between waterfront planning and the praxis of development.

References

Breen, A. and Rigby, D. (eds) (1986), *Urban waterfronts '85: water makes a difference* (Washington, DC: The Waterfront Press).

Careless, J.M.S. (1984), *Toronto to 1918: an illustrated history* (Toronto: James Lorimer).

City of Toronto, Planning Board (1974), *Core area task force: technical appendix* (City of Toronto).

City of Toronto (1978), *Official plan for the City of Toronto planning area part I, amendment number 39* (City of Toronto).

City of Toronto, Planning & Development Department (1981), *Quinquennial review* (City of Toronto).

—— (1983), *Railway lands part II: development concept* (City of Toronto).

—— (1985a), *Railway lands part II: proposals* (City of Toronto).

—— (1985b), *Railway lands part II: final report* (City of Toronto).

—— (1986), *Quinquennial review: overview report* (City of Toronto).

—— (1987), *Quinquennial review: background paper no. 2* (City of Toronto).

Desfor, G. (1988), 'Planning urban waterfront districts: Toronto's Ashbridge's Bay 1889–1910', *Urban History Review*, in press.

Goddard, J.B. *et al* (1985), 'The impact of new information technology on urban and regional structure in Europe', in Thwaites, A.T., and Oakey, R.P. (eds), *The regional economic impact of technological change* (London: Frances Pinter).

Goldrick, M. (1978), 'The anatomy of urban reform in Toronto', *City magazine*, 3, 29–39.

Harbourfront Corporation (1978), *Harbourfront development framework* (Toronto: Harbourfront Corporation).

—— (1984), *A guide to Harbourfront development* (Toronto: Harbourfront Corporation).

Hepworth, M.E. (1986), 'The geography of economic opportunity in the information society', *Information Society Journal*, 4(3), 205–20.

Langton, J.G. (c. 1928), 'Toronto Harbour: its waterfront improvements and industrial advantages' (Toronto: Toronto Harbour Commission Archives, manuscript).

Leinberger, C.B. and Lockwood, C. (1986), 'How business is reshaping America', *The Atlantic*, October, 43–52.

Merrens, R. (1980), *Urban waterfront redevelopment in North America: an annotated bibliography* (Toronto: York University/University of Toronto Joint Program in Transportation, Research Report no. 66).

—— (1988), 'Port authorities as urban land developers: the case of the Toronto Harbour Commissioners and their outer harbour project, 1912–68', *Urban History Review*, in press.

Norcliffe, G.B. (1981), 'Industrial change in old port areas: the case of the port of Toronto', *Cahiers de Géographie du Québec*, 25(65), 237–52.

O'Mara, J. (1976), *Shaping urban waterfronts: the role of Toronto's Harbour Commissioners, 1911–60* (Toronto: York University, Department of Geography, Discussion Paper Series No. 13).

—— (1984), *The Toronto Harbour Commissioners' financial arrangements and city waterfront development, 1910–50* (Toronto: York University, Department of Geography, Discussion Paper Series No. 30).

Schaeffer, R. (1981), *The Board of Trade and the origins of the Toronto Harbour Commissioners, 1899–1911* (Toronto: York University, Department of Geography, Discussion Paper Series No. 27).

Semple, R.K. and Green, M.B. (1983), 'Inter-urban corporate headquarters relocation in Canada', *Cahiers de Géographie du Québec*, 27(72), 386–406.

Smith, N. (1986), 'Gentrification, the frontier, and the restructuring of urban space', in Smith, N. and Williams, P. (eds), *Gentrification of the city* (Boston: Allen and Unwin), 15–35.

Spelt, J. (1973), *Toronto* (Don Mills, Ontario: Collier-Macmillan).

Stanford, G.H. (1974), *To serve the community: the story of the Toronto Board of Trade* (Toronto: Toronto Board of Trade).

Toronto *Globe and Mail* 17, 18 October 1972; 5 May 1984; 22 July 1986; 29 August 1986; 15 November 1986.

Toronto Harbour Commissioners (1912), *Toronto waterfront development, 1912–20* (Toronto: Toronto Harbour Commissioners).

—— (1968), *A bold concept for the redevelopment of the Toronto waterfront* (Toronto: Toronto Harbour Commissioners).

—— (1984), *The debt* (Toronto ; Toronto Harbour Commissioners).

—— (1986), *Port of Toronto News*, 33(3).

Toronto Star 17, 18 October 1972; 3 July 1986; 9, 12 September 1986; 21 November 1987.

World Trade Centre Toronto (1987), *Trade Connections*, 8(1).

7 Public policy and planning of the Rotterdam waterfront: a tale of two cities

David Pinder and Kenneth E. Rosing

Introduction

It can be hypothesised that waterfront redevelopment should be a major feature of the Rotterdam scene in the late twentieth century. To a great extent the world's largest port has achieved its premier position through the relentless pursuit of scale economies (Pinder, 1981), and such a strategy is not conducive to the continued operation of early port areas. In reality the abandonment of the port's older docks has been restrained by two factors. The success of the inland waterway system has meant that otherwise outmoded docks can be used to satisfy demand for barge berths; and, especially in early twentieth-century harbours, the port authority has encouraged port users to modernise *in situ*, rather than close down or migrate downstream. Outstanding examples of this latter strategy are documented in the port authority's house journal, *Rotterdam-Europoort-Delta*.

While it is important to appreciate that the abandonment of apparently outdated docks has not proceeded unchecked, however, the port's retreat has posed major challenges for the city planning system. The viewpoint adopted in this chapter is that the planning system has responded positively, to the extent that challenge has been seen as opportunity. We also stress that, contrary to the trend in many cityports – exemplified by the chapters on London and Hong Kong elsewhere in this volume – substantial efforts have been made to avoid recourse to demand-led planning. Social goals have been given a high profile, and implementation strategies have generally been faithful to these goals. Although at first sight this may seem contradictory for a city rooted so firmly in aggressive commercialism as Rotterdam, it reflects Dutch society's long and strong tradition of linking physical planning and social welfare (Hetzel, 1985). Lastly, however, we argue that analysis of the city's revitalisation programme must not over-emphasise the dominance of social goals. The philosophy on which policy is based varies markedly from one part of the inner city to another, and it is now no exaggeration to claim that Rotterdam is simultaneously pursuing two redevelopment strategies that are distinct in terms of concepts, spatial impact and results. Hence we arrive at our title. This is a tale of two cities or, to be more accurate, two inner cities.

The setting

Rotterdam was founded on the River Rotte in about 1250, just north of that river's confluence with what is now known as the Nieuwe Maas. For centuries the story was one of a battle against the water and against poor navigational conditions, which slowed port development by forcing shippers to use longer and longer routeways through the delta to the sea. But although Rotterdam remained a very unremarkable port, the growth that did occur created an urban form of central significance for this chapter. The medieval city – and, indeed, that of the mid-nineteenth century – was essentially an urbanised triangle, north of the Nieuwe Maas, with its base aligned along the north bank of the river. Within this triangle, the Stadsdriehoek, early port development was interwoven with other urban land uses. In time the latter squeezed out some of the earliest port developments but, by the mid-nineteenth century, the city was still dominated by a dock system running parallel to the river across the base of the urban triangle (Fig. 7.1). This port zone, known as the Waterstad, is one of our 'cities'.

The second was created by economic growth in the late nineteenth century, and most particularly by German industrialisation. Moving to take advantage of new inland and ocean-going transport technologies – and greatly assisted by German investment designed to protect maritime access – Rotterdam participated in the construction of the New Waterway, a ship canal opened in 1872 and substantially improved by new dredging technologies in the 1890s. For the first time this gave the port rapid, safe access to the sea. In commercial circles the view was still widespread that the port should capitalise on improved access by continuing to develop on the north bank, as a number of plans in the city archives testify. But external pressures for bridging the river built up in the third quarter of the century, primarily because of the need for a railway linking Amsterdam and Brussels. Simultaneously the city council had become increasingly interested in the south bank for city expansion, and by 1869 the land between Feijenoord and Charlois had been annexed (Fig. 7.2). A charismatic entrepreneur, Lodewijk Pincoffs, then played a crucial role. Using largely German capital, this enterprising individual created the *Rotterdamse Handelsvereniging* (RHV), and employed this trading company to spearhead port expansion on the south bank. While the authorities constructed road and rail bridges, the RHV dug the Binnenhaven and the Entrepothaven. In addition, state investment was made in the Spoorweghaven and the Koningshaven, both being spin-offs from cross-river railway construction. By 1879 the isolation of the south bank was ended, and port areas technologically superior to anything the Stadsdriehoek could offer were available.

Initially this dramatic change of direction was far from successful. The RHV struggled to survive, partly because in 1879 Pincoffs – the visionary

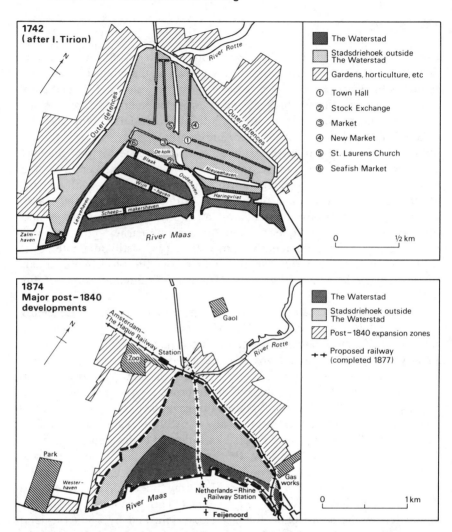

Figure 7.1 *Rotterdam: the Stadsdriehoek, the Waterstad and city structure, 1742 and 1874*

who had led the drive to the south bank – had fled to America following the exposure of major fraud. An 1888 map of Rotterdam shows that development south of the Nieuwe Maas was still unimpressive, but by then the city's economic take-off, powered by a port that was now municipally owned, was underway. More port expansion of exceptional scale was planned; this, together with the needs of the existing port, generated a vast demand for labour. In 1860 the city population was 106,500; by 1880 it was 150,000 and by 1900 it was 320,000. Growth naturally affected both banks of the river – indeed Figure 7.1 shows a belt of expansion that by 1874 had already taken place around the Stadsdriehoek. But the large majority of the construction took place on the south bank, where new harbours were being dug, where space was readily available and where it was anticipated that most port-associated employment would be created. In this way the south bank became the city's proletarian quarter. At times during its development it must have looked like a current third-world city and, when finished, most of the housing in the harbour-related areas was far from adequate. In this respect the area was by no means unique in the Dutch urban system (Grinberg, 1977, 21–32), but the contrast with the north bank was sharp. There – despite a share of working-class housing – the city evolved to monopolise commerce, administration, entertainment and higher-class housing. The tale of two cities had begun.

Retreat

Three phases of port abandonment can be recognised, of which two are of central significance. As early as 1882 two disused and derelict early seventeenth-century docks, the Glashaven and the Bierhaven, were reclaimed by the city authorities to make new streets. Twenty years later the Westerhaven, only fifty years old and just downstream from the Stadsdriehoek, was similarly closed and filled. For modern Rotterdam the chief significance of this latter step was that the Westerhaven district, adjacent to a new public park, rapidly developed into a high-class residential area. Conversion of this district into an office quarter, much of it port-related, occurred this century, and today this valuable urban townscape is protected by a blanket preservation order.

Secondly, and more importantly from the viewpoint of this chapter, on 14 May 1940 remaining port activities in the Stadsdriehoek – activities which contemporary aerial photographs show to have been surprisingly extensive – were totally disrupted by German bombing. The attack devastated the urban triangle and, when clearance was undertaken, some older harbours – especially Blaak – became convenient dumping sites for rubble. Some port-related recolonisation of the Waterstad occurred in the postwar period, but the historic docklands never regained their former importance. West of the main railway line, which bisects the Stadsdriehoek, postwar rebuilding for largely port-related commerce was pursued in conjunction with the development of a new city centre. East of the railway, around the Haringvliet and Groenendaal, some of the land – astonishingly – would not be redeveloped until the 1980s.

Finally, the port's retreat in the postwar era has naturally reflected the imperatives of scale and technological change that have been important around the world. Because bombing accelerated change on the north bank, the impact of this phase has been focused south of the river. Here port activity has virtually ceased upstream of the first twentieth-century harbour, the Rijnhaven. By the early 1990s ownership of virtually the whole

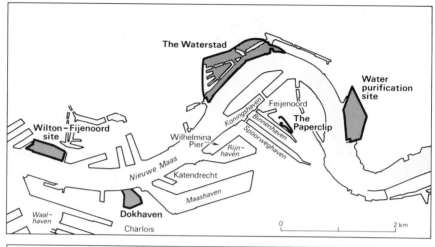

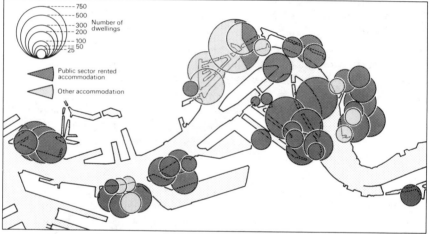

Figure 7.2 *Waterfront revitalisation outside the Waterstad, Rotterdam*

dock system in this area will have been transferred from the municipal port authority, which has no desire to be involved in redevelopment, to the municipality itself. This change of ownership is more important than it might initially appear, because the power structures and legal statuses of the two organisations differ radically. For example most planning controls do not apply to the port authority, but the municipality is subject to the full range of regulations. Among other things this means that there must be local public participation in planning, and this may well have influenced the municipality's preferred housing strategies detailed below (Draisden, 1981).

While this part of the south bank is the focus of recent retreat, it is necessary to note that other outlying localities have also been hit by abandonment. This partly reflects port withdrawal – the Dokhaven 1.8 km downstream is a good example – but it is also a consequence of industrial restructuring. For example, the Netherlands' shipbuilding and repairing industry has been severely hit by global competition, and has concentrated in Vlissingen in the southern part of the delta. As a result, the waterways around Rotterdam are punctuated by former shipyard sites. One of these, the Wilton-Fijenoord yard on the north bank of the river, downstream from the historic core, has been fully incorporated into the housing programme discussed below (Fig. 7.2). Redundant space has also been generated by other forces, including the city's investment in new infra-structure. In this context the most significant aspect of retreat has been the abandonment of an outdated water-purification plant on the waterfront upstream from the Waterstad. This, too, has been incorporated into the revitalisation strategy (van Vliet, 1983).

Revitalisation outside the Waterstad

Since the mid-1970s an accelerating revitalisation programme has been pursued in and around the late-nineteenth-century harbour areas. The most recent aspect of this programme to be announced is a major office, residential and recreational complex in a south bank district known as the Kop van Zuid (Gemeente Rotterdam, 1987, 6–10). If implemented – and there is still some doubt – this development will focus on the Wilhelmina Pier north of the Rijnhaven, with an extension – chiefly on infilled dockland – towards the south east (Fig. 7.2). It has been stimulated by the imminent prospect of inner-city land shortages for large-scale office development on the north bank, but it poses major challenges – including improved cross-river communications to integrate older and newer busi-ness districts.[1] Also, the underlying philosophy is very different to that of the current revitalisation policy outside the Waterstad, which is over-whelmingly concerned with the provision of improved housing (Wang, 1987). This goal is being achieved by the pursuit of two interrelated strategies and, despite the recent publicity accorded to the Kop van Zuid project, it is appropriate that the discussion should concentrate on these socially oriented approaches to revitalisation.

The first has been directed at sub-standard housing in the post-1870 maritime quarters surrounding the port (Gemeente Rotterdam, 1987, 2–5). If policy for these areas had been formulated in the 1960s, there is little doubt that clearance followed by redevelopment would have been central to the preferred strategy. But policy was not decided until the late 1970s, by which time it had become obvious in the Netherlands that municipalities advocating wholesale clearance were treading a hazardous path. The dangers were brought into focus in Amsterdam where the inner-city plans of the renowned city planning department were first halted and then defeated by local community opposition. The shock waves from this confrontation spread rapidly to other cities (van der Sluys and van Evert, 1985, 173–83), leading to the adoption of radically-different strategies.

While these vary from case to case, their common aim is the rehabilitation of existing property rather than its redevelopment. Although demolition is still likely to occur where, for example, property is too decayed to rehabilitate, improvement is the preferred option. In part this reflects new attitudes to the urban environment; townscape preservation is now high on the agenda. A second motivation is that the strategy should benefit cities by minimising population loss through decentralisation to other municipalities. In the Netherlands city income largely comes as a national subsidy and is related to population. In Rotterdax the population total has fallen dramatically: from 730,000 in 1960, to 555,000 in 1984. Although a slight recovery has subsequently occurred (to 574,000 in 1988) a related problem is that the selective nature of out-migration has impaired purchasing power, posing an obvious threat to the continued prosperity of the commercial core. The dominant goal, however, is primarily social. The aim – stated explicitly – is to improve housing conditions while avoiding the community destruction which clearance would cause. Local people may need to be moved from an area during the improvement phase, but 'emergency' housing can often be provided in the vicinity, and the intention is to ensure that as many original inhabitants as possible eventually return to a district after its renovation.

The second strategy is directed at the vacated docks and other redundant spaces such as the Wilton-Fijenoord shipyard and the water-purification site. In these areas policy is dominated by the construction of new housing, mainly in the form of low- and medium-rise flats. By 1990 4,600 new dwellings will have been provided on the south bank of the river, plus 3,400 on north bank sites outside the Waterstad (Fig. 7.2). This building programme is clearly related to the goal of retarding the decline of the city's population, but it is also inseparable from the policy of moulding revitalisation to the needs of low-income groups which now dominate the inner-city population. On the south bank 80 per cent of the provision is publicly financed rented housing for these groups; on the north bank – again outside the Waterstad – the figure is 93 per cent.

In addition, the emphasis on public housing construction assists in solving an important difficulty associated with the rehabilitation of the nineteenth-century housing stock. This is that improvement normally leads to the creation of fewer, larger dwellings, so that it is impossible to rehouse everyone in their original locality. In the south bank area of Katendrecht, for example, where an extensive rehabilitation project is currently in hand, on average three old flats are being rebuilt as two new ones. Old facades are retained, but internal divisions are totally altered. Nearby, unashamedly modern blocks – built on two infilled ninteenth-century harbours – provide accommodation for displaced families with roots in the area, including children who have reached family-forming age.

Four other facets of strategy outside the Waterstad must be noted. Firstly, the pursuit of social goals has been extended to investment in other types of social overhead capital, especially schools for children of pre-secondary school age. In Katendrecht, for example, two new elementary schools have been built, one Catholic and one non-denominational. Secondly, although new housing is dominated by the public sector, and although many public-sector apartments enjoy magnificent views of the port and river, it is noticeable that the few private-sector projects have almost all been allocated prime waterfront sites. Here, as in revitalisation projects around the world, the alliance of capital and influence is evident, albeit on a restricted scale.

Thirdly, in contrast to policy in many other ports and, indeed, to the approach adopted in the Waterstad, redundant water areas have not been treated as sacrosanct because of their landscape and recreational potential. Infilled docks are not uncommon, and it is tempting to link this with the fact that policy aims to provide for groups in society who are unlikely to spring to the defence of water areas on environmental grounds. What can also be argued, however, is that infilling is in large measure a response to physical planning pressures and that there are positive benefits for the community. For example, inadequate sewerage in the southern inner city has been transformed by a project in the Dokhaven (Fig. 7.2). Here a sewage treatment plant has been built on the floor of the harbour, which has then been infilled to create a substantial park surrounded by housing built on the old harbour quays. In Feijenoord and Katendrecht infilling has similarly helped to increase usable space, and has also ameliorated development problems on awkward – especially elongated – sites.

Fourthly, there is always a danger that planning dominated by social housing will generate a monotonous environment. To argue that Rotterdam has avoided this pitfall completely would be to exaggerate. Especially south of the river, however, in a number of building projects the aim has at least been to diversify the morphology and, indeed, to cultivate image and identity. This is most evident in Feijenoord's 'Paperclip' project, where an elongated apartment development has been curved back on itself to exploit the potential of an awkward triangular site. While this project is architecturally and visually interesting, however, it also demonstrates that site constraints may be difficult to overcome completely. For example, the Paperclip's north–south orientation means that the many apartments inside its three curves never receive direct sunlight.

The Waterstad

The strategy for the Waterstad is much more diverse than that discussed above, with the result that, as development has progressed, the area has become increasingly reminscent of many other waterfront redevelopment projects around the world. Private capital is much more in evidence than in reconstruction projects outside the Waterstad; the leisure theme has a high profile; and there is far less emphasis on provision for the needs of an inner-city population (Gemeente Rotterdam, 1984; Grondbedrijf Rotterdam, 1986; Jobse, 1987). Nonetheless, Rotterdamers have not been ignored by the strategy, and revitalisation is proceeding within a framework defined and applied by the city authorities.

Leisure provision – at least to date – has been primarily non-commercial, and has been dominated by investment in new museums and a library. The larger of the two museums – the city's Maritime Museum – lies on the Leuvehaven in the western Waterstad (Fig. 7.3). Although this museum's exhibits are partly housed in new buildings, there are also substantial open-air collections of historic ships and tugs occupying adjacent parts of the Leuvehaven. The second museum – of Inland Shipping – also makes extensive use of available water and is an entirely open-air development. Exhibits are displayed around the Oude Haven – Rotterdam's oldest surviving dock area – and on a fully operational repair slipway. The site, adjacent to the river and slightly to the east of the railway which divides the city centre, is important in structural planning terms because it provides a point of attraction towards the east of the Waterstad. So does that of the public library, which stands close to the Museum of

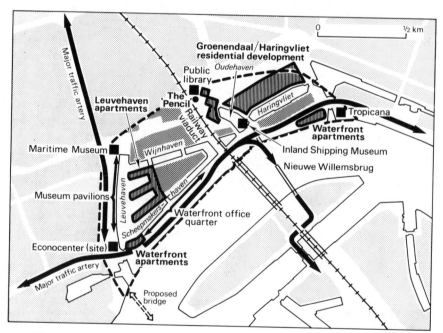

Figure 7.3 *Structural components of the Waterstad plan, Rotterdam*

Inland Shipping a little further from the river. Historically the railway viaduct has resulted in a re-sorting of central business district commercial activities, with the area to the east becoming a rather down-market zone. Land use here has been dominated by commercial establishments requiring relatively low-value land, and the lack of commercial impetus has been a factor underlying failure to redevelop until the 1980s a large area destroyed by the bombing. Attractions such as the museum and the library are intended to improve the district's public image and achieve more effective integration of the two halves of the Waterstad. This use of non-commercial investment for integrative purposes has much in common with the strategy discussed by Edwards (Chapter 8).

Commercial activity based on the leisure function chiefly comprises a modest cluster of bars, small shops and similar outlets in the vicinity of the Inland Shipping Museum. By the early 1990s, however, the commercial leisure dimension will be much more overt, primarily as a result of the completion of two major private-sector projects. The most advanced of these is Tropicana, a leisure-pool complex including a restaurant and shops, located on the waterfront in the extreme eastern corner of the Waterstad. From the city planners' viewpoint this, like the Inland Shipping Museum and the library, is intended to function as a focal point strengthening the structure of the eastern Waterstad. The second commercial project, the Econocenter, is a more diverse scheme steered by a foundation with public and private representation, but financed by the private sector. Central to the plans are a 300-seat 'Omnimax' theatre designed to project a super-screen film of Rotterdam and its port, together with exhibition space. The latter will include a permanent exhibition on the Rotterdam region, with interactive displays on a wide variety of economic activities, from banking to transport. On an adjoining site a 160-room hotel is to be built. Clearly, whereas Tropicana will primarily serve the city population, the Econocenter is aimed chiefly at the tourist and business-visitor markets. This market orientation is closely related to the site allocated to the project, which is one of the prime locations available within the old port area. Econocenter will occupy the western corner of the Waterstad, where it will overlook the riverfront and reinforce the attractions of the nearby Maritime Museum.

Commercial development that is largely unrelated to new leisure functions is also an important facet of the western Waterstad strategy. Commerce, much of it port-related, is a traditional activity in this quarter and was quickly re-established after the wartime bombing. But since the early 1980s the office sector has developed particularly dramatically, mainly as a consequence of investment by pension funds and insurance and shipping companies. By the 1990s over 25,000 square metres of new office space will have been created, thus confirming the Waterstad's status as an employment node within the city. However, the impact of this upswing has not been distributed widely throughout the redevelopment area, partly because the city has required the developers to provide internal car-parking, but also because the spatial impact of office development has been limited by land-use zoning. All the large projects in this sector have been concentrated into a single belt along the waterfront between the Inland Shipping Museum and the Leuvehaven, where they have consolidated a prestige office quarter with roots in the interwar period. In this way the office sector has secured most of the waterfront and, in townscape terms, has created a quarter that is increasingly evocative of the North American city.

Housing, the basis of redevelopment outside the Waterstad, is the third major element of revitalisation policy within it. By 1990 more than 1,800 new dwellings will have been provided. To a degree, new housing once more reflects concern for economically disadvantaged sections of the city population, particularly on the eastern edge of the Waterstad in the Groenendaal–Haringvliet district. Construction here has utilised the last large tract of urban fallow created by wartime bombing and has provided almost 60 per cent of the Waterstad's new housing. What has been built is a mixture of public-sector and state-subsidised rental accommodation, and in part the area has received overspill population displaced by housing-renovation programmes in the city's Oude West district. Yet, despite this overt social dimension, residential development here should not be equated with that outside the Waterstad, the large majority of which comprises simply public-sector housing – the most basic form of rental accommodation. State-subsidised rental property raises the status of the Groenendaal–Haringvliet development above the basic level, and even more significant steps are taken up the social hierarchy as one moves to the river and from the eastern Waterstad into its western half. On the river in the eastern Waterstad, luxury apartments have been built near the Tropicana pool. In the west, finger quays in the Leuvehaven are now occupied by private-sector apartments; many overlook the Maritime Museum and all have water views. Here the ratio between one-bedroom apartments and large units (nearly 1:1;) suggests that provision is biased towards a relatively well-to-do population without children. And on the waterfront once more, developers are now marketing over 300 luxury flats adjacent to the Econocenter.

Two additional aspects of the Waterstad strategy – both environmental – require consideration. The fact that both museums rely heavily on the availability of water reflects a basic townscape-design assumption that water areas shall be retained and maintained to safeguard the maritime atmosphere. In fact maintenance standards are such that the docks remain accessible to small inland waterway barges which come and go at all times and moor, sometimes in ranks four deep, throughout the area while awaiting work. Most of the barges are family-owned and have customary moorings when in Rotterdam. Nationalities tend to group together, creating Belgian, French and Swiss 'villages' which – although individual families are constantly on the move – are remarkably stable. Thus the preserved docks are not simply landscape features but impart a dynamism to the environment that is missing in the redevelopment areas of many ports.

Secondly, while there are examples of architectural style being employed to create a sense of image and identity in the nineteenth-century redevelopment areas, these experiments are eclipsed by the emphasis placed on design in the Waterstad. In sharp contrast to many other port-revitalisation schemes, this emphasis has not meant the replication of vernacular house and warehouse styles. Early in the post war period the policy adopted for the devastated city centre was to rebuild following modern architectural styles, not least to create an image of Rotterdam as a dynamic forward-looking phoenix. By no means all developments in the Waterstad have been visually striking. In the housing field, especially, there is much that is unexceptional. But housing around the Inland Shipping Museum comprises cubes, tipped on one corner and mounted on columns several metres high. Nearby stands a cone-capped apartment tower block, nicknamed 'The Pencil'; and close to this is the public library, dominated by yellow external ducts reminiscent of the Pompidou Centre in Paris. By the Leuvehaven the restrained Maritime Museum comprises two interlocking triangles with corners recalling ships' bows. Along the water-front, office developments include the blue-glass De Maas Tower, and the striking white Nedlloyd building, from the facade of which a diagonal slice has been 'cut'. Whatever the individual's reactions to these buildings – enthusiasm, curiosity, astonishment, dismay – they are a clear statement of the philosophy that change in the Waterstad, while it may exploit the past as a resource, should not result in the creation of a fossilised heritage environment.

Conclusion

It is evident that the strategies pursued in Rotterdam are leading to two radically different outcomes: one essentially homogeneous and geared to social need, the other diverse and attuned to the opportunities presented by redundant space adjacent to a dynamic city centre. Both exemplify Riley and Shurmer-Smith's (Chapter 3) contention that local forces may be vitally important in determining the scale and nature of redevelopment, since they are both creations of a forceful city administration. Outside the Waterstad this administration has dictated almost every detail of the revitalisation process; inside it there has developed a public-authority/ private-sector coalition similar to those found in many other port-rejuvenation schemes. Although private investors in this coalition have been largely responsible for developing many prime sites, particularly for housing and office expansion, this does not mean that demand-led planning has been dominant. The city itself has been a heavy investor; non-commercial leisure functions have been given a high profile; and change has closely reflected the planners' land-use zoning preferences. Moreover, it is arguable that if capital is to capture prime sites it is appropriate that it should do so here. Redevelopment has not displaced an underprivileged population in the Waterstad; that was achieved by the bombing in May 1940.

By adopting these radically different approaches, Rotterdam has arguably come close to achieving the best of both worlds. In its late-nineteenth-century districts a sustained attack has been made on low-quality residential environments, primarily to the benefit of their inhabitants. In the Waterstad it has proved possible to exploit leisure potential, but also to break free of the leisure stereotype and accommodate – without social friction – powerful commercial pressures and residential demand from higher-income groups.

Despite these achievements, however, important issues relating to both strategies can be identified. Policy for the nineteenth-century districts is entirely concerned with housing and the provision of other social overhead capital. Although unemployment rates in these districts are frequently well above 25 per cent, especially among immigrants, the strategy has no economic dimension. Even with its strong social orientation, therefore, it does not meet a number of the criticisms raised by, for example, Church (Chapter 12). With respect to housing policy, the programmes are apparently proceeding smoothly, but there are residents who are permanently displaced despite the goal of local rehousing in refurbished or new accommodation. This raises two issues. Firstly, are those displaced the weaker elements in the local community, such as unemployed immigrants or elderly Dutch people? If so, what forces are responsible and can they be corrected? Secondly, what are the socio-economic consequences for those displaced? Where do they go? Does movement impose costs – temporary or permanent – on them? And does it trigger a more peripatetic lifestyle or lead to integration with a new local community? In the Waterstad, meanwhile, the main issue is whether revitalisation will bring about an internally well-integrated urban quarter. As yet, despite impressive change, the area is clearly differentiated east and west of the railway. Office development, most private housing and the Maritime Museum are all concentrated in the west, where they enjoy the advantage of proximity to the city centre. Locations east of the railway are more remote. The cluster of leisure-related shops and bars associated with the Inland Shipping Museum is, as has been indicated, modest and the museum and library are essentially outposts of non-residential revitalisation. Although the Tropicana will improve east–west balance, the best prospect for effective integration is likely to be removal of the railway as a barrier. The intention is that this will be achieved by the construction of a tunnel under the Waterstad and river, but this project is not due for completion until 1996. By then the

Waterstad's structure will be firmly established, so that effective integration – even in the long term – may be difficult to accomplish.

Finally, it is appropriate to place Rotterdam's approach to waterfront revitalisation in a broader perspective. So far as the Waterstad and the Kop van Zuid project are concerned, policy is not strikingly different to strategies being pursued in many large cityports around the world. Indeed, it is evident that what is proposed for the Wilhelmina Pier in the Kop van Zuid owes much to Baltimore, with which Rotterdam is now twinned. Conversely, however, other studies presented in this volume demonstrate that concern for communities in nineteenth-century residential districts, with the consequent application of policies possessing a strong social orientation, is a very uncharacteristic approach to redevelopment. While it would be wrong to argue that Rotterdam's policy is perfect, its existence and the progress being made call into question the widespread tendency to do little for these inner-urban areas. Against this background the central issue is clear: if Rotterdam is able to devise and implement a strategy to assist inner-urban communities, why do the authorities in so many other cityports fail to recognise or meet the self-same challenge?

Note

1   Cross-river communication has already been marginally improved by the construction of a new suspension bridge, the Nieuwe Willemsbrug, opened in 1982. It is intended that this will be supplemented by a second road bridge linking the central city to the Wilhelmina Pier via the Leuvehaven area.

Acknowledgement

The authors are grateful to Professor G.A. van der Knaap of the Economisch Geografisch Instituut, Erasmus Universiteit Rotterdam, for comments on a draft of this chapter.

References

Draisden, M.D. (1981), 'Fostering effective citizen participation: lessons from three urban renewal neighbourhoods in The Hague', *Planning and Administration*, 8, 40–62.
Gemeente Rotterdam (1984), *Binnenstadsplan Rotterdam 1985* (Rotterdam: Gemeente Rotterdam).
—— (1987), *Rotterdam renewal 2: new destinations for Rotterdam's Meuse banks* (Rotterdam: Dienstenstructuur voor Ruimtelijke Ordening en Stadsvernieuwing).

Grinberg, D.I. (1977), *Housing in the Netherlands, 1900–1940* (Delft: Delft University Press).

Grondbedrijf Rotterdam (1986), *Het oude havengebied en Groenendaal* (Rotterdam: Dienstenstructuur voor Ruimtelijke Ordening en Stadsvernieuwing).

Hetzel, O.J. (1985), 'Government housing policies in the Netherlands since 1945' in A.K. Dutt and F.J. Costa (eds) *Public planning in the Netherlands* (Oxford: Oxford University Press), 141–60.

Jobse, R.B. (1987), 'The restructuring of Dutch cities', *Tijdschrift voor Economische en Sociale Geografie*, 78, 305–11.

Pinder, D.A. (1981), 'Community attitude as a limiting factor in port growth: the case of Rotterdam', in D.A. Pinder and B.S. Hoyle (eds) *Cityport industrialisation and regional development: spatial analysis and planning strategies* (Oxford: Pergamon Press), 181–99.

van der Sluys, F. and van Evert, G. (1985), 'Planning for urban renewal in The Hague', in A.K. Dutt and F.J. Costa (eds) *Public planning in the Netherlands* (Oxford: Oxford University Press), 161–83.

van Vliet, M. (1983), *DWL-terrein: van waterfabriek tot nieuw woongebied* (Rotterdam: Dienstenstructuur voor Ruimtelijke Ordening en Stadsvernieuwing).

Wang, W. (1987), 'Herbruik van oude havengebieden te Rotterdam', *Bouw*, 8, 48–53.

8 Public policy, physical restructuring and economic change: the Swansea experience

J. Arwel Edwards

Introduction

In the United Kingdom interest in waterfront revitalisation has tended to focus on ports such as London (Chapter 12) and Liverpool (Adcock, 1984), where the redundant space problem is extreme. This preoccupation may be understandable, yet it should not be allowed to obscure the fact that many smaller ports are also grappling with the challenges posed by redundant space. This is particularly true around the Bristol Channel and Severn Estuary, a maritime region with a long history of inland, coastal and overseas water-borne trade (Hallett and Randall, 1970; Hilling, 1984). This region experienced a general decline in port activities during the interwar period, and after 1945 contraction and closure accelerated. Since the early 1970s, however, there has been a widespread resurgence of interest in its waterfront and dock areas, not as a consequence of improvements in trade, but because of their potential for new land uses and activities. Fourteen separate port-redevelopment schemes have been proposed, by far the greatest spatial concentration in the UK, and participants in the projects include a varied range of private and public agencies (Fig. 8.1). Seven schemes – at Bridgwater, Bristol, Gloucester, Cardiff Docklands, Cardiff Bay, Penarth and Swansea – are already in progress; the others – at Pembrey–Burry Port, Llanelli, Porthcawl, Barry, Newport, Lydney and Ilfracombe – are under consideration. In addition, several proposals for the construction of barrages, including one across the Bristol Channel, have been put forward. Currently the most ambitious detailed project concerns Cardiff Bay and would involve the enclosure of more than 800 hectares of water and developable land (Edwards, 1988a).

In this chapter the results are presented of investigations in one of the region's leading medium-sized ports, Swansea. The selection of Swansea for detailed study is appropriate for a number of reasons. Compared with many waterfront redevelopment projects, the local authority has played an unusually dominant role, being the landowner and promoter of redevelopment. The authority's policies show a strong concern for social and environmental change, as well as for economic recovery. Also, there is a long-term political and financial commitment to the policies' success. At the same time, it is believed that revitalisation of the Swansea waterfront should be dependent on co-operation between public and private sectors, and a distinctive managerial framework has been developed to achieve this.

After a brief discussion of the local setting, attention focuses on the dominant, interrelated, facets of change: physical decline and regeneration, and economic aspects of the revitalisation process. Many of the findings draw on an investigation of marina development (Edwards, 1985) and on a study of decline and recovery in the city's redundant port zone (Edwards, 1987).

Swansea and its Maritime Zone

There are two dock complexes in Swansea: an older grouping to the west of the River Tawe and a more modern one to the east. This paper is primarily concerned with the western docks, where development began with the opening of the North Dock and Half Tide Basin in 1851, followed by the South Dock and Tawe Basin in 1859 (Fig. 8.2). In the twentieth century the experience of these early port facilities is one that has become very familiar. Faced with a variety of operational difficulties and competition, the North Dock was closed as early as 1937. The Half Tide Basin managed to survive until 1966 when it, too, closed; and by 1969 the South Dock and Tawe Basin had experienced a similar fate. Ownership of land in the abandoned western docks, as well as most adjacent land leases and buildings, was acquired by the City of Swansea from the British Transport Docks Board in 1971. By then all the docks – with the exception of the

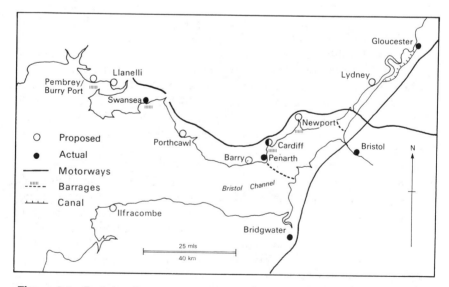

Figure 8.1 *Port development schemes in the Bristol Channel-Severn Estuary*

South Dock – had been completely infilled. The City Engineer, who had responsibility for planning matters, proposed that the land be used for an inner-urban relief road and industrial sites, proposals similar to those put forward for Bristol at about the same time. However, these proposals had not been accepted when local government reorganisation took place in 1974.

In 1974 the city council, through its newly created planning department, undertook an appraisal of the city's economy and environment which had a considerable bearing on the redevelopment process. The appraisal noted that the traditional economic bases of the city and surrounding region – the coal and metallurgical industries – were clearly in decline and that unemployment was increasing. Although a range of new secondary and tertiary activities was growing in importance, it was evident that inter-regional movement of firms to Swansea would not provide sufficient new jobs. Locally generated growth was, therefore, identified as essential for successful restructuring of the city's economy. The appraisal also drew attention to the poor state of the physical environment and the damage caused as a result of continuous industrialisation and pollution since 1715. Parts of the local region were being successfully upgraded and transformed as part of the Lower Swansea Valley Project, and it was decided to extend the concept of improvement applied there to the dock areas.

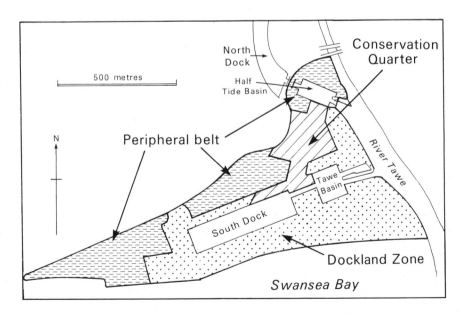

Figure 8.2 *Former docks and constituent sub-areas in the Swansea Maritime Zone*

Subsequently twelve major policy documents, and many detailed plans, concerned with the redevelopment fund of what might be termed the Maritime Zone have been issued (Edwards, 1988b).[1] These have highlighted the existence of three distinctive sub-areas. The first is an extensive 'Dockland Zone' that covers the former South Dock and Tawe Basin, as well as land to the south-east that is occupied by manufacturing (Fig. 8.2). The second is a 'Conservation Quarter' north of the Tawe Basin. Originally occupied by small workshops and businesses closely linked to port activities, this area is therefore comparable in character to Hilling's 'maritime quarter' or 'sailortown' (Chapter 2).[2] Finally, there is a discontinuous 'Peripheral Belt', comprising extensive tracts of land previously occupied, in the north, by the Half Tide Basin and, to the south-west, by railway sheds, sidings, the old Victoria Station and a limited amount of housing. Separate planning strategies, which are discussed later, have been applied to each of these sub-areas, but their nature has been determined by common underlying objectives adopted by the city council. The aim has been to establish an environment that is not only conducive to incoming private investment, but which also provides a more attractive physical setting and opportunities for local businesses and residents.

To a certain extent the combination of measures taken to achieve these goals sets Swansea apart from comparable schemes elsewhere. To accelerate the decision-making process, the conventional corporate-management type of structure, characteristic of local authorities, was replaced at critical stages with a quasi-Urban Development Corporation approach. Small all-party committees were established, able to be convened at short notice and given plenary powers. However, as was noted above, in order to retain maximum control over the situation the council took control of the land. This was generally achieved through agreement, but compulsory purchase was used where necessary.

The council also made a long-term financial commitment to renewal initiatives; indeed, 8.5 per cent of its capital expenditure since 1974 has been directed to the Maritime Zone, and considerable success has been achieved in attracting national and international aid, particularly from the

Table 8.1 Sources of grant aid provided for the Swansea Maritime Zone to January 1988 (in million £)

European Regional Development Fund	2.12
Urban Development scheme	1.66
Urban Aid Programme	0.53
Welsh Development Agency	0.31
Industrial Development Act	0.15
Total	4.77

Source: City of Swansea Development Department

European Regional Development Fund (Table 8.1). Much of the finance has been spent on land assembly and clearance (£2.2m), infrastructure improvements (£5.3m), construction work (£2.1m) and conservation and enhancement (£2.2m). Beyond this, as Williams (1988) states, it was agreed that the pattern of change should be determined by constructive land-use planning, and that each plan should be part of a comprehensive strategy, not an end in itself. Decisions were to be influenced more by design criteria than by price. Finally, considerable emphasis was placed on maintaining credibility to retain the confidence of both the public and the potential investor (Osborne, 1987a; 1987b).

Dereliction and physical rejuvenation

In 1974 disused land and water surfaces predominated in the Dockland Zone: the Tawe Basin had been filled, and in the partially filled South Dock only a metre of brackish water remained. Indeed, the Maritime Zone as a whole was a blighted, decaying area in an inner-urban location 400 metres south of the city's thriving central business district (Fig. 8.3). The small amount of land still in use was given over to four activities of approximately equal extent: manufacturing north and south of the Tawe Basin, distribution and whole-saling around the South Dock, commercial and office functions in the Conservation Quarter, and housing in a peripheral western location. Yet, by 1988, land-use changes had transformed the entire Maritime Zone. Most vacant land and buildings had been replaced by new residential, industrial and commercial land uses, while formerly redundant water areas formed the focus of leisure-oriented commercial development (Fig. 8.3).

This transformation was accomplished by implementing contrasting policies in each of the Maritime Zone's three sub-areas. The most radical changes occurred in the Dockland Zone, around the South Dock and Tawe Basin. Prior to redevelopment, the short-term leases of most existing businesses here were terminated and the firms moved out of the decaying, temporary buildings. The magnitude of change was such that, of thirty-five firms present, only two – both manufacturing concerns which owned their own sites – remained in the same premises throughout the study period. Being the principal landowner in the area, the local authority was closely involved and took a sympathetic interest in the relocation process, assisting in the identification of alternative sites and with the actual removal. It also provided financial compensation for the disturbance and helped with the provision of temporary sites for those firms which it wanted to return to the redeveloped Dockland Zone, although only one firm is known to have returned to the area after redevelopment.

In contrast, there was no compulsory relocation of firms from the Conservation Quarter. As the name suggests, the emphasis here was on

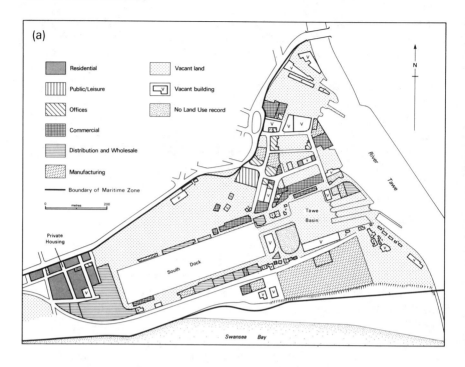

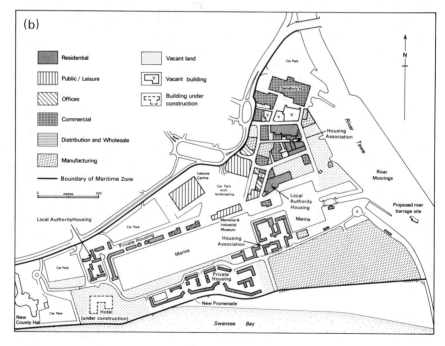

Figure 8.3   *Land use in the Swansea Maritime Zone, (a) 1974 and (b) 1988*

improvement of the existing physical and economic environment. Of the forty-eight firms recorded there in 1974, twenty-five remained in 1986, although some intra-area movement had occurred. The firms which stayed cited a combination of reasons for remaining, including low rents (twenty-four firms), expectations of improvement in the area's status and environment (fourteen), proximity to the city centre and professional offices (twelve), and the need to be near the docks, the Dock Office or financial institutions (eight).

Acquisition and clearance was once again the dominant policy in the Peripheral Belt. Here, however, the displacement of economic activities was less significant than in the Dockland Zone, primarily because most of the land in question was previously linked with the disused railway. Some social disruption did occur as a result of housing demolition in the extreme south-west of the Belt, but against this must be set the fact that the demolished housing was in extremely poor condition.

Rejuvenation of the Maritime Zone has not been based on the traditional activities of the past, but on the acquisition of new functions, especially in fields of leisure and recreation. Once more, the local authority has played an important role, opening in 1977 a large leisure complex in the Peripheral Belt and an Industrial and Maritime Museum on the north side of the South Dock (Fig. 8.3b). With 704,000 and 202,000 visitors respectively by 1986, these developments have been particularly influential in bringing local residents and visitors to a part of Swansea that would otherwise have been ignored, alerting them to the changes taking place and helping modify negative perceptions of the area. The city council's investment has also been important as a symbolic commitment to what was previously considered an area with few prospects for the future, a commitment, moreover, that is continuing. The council has recently agreed to finance the construction of a sea wall and promenade that will not only open the foreshore to the public, but will also link new developments in this area to the city centre (de la Hay, 1988).

The most significant private-sector development in the leisure sphere was the opening in 1982 of a 550-berth marina in the South Dock and Tawe Basin. Being the first of its size and kind in the Bristol Channel–Severn Estuary region, the marina has attracted large numbers of privately owned pleasure craft, as well as vessels of historic interest and floating exhibits. Without doubt, it has been the focal point for the entire redevelopment. By August 1986 ten new firms had been established near the marina – seven of them directly dependent on its operation, eight of them in the service sector – and by March 1988 a further fourteen firms had moved in (Table 8.3a). In addition a 120-bed hotel is currently nearing completion (Fig. 8.3b) and by the 1990s will further enhance the high-order leisure functions of the Dockland Zone.

Following close behind these developments – although on a smaller scale – there has been a revival in the Conservation Quarter; in 1986 forty-five new firms not present in 1974 were recorded, twenty-seven of which had been established since 1981. Three were manufacturing concerns, but the majority of new enterprises were in the service sector, and it is clear that many businesses were dependent on the visitors attracted to the area for recreational purposes, although the importance of residents in new housing (described below), and the proximity of the city centre, should not be overlooked. Typical of these new establishments are small shops, wine bars and pubs, restaurants and cafés, estate agents, amusement arcades and discos.

Here too the local authority has played an influential role. By making available premises at low rents, assisting in the conversion of premises and sponsoring individual enterprises, it has given considerable encouragement to the development of specific cultural, craft and artistic ventures. A garage has been transformed into a small theatre and workshops, an old church into an art gallery and workshops. The workshops have been occupied by glass studios, potters, artists and a film centre. Assistance to voluntary organisations has been given through the provision of council-owned premises on short leases.

In contrast to the developments associated with recreational functions, other manufacturing, wholesaling and office activities – the mainstay of the economy prior to redevelopment – have experienced little physical expansion in most of the Maritime Zone. Manufacturing which survived the clearance programme continues largely as before, and the local authority has constructed five small industrial premises south of the Tawe Basin. But wholesaling and distributional activities have completely disappeared, while private-sector offices are no longer to be found outside the Conservation Quarter, where their presence has been consolidated rather than expanded.

An important objective of the restructuring process has been to re-establish the area as an attractive residential location, and not just a destination for recreation. Housing development has been undertaken by three separate agencies: the local authority, a housing association and private firms, with the housing association (521 units) and the private sector (410 units) accounting for by far the largest proportion of the 1,129 dwellings completed. As with commercial development, the marina has again been the focus for investment, with virtually all land adjacent to the South Dock being given over to private or housing association dwellings.

The local authority has, therefore, only been responsible for the construction of a relatively small amount of housing. This comprises replacement dwellings (forty-nine units) at the western end of the Dockland Zone, and sheltered housing for the elderly and disabled (149 units) north of the Tawe Basin. Despite this low level of direct involvement, however, the city council has exerted an influence in other ways that have brought benefit to the local population. Private developers, for example, were persuaded to let the council nominate residents for some of the new homes from the housing waiting lists. Similarly, the housing association agreed to make a proportion of its sale properties in Maritime Village (between the Marina and the Tawe Basin) available to first-time and elderly buyers with limited resources through an equity-sharing scheme.

Finally in the context of land use, it is important to remember that the dynamics of any area cannot be considered in isolation, but affect – and are affected by – changes elsewhere, especially in contiguous zones. This is particularly pertinent here, where developments in the Peripheral Belt cannot be ignored. The catalytic function of the leisure complex, which dominates the central section of this belt, has already been mentioned. But the Peripheral Belt also became the chosen location for a large Sainsbury food supermarket (built on the original Half Tide Basin in the north) and (in the west) for a major public administration centre, West Glamorgan County Council's new county hall.[3] While it can be argued that the Peripheral Belt was in many ways a convenient location for these activities, not least because all require car-parking space that was amply available, their functional role in the revitalisation process is difficult to overstate. All have contributed to the upgrading of the area, have brought in many more people, and may well have given other activities the confidence to establish themselves in the district. What must also be emphasised is that in each of these developments the constructive role of the local authority has been crucial. By making land available, arranging the necessary planning permissions and generally facilitating change, the council has sought to ensure that no opportunity was lost to stimulate upward transition in this area.

Economic impacts

Research into economic change has focused on employment trends and, although other impacts require further detailed investigation, the general pattern and direction of development can already be identified.

Employment trends, 1974–86

Changes in the nature and scale of employment have been as far reaching as those affecting the physical fabric and the environment. In many ways they have reflected general processes – discussed by other chapters – that are commonly observable in the inner-urban areas of other advanced countries. These processes include deindustrialisation (Blackaby, 1978; Martin and Rowthorn, 1986), evolution towards post-industrial economic and social structures (Bell, 1973; Ochel and Wegner, 1987) and the growth of female and part-time employment, coupled with contraction in the male labour market (Champion *et al*, 1987). What is also evident, however, is that the local authority has acted as a catalyst that has accelerated change

Table 8.2 Firms and permanent employment in the Swansea Maritime Zone, 1974–1986

(a) Dockland Zone

Year	No. of firms	MFT	MPT	FFT	FPT	Total
1974	35	807	17	200	77	1101
1976	17	402	15	142	42	601
1981	6	216	0	77	26	319
1986	13	216	15	97	33	361

(b) Conservation Quarter

Year	No. of firms	MFT	MPT	FFT	FPT	Total
1974	48	535	43	167	59	804
1976	49	575	41	147	63	826
1981	53	624	41	144	101	910
1986	80	525	72	217	96	910

(c) Dockland Zone and Conservation Quarter

Year	No. of firms	MFT	MPT	FFT	FPT	Total
1974	83	1342	60	367	136	1905
1976	66	977	56	289	105	1427
1981	59	840	41	221	127	1229
1986	93	741	87	314	129	1271

(d) Total Maritime Zone (Peripheral Zone included)

Year	Total
1974	1905
1976	1427
1981	1229
1986	2516

MFT = Male full-time employment   FFT = Female full-time employment
MPT = Male part-time employment   FPT = Female part-time employment

Data relating to full-time and part-time employment, and to male/female employment, are not fully available for the Peripheral Zone. A breakdown comparable to those for the Dockland Zone and Conservation Quarter cannot, therefore, be provided.

Sources: 1974, 1976, 1981 data: Swansea City Council; 1986 data: Edwards (1986).

through the pursuit of its strategy for the Maritime Zone. To a great extent this strategy has been supportive, but it has also generated dislocation and employment decline as a result of enforced business relocation. In this respect Swansea well illustrates the adverse consequences of land-use and employment change discussed by Tweedale (Chapter 12) and Clark (Chapter 13), although the viewpoint put forward here is that the costs of this process are outweighed by the gains of upward environmental transition.

Analysis of *permanent* employment trends in the Maritime Zone as a whole requires recognition of three distinct phases. Between 1974 – when the revitalisation programme was initiated – and 1976, land clearance and business relocation caused a 25 per cent fall in total employment, from 1,905 to 1,427 (Table 8.2d). This sharp contraction was followed by a period of slower decline, causing an additional 14 per cent loss by 1981. It was, therefore, only in the 1980s – following local-authority investment in essential infrastructural improvements – that employment recovery was initiated. Yet by 1986 permanent employment was 32 per cent higher than in 1974, and was twice the 1981 total. *Temporary* employment, meanwhile, also rose dramatically in the 1980s as rebuilding began and construction workers were recruited. By 1987 the building industry had added more than 500 male jobs to the local labour market. This was equivalent to 20 per cent of the labour demands of other employers in the Maritime Zone and – perhaps more significantly – to 63 per cent of their male employment.

In the late 1980s construction continues to make a major contribution to employment, but it cannot be relied upon as a mainstay for the 1990s, when reconstruction is complete. Moreover, when permanent employment is examined in greater detail, it is evident that fundamental structural shifts have created for the 1990s a set of labour-market requirements that is very different to that of the 1970s. These structural shifts have in turn been linked with major changes in the balance of male and female labour, and with the evolution of the geography of employment within the area.

Deindustrialisation and enforced relocation have impacted most deeply around the South Dock and the Tawe Basin, the Dockland Zone originally biased towards manufacturing and wholesaling. Here, total employment fell by 71 per cent between 1974 and 1981, and full-time jobs for men accounted for three-quarters of the losses (Table 8.2a). As has been indicated, in the 1980s this slide was halted by the in-migration of small businesses, many of which are marina-related. But a major employment recovery has yet to be achieved. By August 1986 new firms had created only forty-five new jobs, thirty of which were for men. In net terms, male full-time employment in 1986 was no higher than in 1981 and, although a modest expansion of total employment had been achieved, part-time work accounted for half the gains.

In the Conservation Quarter the local authority's rejection of clearance, and the Quarter's bias towards the service sector, have generated an entirely different outcome. Male employment – which is dominant despite the bias towards services – has fluctuated but has never slumped; female employment has expanded substantially in the 1980s; and total employment in 1986 was 13 per cent higher than in 1974 (Table 8.2b). Thus, so far as the labour market is concerned, there has been a clear shift towards the Conservation Quarter as the revitalisation programme has progressed. In 1986 this district accounted for 72 per cent of total employment in the Dockland Zone and the Conservation Quarter, compared with 32 per cent in 1974. What must also be stressed, however, is that the Conservation Quarter's relative success has been insufficient to offset completely the employment losses experienced in the Dockland Zone. Consequently the growth in total employment recorded in the 1980s in the entire Maritime Zone has been entirely dependent on the development – for the first time – of large-scale employers in the Peripheral Zone. Without this development, employment in 1986 would have remained a third lower than in 1974 (Table 8.2c and d).

In addition to its leading role in overall recovery, the emergence of the Peripheral Zone as a source of employment prompts three observations. Firstly, it has strongly reinforced the service sector as the Maritime Zone's dominant employer. Only the Welsh Glass works (with 150 employees) has added to the manufacturing labour-force. Secondly, the private-sector element in service-sector growth – the Sainsbury food supermarket – has generated job opportunities that are not typical of the area as a whole. Out of a total workforce of 250, 85 per cent are female and 75 per cent are part-time employees. The latter undoubtedly reduce the overall economic impact of the development, yet the types of job on offer – essentially involving low-skilled repetitive work – are suitable for workers who, through limited education or other adverse circumstances, are not normally in demand in areas that have been revitalised. Thirdly, while the private sector is present, it is public-sector employment that has dominated growth in the Peripheral Zone. This has been achieved partly through the construction of the leisure centre, but primarily through the decision to build West Glwmorgan's county hall in this locality. With a labour force of 940, the county hall is easily the largest employer in the entire Maritime Zone. From the viewpoint of the city economy, it is necessary to appreciate that the large majority of county hall employment has been relocated to this site, and is therefore not new. But the economic implications are still far-reaching, especially with respect to employee expenditure in the locality.

Other economic impacts

In the private sector the development that has had the clearest impact is the marina. A recent survey (Edwards, 1985) indicated that annual expen-

Table 8.3 Estimated expenditure by boat-owners using Swansea marina, 1985 (in thousand £)

	Fuel	Cateri,g/ provisions	Chandlery	Total	(%)
Owners with a permanent berth in Swansea and resident in:					
West Glamorgan	29	97	40	166	(38)
Rest of Wales	28	102	27	157	(36)
West Midlands	3	12	5	20	(5)
Rest of UK	6	13	6	25	(6)
Owners with no permanent berth in Swansea (visitors)	5	49	12	66	(15)
Total	71	273	90	434	(100)
(%)	(16)	(63)	(21)	(100)	

Figures exclude berthing charges and major chandlery purchases, such as sails and radar equipment.
Source: Field survey (Edwards, 1985)

diture by boat-owners exceeded £400,000, of which 62 per cent came from outside the local West Glamorgan sub-region (Table 8.3). Almost two-thirds of all expenditure was associated with subsistence items, a proportion having clear implications for restaurants and low-order retailing, while fuel and chandlery accounted for the remainder. Two points relating to these results must be stressed. Firstly, in the mid-1980s marina development was far from complete, and the project's economic impact is undoubtedly increasing as it matures. Secondly, the expenditure breakdown detailed in Table 8.3 relates only to day-to-day items. Berthing charges – estimated to have brought the marina company a gross income of almost £200,000 – were additional. So too were major items of chandlery, such as sails and radar equipment, and the purchase of vessels. Even though these major items are almost all produced elsewhere and are 'imported' to the local economy, causing economic 'leakage' effects, they have become significant for the marina-related service sector. For example, Swansea now has a role as a yacht sale–resale centre for a large part of south Wales, and its influence in this respect also extends to the south coast of the Bristol Channel. This generates sub-regional income through commission charges, vessel-inspection services and vessel servicing and refurbishment.

Tangible benefits for the local authority accrue at least partly in the form of higher rental income. In 1974 this amounted to only £28,000 but by 1987 it had increased to £203,000, of which 80 per cent was derived from

Table 8.4   Taxation income (rates) from the Swansea Maritime Zone, 1974 and 1986 (as a percentage of city total)

		Domestic	Commercial	Total
1974	Total Maritime Zone	0.04	1.19	1.23
1986	Dockland Zone and			
	Conservation Quarter	0.48	0.63	1.11
	Peripheral Belt	0.00	1.78	1.78
	Total Maritime Zone	0.48	2.41	2.89

Source: City of Swansea Finance Department

the marina-dominated South Dock development. More generally, the Maritime Zone's contribution to total city income from local property taxation (rates) rose from 1.23 per cent in 1974 to 2.89 per cent in 1986 (Table 8.4). One factor in this gain was the completion of housing projects: these contributed 0.48 per cent of city tax income in 1986, compared with only 0.04 per cent in 1974. But – as with employment – the major gain in local taxation resulted from developments in the Peripheral Zone. Without this growth, the main commercial tax-paying element of which was the Sainsbury supermarket, the Maritime Zone's contribution to the city budget would still be less than in 1974.

It is evident that opportunities exist to extend these brief examinations of economic impact in the private and public sectors. As a final point, however, it is necessary to stress that further work should attempt to assess the balance of benefits and costs. Already, for example, costs can be identified in the form of traffic congestion in the Conservation Quarter; late-night noise from leisure-related activities; and rising property prices and their attendant social implications. But it is also arguable that the cost–benefit approach should be extended to the public sector, to place its investment in a clearer perspective. In particular, how much of the city's heavy investment in infrastructure can be recouped in straightforward economic terms, and how much must be assigned to less quantifiable – yet still vital – gains such as environmental upgrading and port–city re-integration?

Conclusion

As the problem of achieving effective waterfront revitalisation spreads to more and often smaller cityports, and as it becomes more fashionable to downgrade the competence of local administrations, a pressing need arises to assess objectively the role which local authorities are able to play in urban regeneration. The Swansea experience – which substantiates the emphasis placed by Riley and Shurmer-Smith (Chapter 3) on the influence of 'bottom-up' forces – is that a local authority can in many ways play a leading and generally effective role, particularly if its commitment is demonstrably of a long-term nature. Long-term commitment arguably gains the confidence of other 'actors' in the revitalisation process, and in Swansea's case was signalled by substantial pump-priming and by the assertion of high standards for restructuring. These standards began with the creation by the local authority of high-quality decision-making structures tailored to the needs of the problem.

In terms of physical improvement and general urban development, there is no doubt that the outcome of this local-authority orchestrated programme has been essentially successful. The Conservation Quarter, the only area with real architectural merit, has been set on an upward spiral; in the Dockland and Peripheral Zones much larger swathes of old industrial and derelict land have been cleared; and substantial private and public investments have brought into being an environment far superior to its predecessor. Moreover, this new environment touches the lives of a much larger proportion of the population than was formerly the case, chiefly because of the drawing power of developments such as the supermarket, the leisure centre, the marina and the museum. These innovations have been primarily responsible for the reintegration of the city and its abandoned dockland.

Success in this direction does not, however, imply that progress along other avenues has been equally good. As has been indicated, more economic research is required. But while, for example, the marina has made new direct and indirect contributions to local development, traditional forms of employment have either disappeared or have been relocated to the disadvantage of local residents. Replacement jobs have not matched the skills of displaced workers, and recent job 'growth' has been achieved primarily by the inward relocation of employment rather than by its creation. The question that arises, therefore, is whether imperfect progress in the economic sphere cancels out environmental and other planning gains. In Swansea's case it is argued that this has not happened. Against the enforced loss of some 800 Dockland Zone jobs, many of which would have disappeared through free-market deindustrialisation, must be set the fact that more than sixty hectares of redeveloped land have been reabsorbed into the city's functional structure. What is recognised, however, is that the cost–benefit equation must be examined in many more localities before a reliable overall picture can emerge. One largely-favourable outcome does not provide a general rule.

Notes

1   It should be noted that the Maritime Zone defined here excludes the North Dock mentioned earlier. Policy has focused on the more remote triangle of

land extending south and south-west of the Half Tide Basin (Fig. 8.2), and it
is on this district that the remainder of the chapter concentrates.

2   In policy documents this area and the Dockland Zone are known collectively
as the Maritime Quarter. This term has not been used in this chapter since
maritime quarters, as defined by Hilling (Chapter 2) and others, do not
include abandoned docks. Swansea's Conservation Quarter is on its own a
maritime quarter, as defined in this book.

3   West Glamorgan County Council is an administrative authority created by
local government reform in 1974 and is distinct from the city council. Its
jurisdiction extends well outside Swansea, but since West Glamorgan was
established its administration has been based in the city.

Acknowledgements

The assistance provided by Trevor Osborne and David Williams of the Development Department, City of Swansea, is gratefully acknowledged.

I should also like to express my thanks to Guy Lewis and Paul Taylor, carto-
graphers, and Alan Cutliffe, photographer, Department of Geography, University
of Wales, Swansea.

References

Adcock, B. (1984), 'Regenerating Merseyside's docklands: the Merseyside
Development Corporation 1981–84', *Town Planning Review*, 55(3), 265–89.
Bell, D. (1973), *The coming of post-industrial society* (New York: Penguin).
Blackaby, F. (ed.) (1978), *Deindustrialisation* (London: Arnold).
Champion, A.G., Green, A.E., Owen, D.W., Ellin, D.J. and Coombes, M.G.
(1987), *Changing places* (London: Arnold).
de la Hay, C. (1988), 'Swansea: victim of wartime devastation and failed industry?',
Landscape, 6, 36–43.
Edwards, J.A. (1985), *The identification and location of potential users of the
Swansea Yacht Haven in the West Midlands*, report to Economic and Social
Research Council, Department of Geography, University College, Swansea.
—— (1988a), *Port developments in the Bristol Channel*, unpublished ms submitted
for publication.
—— (1988b), 'Marina and maritime quarter developments in Wales', *Cambria*
(forthcoming).
Edwards, S.C. (1987), *The local impact of the redevelopment of Swansea's Maritime
Quarter*, unpublished undergraduate dissertation, Department of Geography,
University of Southampton.
Hallett, G. and Randall, P. (1970), *Ports and maritime industry in South Wales*
(Cardiff University College, Cardiff).
Hilling, D. (1984), 'The restructuring of the Severn estuary ports', in B.S. Hoyle
and D. Hilling (eds), *Seaport systems and spatial change* (London: Wiley),
11–22.

Martin, R. and Rowthorn, B. (1986), *The geography of deindustrialisation* (London: Macmillan).

Ochel, W. and Wegner, M. (1987), *Service economies in Europe* (Boulder, Colorado: Westview Press).

Osborne, T.M. (1987a), *Forgotten towns – case study of Swansea*, paper given at 'Forgotten Towns Conference', 26 November, sponsored by the Royal Town Planning Institute and the District Planning Officers' Society.

—— (1987b), *Tourism and the local government role – the case study of Swansea*, paper given at Local Government and Tourism Ninth National Seminar, 17 October.

Williams, D. (1988), *Swansea Maritime Quarter – a study of dockland redevelopment*, MSc Thesis, University of Wales, Swansea (forthcoming).

9 Urban revitalisation, public policy and the redevelopment of redundant port zones: lessons from Baltimore and Manchester

Christopher M. Law

This chapter examines the role which the redevelopment of port zones, influenced by public policy, can play in the revitalisation of urban areas. A fundamental assumption is that investigations of redundant port space should not be separated from more general analyses of inner-urban change. During the postwar period the core areas of major cities in North America and Britain have experienced decline as witnessed by population decrease, rising unemployment, increasing poverty, reduced employment and growing competition with centres in the outer city. The decline of port and port-related activities has contributed to the problems of the core, but at the same time vacant waterfront lands offer opportunities which can greatly assist the policies of revitalisation. The exact nature of these opportunities will vary from one city to another depending on the economic character of the urban area, the size and form of the redundant zones and their location within the urban area. The chapter will discuss these issues and illustrate them by reference to two case-studies: Baltimore and Manchester.

Problems of the urban core

Urban areas are subject to a constant process of change. Whilst the growth of population and economic activities can in principle be accommodated by redevelopment to higher densities, during the twentieth century the predominant mode of development has been peripheral expansion and the decentralisation of people and jobs. Initially this had little impact on the compact high-density urban cores developed during the nineteenth and early twentieth centuries, and the monocentric character of cities was therefore maintained. However, by the mid-twentieth century extensive suburbs had been developed around major cities in North America and Britain, and a decisive shift was taking place in the preferred forms of transport, away from railways and buses towards cars and trucks. This enabled suburban and exurban areas to develop at even greater distances from the city centre. To meet the needs of these suburban residents, shopping centres evolved, and there has also been a significant shift of industry and warehousing to the outer city, where large sites are available which are usually cheaper and also accessible to national and regional highways. Finally, offices have begun to decentralise towards accessible sites in the outer city and near preferred residential locations. Overall the spatial structure of metropolitan areas has been changing from a monocentric form to a polycentric one (Leven, 1978; Muller, 1981).

This process of decentralisation has impacted severely on core areas (Law, 1988a). The city centre has lost industry, warehousing and transport activities. In the United States retailing has declined significantly, in many cases by over a half (Robertson, 1983). In Britain retail decline in major city centres has been less because, until the mid-1980s, planning policies constrained the growth of centres in the outer city. The experience of office development in the city centre has varied considerably, as will be discussed below. In the surrounding inner city, population has declined as the average size of households has fallen, and as residential areas have been redeveloped to lower densities. There has also been a tendency for the higher-income groups to leave the inner city in favour of newer lower-density housing areas in the suburbs, so leaving in this area a concentration of the poor, the unskilled, the unemployed and those suffering personal problems. Industry and warehousing have also declined in this zone. In part, jobs have decreased as those firms that remained have increasingly mechanised production (Fothergill *et al*, 1985). But employment has also fallen as firms have closed or relocated to the suburbs, while few new firms have been attracted to the area because of the obsolescence of factories and the environment. The decline of port and port-related activities has also contributed to the problems of the urban core, both in terms of the number of jobs lost and of the large amount of vacant and derelict land left behind. There has often been a process of cumulative decline with a lack of investment producing further obsolescence, which has in turn discouraged investment. Another influence has been the fact that it is frequently more expensive to redevelop a brownfield site than a greenfield one.

Whilst these general trends are evident in most cities, there is also a variety of experience so far as the extent of the downward spiral is concerned. For example, in some cities business, government, health and education functions have grown strongly, encouraging a huge increase of office space in the city centre and the gentrification of inner-city areas. However this experience has bypassed other cities – often those which have an industrial character, are located in regions of economic decline, and are overshadowed by other cities in the urban hierarchy. This contrast of experience highlights the need to focus on revitalisation strategies.

Revitalisation policies

Whilst some academics have suggested that the decline of the core is an inevitable process which should be accepted, national and local governments have sought to stem and even reverse the decline. Their motives have been various. In the United States the loss of local taxes can produce serious problems for central cities, which can be solved by regeneration. A concern for social justice has clearly been a major motive for most governments, whilst the fear of unrest has been important from time to time. The core area still plays a major role in the life of the metropolitan area, in terms of business, government, culture and public transport, and to protect these functions some support may be necessary. In addition there may be a desire to maintain or create a strong, dynamic and visually-attractive core which can give a focus and identity to the region. Some have labelled intervention motivated by these considerations 'boosterism'.

Revitalisation policies can be classified in various ways, but one typology is based on whether they are market- or socially led. The former attempts to capitalise on the advantages of the core, which are usually found in the city centre, and encourage activities such as office development and tourism. In the United States public–private partnerships have been important contributors to this approach, and this is now spreading to Britain (Fosler and Berger, 1982). Within this approach public money is seen as necessary, and is often described as pump-priming investment, to fund basic works which are essential before private investment will be profitable. Social approaches to revitalisation, meanwhile, have typically emphasised the needs of residents for better housing, community facilities and jobs. Public funding is again necessary, but tends to occur in the inner city rather than the city centre. In practice aspects of these two approaches may be combined, as exemplified by the attempt to target newly created jobs for the local population rather than for residents of the outer city.

Revitalisation policies may be initiated by national or local governments or by joint public–private organisations, and may be implemented either directly or indirectly by special agencies. Examples of the latter include redevelopment agencies in cities of the United States and – increasingly – urban development corporations in Britain. The task of urban revital-isation is likely to take many years so that, even if the objectives could be specified precisely, it is frequently too early to make a comprehensive evaluation of individual projects. However, preliminary and comparative evaluations are useful in facilitating the diffusion of ideas and best prac-tices, and in assisting policy-formulation for the later stages.

The redevelopment of redundant port zones

Forces causing the decline of port and related industrial activities have been explored in early chapters and need not be considered here. So far as port authorities are concerned, a common initial reaction was that the redundant port zones had little value, since they consisted of derelict and decaying buildings in areas often dominated by industry and working-class housing. One frequent reaction to this situation was to transfer the docklands – and the problem – to public authorities, as Clark emphasises in Chapter 13. However, it gradually emerged from early waterfront re-development schemes that the mix of land and water provided sites that were attractive to many activities (some water-related, some water-enhanced and some unrelated to water) which could be developed with advantage providing that basic works were undertaken to improve these areas. This basic investment inevitably involved the public sector, which was interested in these areas because of its role in urban revitalisation, and of the need to reintegrate redundant port zones into the urban area.

The opportunities provided by redundant port areas will obviously vary from one example to another. Some are very extensive, as with the London Docklands, whilst others are much smaller, as the Manchester example discussed below illustrates. Some have dock basins, some wharves and others finger piers. They may form narrow elongated zones, as at Liverpool, or alternatively can be compact. Redundant port space may lie so close to the city centre that it can be incorporated into it. But it may also be situated in the surrounding inner city, and some might even be on the edge of – or beyond – the city as Pinder and Husain (Chapter 14) demonstrate. Another important variable is that of city dynamism. If redundant dock-lands occur in strong, dynamic, rapidly growing areas where there is a shortage of land, the task of revitalisation is likely to be easier than if the setting is a declining economy where there is already much vacant space. In addition, the opportunities afforded may depend on how much of the port area can be planned as an entity. In some cases, land may only become available in small parcels and the redundant areas can never be seen as a whole. In others the port-authority land can be planned as a unit, while other vacant port-related land, such as disused railways, is developed separately by its owners. Exceptionally, redundant space and ownership may be so concentrated that comprehensive redevelopment is feasible. This wide variety of circumstances makes it difficult to generalise about the processes of waterfront redevelopment, even though recurrent outcomes – such as leisure and recreation – can be identified (Chapter 15).

The motivations of public authorities to the redevelopment of redundant land will also vary. Whilst all will seek to incorporate waterfront redevelopment into the process of urban revitalisation, as we have seen, attitudes as to how this should be achieved are not uniform. Some authorities simply seek to reuse the land as quickly as possible, and through this increase local tax income. This is an important consideration in the United States, particularly as ports there are tax-exempt. Other objectives raise major issues of the type explored in Chapters 11, 12 and 13. In the labour-market context, a common goal is to create jobs to replace those lost – but of any type and for whom? Many waterfront areas have been used for housing – but should this be for locals at prices they can afford or for anyone, including a new middle class who might add social mix to an area? Another objective may well be to improve the leisure amenities of the area – but how much? Is a narrow strip of public access to the waterfront sufficient, or should there be provision for major parks? If recreational facilities and attractions are provided, should they be for locals or to draw in tourists? In some cases, where historic buildings are found, there may be a conservation objective. In addition, although public authorities may be willing to subsidise redevelopment, they may seek to do this with least cost to themselves, so ensuring a large private-sector involvement. This approach has been of long-standing importance in the United States, but is now increasingly significant elsewhere. Finally, some public authorities may seek, through waterfront redevelopment, to transform the image of their area via an environmentally impressive project.

One of the main thrusts of the remainder of this chapter is that – as has been indicated – the opportunities afforded by redundant port zones will depend on their location. Whether they occur in a thriving or declining urban economy – and whether they are located adjacent to the city centre or embedded in the inner city – may be crucial to subsequent development. The two case-studies explored below offer contrasting examples of the power of these factors. Baltimore's Inner Harbor is part of a prosperous and growing metropolitan region and is located very close to the central business district. Manchester Docks are located two or three kilometres from the city centre in the inner city, within a metropolitan region which has experienced stagnation for many decades and decline in recent years. In seeking to draw conclusions from the comparison of Baltimore and Manchester, however, some caution is necessary because the process of revitalisation has not proceeded concurrently in these cities. In Baltimore redevelopment has been taking place for over twenty years. By the early 1980s it was widely acclaimed as a success and held up as a model, both of waterfront renewal and urban revitalisation. Many policy-makers, consultants, practitioners and academics have visited the city so that its example has been diffused around the world. In contrast, the development of Manchester Docks only began in 1981, so that the project is still in its early stages.

Baltimore's Inner Harbor redevelopment

Baltimore is a port and city on the north-east coast of the United States which was founded in 1729 (Olson, 1976). Although its population was 2.2m in 1980 it has been overshadowed during its history by the neighbouring cities of Washington, seventy-two kilometres to the south west, and Philadelphia, 152 kilometres to the north east. Whilst this has prevented higher-order functions – including head offices – from developing, the city has benefited in recent years from some overflow of activities from Washington. For most of its history Baltimore's character has been predominantly industrial, and of a branch-plant nature. Its port has remained prosperous and there are many port-related industries, including iron and steel at Sparrows Point and shipbuilding. However, almost inevitably there has been a movement downstream of these port and port-related activities, so that by the late 1950s the Inner Harbor, the original site of the city, was becoming derelict.

The Baltimore metropolitan region is typical of many American cities (Olson, 1980). Whilst the population of the region nearly doubled between 1940 and 1980, within the central city the number of people decreased from 950,000 in 1950 to 787,000 in 1980 (Law and Grundy, 1984). Expansion in the outer city was encouraged by the construction of a beltway and inter-city highway links, following which out-of-town shopping and – later – office centres were built. Within the central city, average incomes are lower, and the unemployment rate is higher, than for the entire metropolitan area, and there is now a non-white majority. Already by the mid-1950s there was evidence of retail decline in the city centre, and the poor state of housing in the inner city was also generating concern. It was on the basis of these two issues that redevelopment planning was initiated in Baltimore. Strong planning has been facilitated by a political structure which gives great power to the mayor, and by the fact that Baltimore's mayors have held office for long periods. The most recent and influential mayor was Donald Shaeffer, who was in office from 1972 to 1986. It has also been suggested that Baltimore's proximity to Washington has helped it to take advantage of Federal funds such as Urban Development Action Grants, introduced in 1977, and other national urban policies evolved during the 1960s and 1970s.

Although the Inner Harbor project is the largest, most dramatic and perhaps the most successful scheme undertaken by the city authorities, it is by no means the only one. It was preceded by the Charles Center project discussed below. In 1979 the Market Center Development Corporation was established to revitalise the downtown retail district, and in 1984 the Charles Street Management Corporation was established to revitalise a once-grand street. Elsewhere in the inner city, Baltimore is noted for its efforts to rehabilitate housing, including a programme of homesteading, in which derelict properties are sold very cheaply to home owners on condition that they are rehabilitated within two years. This has a parallel in a programme for retail premises known as 'shopsteading'. Waterfront revitalisation is, therefore, a dimension of an extensive attack on urban decline.

The first proposals for urban renewal came not from the city authorities but from the private sector (Lyall, 1982). In 1955 the Committee for Downtown, representing retailers in the city centre, and the newly formed Greater Baltimore Committee, initiated a planning study of the central area which confirmed the malaise being experienced, and proposed the redevelopment of a small rundown area between the retail and office

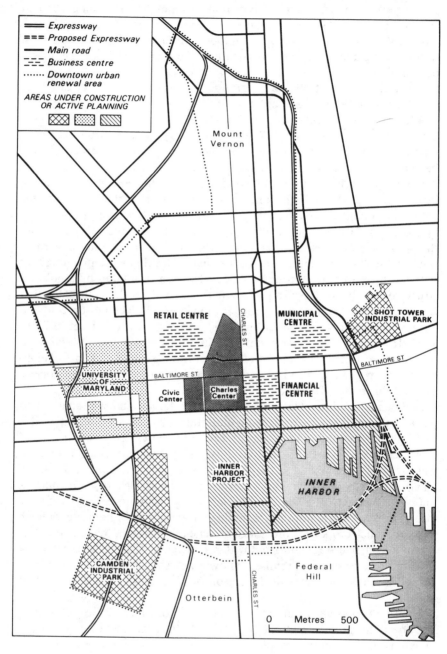

Figure 9.1 *Baltimore city centre and inner harbour*

quarters (Fig. 9.1). In 1959 the city accepted this Charles Center project and established a management office to undertake the programme. The city bought the land, cleared it and then sold plots to developers according to the plan. Over 200,000 square metres of offices were constructed, 40,000 square metres of retail premises, a hotel, a theatre and 300 apartments (Millspaugh, 1964).

The early success of the scheme, coupled with the fact that after Federal grants the project was very cheap, encouraged the city to consider a similar programme for the Inner Harbor, then in a state of decay and becoming the haunt of tramps and drug addicts. In 1964 the Greater Baltimore Committee produced a plan for the Inner Harbor which envisaged 22 hectares of park; offices; housing which would bring the middle classes back downtown; and public and tourist buildings. The scheme was accepted by the city in 1965, which then established Charles Center–Inner Harbor Management Inc. to manage both projects. This is a city agency which has more autonomy and independence than a department of local government. Several years were spent obtaining Federal grants and undertaking basic works, including the clearance of the site and the rebuilding of harbour walls. It was only towards the end of the 1970s that the various elements of the scheme began to come together and its success was seen. In the period from the mid-1960s to the early 1980s, the emphasis of the scheme shifted more to recreation, leisure and tourism. This was in part a reflection of, and a reaction to, national trends. Thus many cities at this time were building convention centres and the city decided to construct one and locate it close to the Inner Harbor. The initial project for the Inner Harbor was for a 100-hectare site (Fig. 9.2), but this has subsequently been extended both eastwards and westwards to include other empty and derelict areas. A chronology of the main events associated with the project is given in Table 9.1.

Baltimore: achievements and evaluation

The core area of the project, around the Inner Harbor, is devoted to leisure and tourist activities. These include a marina, a maritime museum including the historic *USF Constellation*, a waterfront park, a two-pavilion festival marketplace by the Rouse Company called Harborplace, a science museum, an aquarium, a high viewing-point at the top of the World Trade Center, the Convention Center, numerous hotels and an amusement centre. In addition, two stadia are now planned for the Camden Yards district just west of the Convention Center. Retailing associated with tourism has developed in the area, initially in Harborplace, but more recently in The Gallery. The City Fair was moved to the Inner Harbor in 1973, and subsequently many other events have either been started or

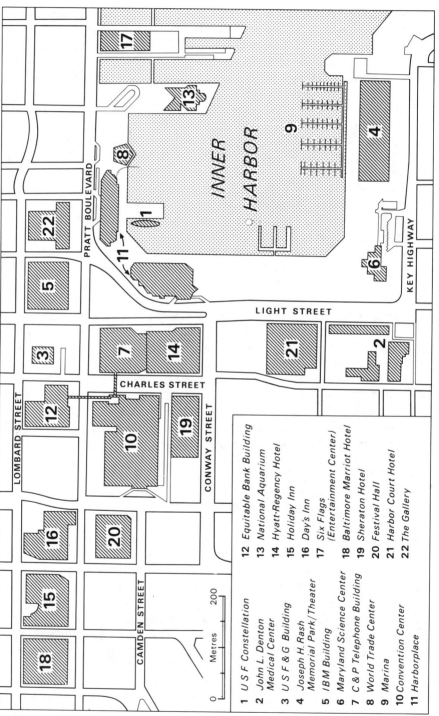

Figure 9.2 Baltimore's Inner Harbor Project

1 U S F Constellation
2 John L. Denton Medical Center
3 U S F & G Building
4 Joseph H. Rash Memorial Park/Theater
5 IBM Building
6 Maryland Science Center
7 C & P Telephone Building
8 World Trade Center
9 Marina
10 Convention Center
11 Harborplace

12 Equitable Bank Building
13 National Aquarium
14 Hyatt-Regency Hotel
15 Holiday Inn
16 Day's Inn
17 Six Flags (Entertainment Center)
18 Baltimore Marriot Hotel
19 Sheraton Hotel
20 Festival Hall
21 Harbor Court Hotel
22 The Gallery

Table 9.1 Baltimore's Inner Harbor project: chronology

Reference numbers in brackets refer to Figure 9.2

Year		Year	
1962	Mayor calls for Inner Harbor study	1977	World Trade Center – 32-storey pentagonal office block with high viewing point (27,880 m^2) (8)
1964	Inner Harbor plan by Greater Baltimore Committee	1978	Marina (9)
1965	Charles Center–Inner Harbor Management Inc. formed to administer both projects	1979	Convention Center (102,230 m^2 exhibition space) (10)
1968	Acquisition and clearance of site began following receipt of Federal Grant	1980	Harborplace – a festival market place (13,200 m^2) (11)
		1980	Equitable Bank Building (33,450 m^2) (12)
1972	USF Constellation (warship built 1797) moved to permanent mooring in harbor (1)	1981	National Aquarium (13)
		1981	Hyatt Regency Hotel (500 rooms) (14)
1972	John L. Denton Medical Center agreed. First phase of Lutheran Church complex for elderly (2)	1984	Holiday Inn (374 rooms) (15)
		1984	Days Inn (256 rooms) (16)
1973	United States Fidelity and Guarantee Company's Office Building (40 storeys, 42,759 m^2) (3)	1985	Six Flags (Entertainment Center in old power station) (17)
1973	City Fair (September) moved to Inner Harbor	1985	Baltimore Marriot Hotel (360 rooms) (18)
1975	Joseph H. Rash Memorial Park (sports complex) (4)	1985	Sheraton Hotel (350 rooms) (19)
1975	IBM building (29,740 m^2) (5)	1985	Festival Hall annex to Convention Center (20)
1976	Maryland Science Center (Museum) (6)	1986	Harborcourt (hotel, offices and appartments) (21)
1977	C & P Telephone Building (26,950 m^2) (7)	1987	The Gallery (retail, offices, hotel) (22)

relocated here. The Tall Ships Festival has used the Inner Harbor in 1976 and 1986.

The redevelopment of the Inner Harbor has greatly enlarged Baltimore's role as a tourist centre and, for the first time, put it in the top league. The Rouse Company claimed that within two or three years of the opening at Harborplace, it was being visited by over 18 million people a year, more than the number of visitors to Disneyland. By 1985 the number of delegates using the Convention Center had risen to 200,000 and its success is illustrated by the increase in the number of hotels. Between 1981 and 1987 the seven hotels built around the Inner Harbor added 2,448 bedrooms to the accommodation available in the city. Surveys by the Office of Promotion and Tourism show that the number of summer visitors to Baltimore's central area from outside the city increased from 2.25 million in 1980, to 6.8 million in 1984 and 7.5 million in 1986. Moreover, their expenditure rose even more rapidly: from $125 million in 1980, to $400 million in 1984 and to $650 million in 1986. In labour market terms, the total number of jobs estimated to have been created by tourism rose from 16,000 in 1981 to 20,000 in 1984, and will almost certainly have increased since then.

While tourist-related development has been impressive, offices form a second important land use. Several office blocks or towers have been built since the early 1970s and have attracted to the city investment in sectors such as finance and insurance, computers and telecommunications (Table 9.1). More recently they have formed part of mixed developments in which offices are combined with a hotel, or retailing, or apartments, as at Harborcourt and The Gallery.

A third area of interest concerns housing, which was included among the objectives of the 1964 plan. The first dwellings to be built were for the elderly, attached to a Lutheran church near the south-west corner of the Inner Harbor, and completed in 1972. Older housing in the adjacent areas, particularly in Federal Hill, has been improved and new houses built on vacant plots. Today there is evidence of gentrification in this area, and in 1986 a multi-purpose tower block, Harborcourt, was completed containing a hotel, offices and 179 luxury apartments. Whilst no other housing has been built around the Inner Harbor, further downstream at Fells Point older housing has been improved and vacant warehouses have been converted to dwellings, again with evidence of gentrification.

Given the nature of these changes it may be tempting to assume that revitalisation in Baltimore springs essentially from the buoyancy of market forces. The evidence is, however, that public investment − whether provided by the City, State or Federal Governments − has played a critical role in the redevelopment of the Inner Harbor. Funds were necessary to undertake the basic infrastructural works, including clearing the piers and warehouses and improving the waterfront. They were also necessary for the 'economic generators' such as the convention centre, aquarium and science museum. (Walter Sondheim, quoted in the *Financial Times*, October 9 1987). Indeed, up until about 1980 it was difficult to attract private investment. For example, the Hyatt Regency Hotel, opened in 1981, required a $10 million Urban Development Action Grant. However, once the success of the project was perceived, and a critical threshold level was reached, then private investment poured in. This is evidenced by the number of hotels built, and by an abrupt change in the public–private investment ratio. Between 1983 and 1987, 95 per cent of all investment was from private funds, compared to only 55 per cent between 1968 and 1983.

One interpretation which may be placed on this turnround is that success has been fostered by the Inner Harbor's location adjacent to the city centre. But it is also arguable that the project has in turn had a considerable impact on the surrounding area, particularly the city centre and – in a more general way – the whole metropolitan area. As the development has reached maturity it has, for example, transformed the image of Baltimore, encouraging many more investors and firms to be keen to come to the city. One example of this is the boom in office building between 1984 and 1986, when 205,000 square metres of offices were constructed. Spillover in favour of the city centre is also evidenced by the new hotels plus catering and retailing establishments now located in the zone which link the project area with the core.

While it is right to emphasise achievements, however, it is also essential to ensure that economic progress is placed in a realistic perspective, particularly with respect to social need. Much of the acclaim which Baltimore has received for its work in urban revitalisation is due to the dramatic transformation of the Inner Harbor. Whilst this scheme has undoubtedly impacted upon the rest of the city, many visitors to Baltimore have been so impressed by the Inner Harbor and the propaganda of the city authorities that they have failed to see that most of the problems of the inner city remain, and that the shift to the outer city, whilst slowed, has not been halted. In the mid-1980s, twenty years after the inauguration of the Inner Harbor project, there were still large areas of poverty in the zones immediately around the city centre. The programme's spread effects, in terms of physical restructuring and the reduction of social deprivation, must not be exaggerated.

The redevelopment of Manchester Docks

Manchester is an inland port which came into being in 1894 as a result of the completion of the Manchester Ship Canal. This canal was built to enable traffic, particularly the dominant cotton trade, to bypass the port of Liverpool which was thought to be overcharging. The port consists of three parts (Fig. 9.3):

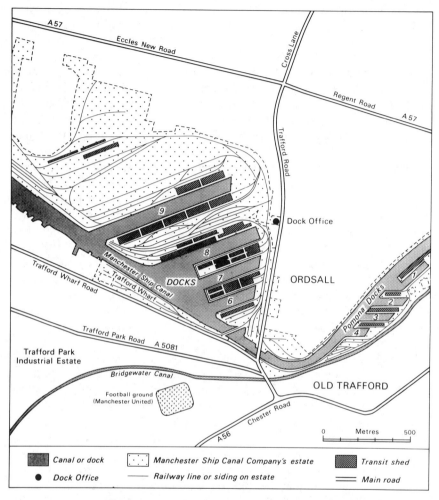

Figure 9.3   *Manchester Docks in the 1960s*

(1)   the Pomona Docks off the River Irwell, formerly used for coastwise traffic;

(2)   Salford Docks, the main docks located in the separate municipality of Salford; and

(3)   Trafford Wharf on the south side of the canal, where in 1896 the pioneering Trafford Park Industrial Estate was established with its own railway system linking the area to the docks.

For many decades Manchester Docks remained prosperous, serving the Greater Manchester region (population nearly three million) including many industries which were built immediately adjacent to the canal and docks. While manufacturing concentrated around these facilities, most of the commercial functions for the port were undertaken in the city centre, three kilometres away. For many decades the only office activities at the port were the Dock Office and Customs House. The surrounding area was either industrialised, as at Trafford Park, or consisted of working-class housing, as in adjacent Ordsall (Law, 1988b). For decades the only exceptions to this generalisation were the sports grounds of Manchester United and the Lancashire Cricket Club in Old Trafford. However, in the 1960s and 1970s over 100,000 square metres of offices were built in this latter district as part of a process of office decentralisation from the city centre.

In 1972 Manchester Docks handled two million tonnes of cargo. By 1985 port throughput was virtually zero, a contraction reflecting several factors. There was considerable industrial decline in the region; the growth of the motorway network undermined the port's hinterland; the increasing size of ships meant that many could not proceed up the canal. Most importantly, containerisation in Britain in the 1970s resulted in consortia which were frequently based at southern and eastern ports such as Felix-stowe, London and Southampton. In April 1984 the Manchester Ship Canal Company (MSCC) proposed closure of the canal's upper reaches, with the intention of concentrating its operational port activities in the lower reaches where trade remained prosperous, mostly based on oil. Closure now appears unlikely, with government help being sought to reduce basic operational expenses, but the MSCC has abandoned any hope of reviving trade in the Manchester Docks. These trends were becoming obvious by 1979–81 when the MSCC began to make some initial decisions concerning the future of the docks.

General urban policy in Greater Manchester

At this time the economic outlook of the region, and in particular of the inner city, did not look bright (Law *et al*, 1984). The population of the inner-city areas of Manchester and Salford had fallen from 619,000 in 1951 to 296,000 in 1981. Between 1971 and 1981 employment fell from 365,000 to 299,000, a decrease of 18.1 per cent, and relative poverty increased. In 1981 inner-city unemployment was 20.4 per cent, compared to 11.4 per cent in the Greater Manchester region. Meanwhile, the city centre had also experienced decline: here the number of jobs fell from 167,000 in 1961 to 106,500 in 1981 (Law, 1986).

There have been several initiatives to revitalise the inner-city areas of Manchester and Salford. In 1978 an Inner City Partnership was estab-lished, receiving funds from the Government's Urban Programme – currently around £23 million a year. In 1981 an Enterprise Zone (EZ), covering parts of Trafford Park and Salford Docks, was designated provid-ing tax and planning advantages – most notably a rate-free period of ten

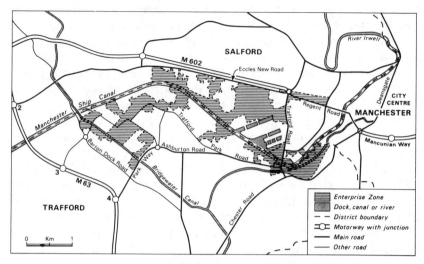

Figure 9.4   *The Salford/Trafford Enterprise Zone*

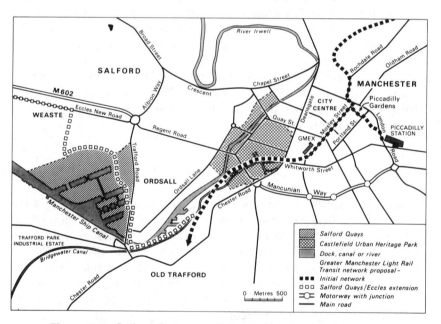

Figure 9.5   *Salford Quays in relation to Manchester city centre*

years – with the objective of speeding up development (Fig. 9.4). There
have also been several initiatives to revitalise the city centre. These have
included the conversion of the former Central Station into the G-MEX
exhibition centre, and the creation of an urban heritage park at Castlefield,
with museums and transport artefacts (Fig. 9.5). Attempts to improve

accessibility to the city centre by constructing a light rail transit system received government approval (for Phase 1) in January 1988. Other recent initiatives have included the establishment in 1987 of the Trafford Park Development Corporation to regenerate the industrial area, and the establishment in 1988 of a Central Manchester Development Corporation.

Strategy evolution for the Docks

Initial proposals for dock redevelopment emanated from the owners, the MSCC. In the late 1970s they began to fill in the Pomona Docks and seek industrial uses for the land. They also began to seek users for the land north of Dock 9, which had been used for storage. When in 1980 the government proposed Enterprise Zones, this land – and that south of Dock 6 – was proposed by the MSCC and Salford city council, receiving designation in 1981. By 1983 it was obvious that the main part of Salford Docks was unlikely to be used as a port again, and the MSCC began to consider other uses. However, they believed that before these could be found, considerable sums of money would have to be spent on improving the infrastructure, rebuilding dock walls, etc. Without the prospect of new uses this could not be borrowed and, as a private company, they would not receive government funds. Accordingly, in 1983 they sold 94 hectares of Salford Docks (excluding the EZ land north of Dock 9) to Salford city council for £1.5 million, so that government money could be obtained for its redevelopment.

By 1983 news of the success of places like Baltimore and the role of tourism in revitalisation had reached Britain, but the inner-city location of the docks suggested that this type of activity was unlikely to be successful. In order to initiate at least some redevelopment the city council offered the land around Dock 6 to a developer, Urban Waterside, providing it could attract £4.5 million of investment within three years. The council also commissioned Shepherd Epstein and Hunter to produce a plan for the docks. In 1985 this proposed that dams be built across Docks 7, 8 and 9 to create basins, thus excluding the polluted water of the ship canal. There would also be spine roads, a high standard of environment and public access to the waterfront (Fig. 9.6). Salford city council decided that there should be a balance of uses: one-third residences, one-third leisure and recreation, and one-third employment activities. Grant aid was sought from the government and, at the end of 1985, a rolling programme of derelict land clearance grants and urban programme money, amounting to £25 million over six years, was agreed. Salford city council was to contribute £1 million a year and additional finance was to be sought from the Manpower Services Commission and the European Community. The whole project was to be known as Salford Quays.

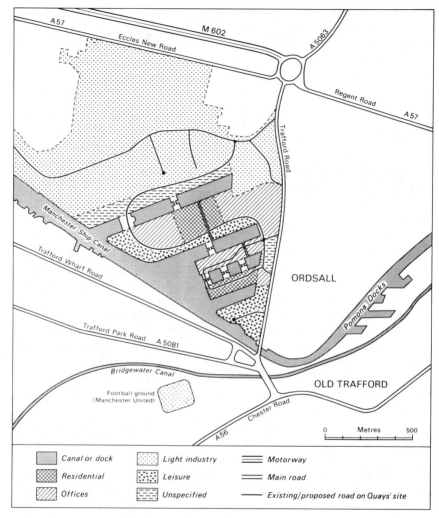

Figure 9.6 *Proposals for Salford Quays*

Results and evaluation

The Salford Quays project is managed by a small group of chief officers based in the Civic Centre, but with a local project office for the organisation of basic works. Development is proceeding from south to north and the middle of 1987 appears to have been a turning-point for the project, a point perhaps equivalent to the threshold that was critical in Baltimore. By this time £15 million of public money had been spent or committed, and £90 million of private finance, a leverage ratio of 1:6. Initial construction, including a multiplex cinema, a hotel, some dwellings and the first phase of offices at Waterfront 2000, were complete and further investment was committed. This created confidence which attracted further developers to the project. Although still in its early stages, the transformation of the derelict docklands has been widely acclaimed, with frequent visits by government ministers and royalty. It is, of course, still too early to make a full evaluation of the scheme, but a number of preliminary observations can be made.

The most fully developed part of the former docklands is that covered by the Enterprise Zone. By the end of 1986 this section of the EZ had 270 firms and 2,700 jobs, of which about one-third were in manufacturing, one-third in distribution and one-third in offices (including high tech). Surveys of the firms in the EZ by Salford city council suggest that the skill content was high: 76 per cent of the jobs were classified as skilled. Also, the uptake of land appeared encouraging: by the end of 1986, 80 per cent of the available area was developed or committed. However, these impressive figures should be treated with caution. High-skill jobs are not likely to be well matched to the local population. Secondly, only 25 per cent of the firms were new; the remainder were either relocations (61 per cent) or new branches (14 per cent). Overall it would appear that the zone has attracted either existing or new developments from other parts of Greater Manchester and that there has been very little extra employment generated for the region by the EZ. In the context of the larger area, 2,700 jobs – many of them not new – is small compared to the employment losses sustained in recent years. As in Baltimore, there is a need to distinguish between physical change and its socio-economic consequences for the community.

Caution may also be appropriate with respect to leisure and recreation functions. Progress in this sphere at present amounts to a cinema, a hotel, a small marina and a proposed pub–restaurant. Suggestions for substantial tourist attractions have not so far produced any actual results on the ground, although there is obviously time for this to happen. In addition to the time factor, difficulties in attracting tourist developments may well reflect the general character of the area and competition from the attractions of the city centre. Here it is necessary to recall that, in contrast to Baltimore, the docks and the conurbation centre are by no means adjacent. Locational relationships could well be significant in retarding this type of economic take-off. Indeed, a new tourism study will attempt to reduce this problem by linking Salford Quays into developments in the Manchester core. Specific proposals are likely to include boat trips along the River Irwell and a branch of Manchester's planned light rail rapid transit system.

More encouraging signs have come from residential development, even though it is at a very early stage. The plan for Salford Quays envisages 381 dwellings, of which only 19 had been completed by mid-1987. There was a great demand for these units, and prices ranged from £37,000 to £66,000. In December 1987 when the first 11 units of the Grain Wharf Scheme, priced at £44,000, were completed they were sold on the first day. This can be compared with a small private estate in Ordsall, 200 metres away from the Quays, where houses priced at £20,000 have remained unsold for two years. There is thus likely to be a middle-class occupation of the Quays in contrast to the working-class nature of the surrounding housing. Salford city council welcome this gentrification, arguing that it will introduce social mix into the area.

Encouraging signs are also evident in the context of office development. So far most office decentralisation in Manchester has been southwards, but proposals for Salford Quays would push the process northwards. Once again, only a few offices have been let, but these have gone to computer firms at rents around £75 per square metre. This price is nearly equal to those asked in prime areas of the city centre, and is twice those of Old Trafford, where some of the southward decentralisation has occurred. In contrast to leisure-based activities, therefore, distance from the conurbation core does not appear to be a significant handicap. Instead it appears that Salford Quays is seen as a prestige location, with the advantages also of car parking and good accessibility (via the nearby M602 motorway).

Lastly, it is arguable that, even in its early stages, the project is creating spillover effects reminiscent of Baltimore. On the south side of the canal, at Trafford Wharf, some of the EZ has already been developed for high-tech offices. Similarly, the newly formed Trafford Park Development Corporation proposes a Wharfside Village here consisting of offices. And various ideas have been suggested for the Pomona Docks, from offices to housing. These are being held in abeyance, awaiting the outcome of the tourism study, but following its publication delay is unlikely to be protracted.

Conclusion

The public sector plays an important role in the redevelopment of redundant port zones, not least in providing funds for basic works. It frequently owns the land, or is in a position to influence development. However, it is not a free agent, and must usually seek investment from the private sector. In this sense in Britain there is a contrast with the programme of slum clearance from the mid-1950s to the mid-1970s, when redevelopment was predominantly public-sector-led and concentrated almost entirely on housing. Under the Thatcher Government this type of redevelopment is not favoured, and local authorities like Salford can only receive support providing they involve the private sector. The urban development corporations which are responsible for dockland redevelopment in London and Liverpool are also under this imperative. In the United States, the local government units are under pressure to attract private investment in order to increase local taxes. There is thus an increasing convergence between the United States and Britain towards schemes which are market-led.

Social objectives often appear watered down and there may be only a slight bending of proposals towards the needs of local inhabitants. The social tasks are expressed in terms of bringing derelict land back into use and strengthening the general urban economy. Neither the Baltimore nor Salford projects have had objectives which involved the local community. The examples investigated suggest that market interest is likely to be low in the early stages, but once basic works have been undertaken and a threshold of development reached, interest will quicken. Yet in this situation most local residents suffering from poverty and unemployment can only hope to benefit indirectly as the problems of the wider city are solved. Also, developments in the redundant port zones will respond to market conditions, which will inevitably evolve and change over time. In this situation the local-authority planners must be flexible, taking advantage of the opportunities as they appear. Flair, imagination and good marketing are essential characteristics for local planning today, as the examples of Baltimore and Salford show.

Postscript

Interest in Salford Quays as a redevelopment site has continued to increase since the completion of this chapter. Information on developments during 1988 is given in the author's forthcoming paper 'From Manchester Docks to Salford Quays: a progress report on an urban redevelopment project', *Manchester Geographer*, NS9 (1988).

References

Fosler, R.S. and Berger, R.A. (1982) (eds), *Public–private partnership in American cities: seven case studies* (Lexington, Kentucky: Lexington Books).

Fothergill, S., Kitson, M. and Monk, S. (1985), *Urban industrial change: the causes of the urban–rural contrast in manufacturing employment trends* (London: HMSO).

Law, C.M. (1986), 'The uncertain future of the city centre: the case of Manchester', *Manchester Geographer*, NS7, 26–43.

—— (1988a) (ed.), *The uncertain future of the urban core* (London: Croom Helm).

—— (1988b), *The redevelopment of Manchester docks*, Discussion Paper No. 32, Department of Geography, University of Salford.

Law, C.M. and Grundy, T. (1984), *The Greater Baltimore area*, Comparative Study of Conurbations Project Working Paper No. 7, Department of Geography, University of Salford.

Law, C.M., Grundy, T. and Senior, M.L. (1984), *The Greater Manchester Area*, Comparative Study of Conurbations Project Working Paper No. 1, Department of Geography, University of Salford.

Leven, C.L. (1978), 'Growth and non-growth in metropolitan areas and the emergence of polycentric form', *Papers, Regional Science Association*, 48, 101–12.

Lyall, K. (1982), 'A bicycle built for two: public–private partnership in Baltimore's renaissance', in R.S. Fosler and R.A. Berger (eds) *Public–private partnership in American cities* (Lexington, Kentucky: Lexington Books), 17–57.

Millspaugh, M. (1964), *Baltimore's Charles Center: a case of downtown renewal* (Washington DC Urban Land Institute).

Muller, P. (1981), *Contemporary suburban America* (Englewood Cliffs, New Jersey: Prentice-Hall).

Olson, S. (1976), 'Baltimore' in J.S. Adams (ed.) *Contemporary Metropolitan America: Vol. 1 nineteenth century ports* (Cambridge, Massachusetts: Ballinger), 1–93.

—— (1980), *Baltimore: the building of an American city*, (Baltimore, Maryland: Johns Hopkins University Press).

Robertson, K.A. (1983), 'Downtown retail activity in large American cities 1954–1977', *Geographical Review*, 73, 314–23.

10 Market forces ascendant: dynamics of change on the Hong Kong waterfront

Roger Bristow

Redevelopment on the Pacific Rim

It is already widely anticipated that the economic centre of the world in the twenty-first century will shift to the countries of the Pacific Rim. It should come as no surprise therefore that, while waterfront redevelopment on the western seaboard of the United States is better known (see Tunbridge Chapter 5), the major economic advances in Far Eastern nations have also induced spectacular changes in their cityports. Waterfront infrastructures there have readjusted rapidly to the twin impacts of technological change and rising economic wealth and expectations. Land-hungry territories like Japan, Singapore and Hong Kong have recently resorted to major reclamation programmes that will allow expansion and development of new infrastructure to facilitate business, port and airport growth. Indeed, throughout the Far East, trade growth and the rapid emergence to dominance of the long-distance container trades have induced port-facility transformation as radical as anywhere in the world.

Hong Kong portrays nearly all these trends. With an economy which has had growth rates in excess of 10 per cent per annum in recent years, the port recorded the world's highest annual container throughput in 1987. This was in itself an impressive achievement for a port with only six berths, but even more remarkable is that it is committed to doubling its capacity by the mid-1990s. The territory has also seen major waterfront change as uses have migrated or withdrawn to be replaced by substantial residential, commercial or public complexes. Finally, its harbour shoreline has been irrevocably altered by successive waves of reclamation, a process that began with the foundation of its major city in 1841.

Hong Kong is often held up as the outstanding example that illustrates the benefits to be derived from applying free-market economics. Indeed its government is locally known for pursuing 'positive non-interventionism' as its guiding principle in public policy-making. Yet, even here, close analysis of land-development processes betrays a subtle blend of both public and private inputs which have provided Hong Kong with its dynamic built environment, and which have elevated the territory to its present status as a world-class international city. The redevelopment of the Hong Kong waterfront, therefore, is not only interesting because of the nature, magnitude and outcomes of the processes involved, but because in more general terms it represents the result of a unique approach set within a distinctive cultural and decision-making milieu, a situation which separates it from other procedural and cultural environments described elsewhere in this book. Hong Kong, while international in outlook, remains essentially a Chinese city on to which British bureaucratic procedures and Western cultural and business practices are merely attached rather than absorbed. It represents therefore both a general and a very specific set of perspectives on the subject of waterfront redevelopment in the world of the late 1980s. Here we examine those perspectives in order to discern the underlying development processes involved and to assess their significance for waterfront-redevelopment programmes elsewhere.

Dynamics of change on the Hong Kong waterfront

Trade has always been the centrepiece of the Hong Kong economy. The territory's location and its natural harbour make it one of the great international ports of the world (Chiu, 1973), and only Singapore rivals it in importance as a trade hub in East Asia. In earlier times with deep-water wharves rare – cargo-handling was traditionally overside to lighters – waterfront sites were occupied by maritime services such as shiprepairing, refuelling, warehousing (godowns) and limited naval defence operations. More recently, however, the complex web of pressures that exist on the limited shoreline of the harbour area has brought about radical change.

The onset of this period of change can be traced to the introduction of trans-Pacific container services in the early 1970s (Wong, 1986). Indeed, the subsequent rapid expansion of container handling was crucial to the livelihood of the territory as a major player in international trade. Despite some government initiatives in the 1960s (Container Committee, 1966 and 1967), the real impetus to provide suitable terminal facilities in Hong Kong came from the private sector. The same applies to the subsequent expansion of the Kwai Chung container terminal in 1985 and 1987–8, although this was done with public approval and support (Marine Department, 1986). For the 1990s, yet further major expansion has been suggested by both the government (Marine Department, 1986) and the private sector (Lau and Westlake, 1987; *Far Eastern Economic Review*, 1987a, 1987b and 1988b). This would involve major reclamation, with some options requiring substantial investment in the Western Harbour near Peng Chau to provide sites for container berths, a new international airport, housing and other services (Fig. 10.1).

The magnitude of such investment intentions is everyday evidence of the development pressures which underpin the visible manifestations of

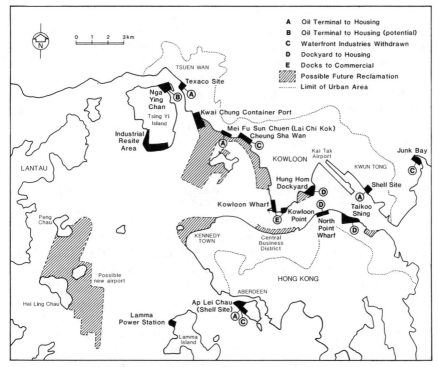

Figure 10.1 *Waterfront redevelopment sites and potential future reclamation areas in Hong Kong harbour*

change on the waterfront and elsewhere in Hong Kong. Changes of land-use and activity patterns occur with great rapidity and frequency and are often large scale. The incentive fully to utilise scarce economic resources is great and, with minimal intervention from government, private capital is able to redeploy its assets rapidly and with ease. The result is a built environment which is in a constant state of readjustment and redevelopment. Given the attractiveness and value of waterfront locations in Hong Kong, it is not surprising that sites there have been the focus of development pressures and change, yet it is a set of changes that must be seen within the dynamics of change throughout the territory.

The major determinants of urban form in Hong Kong have been the twin pressures of land shortage and population growth. According to Pun (1986, 231):

Population size is a more important source of planning problems in Hong Kong than in any other city. The small and almost fixed land resource further aggravates these problems. One school of thought considers that the situation has been worsened by the past concentration of population and activities in the largely unplanned development on the relatively flat strips of land around Victoria Harbour.

It is perhaps not surprising that with only 20 per cent of its limited land area being easily developable, and its population having increased from below one million at the end of the Second World War to nearly six million now, urban densities around the harbour have risen to as high as 16,000 persons per hectare. Hong Kong is therefore a high-density city which brings problems for the planner, but opportunities for the developer. Land is extremely valuable, and obsolescence of buildings and land uses can lead to rapid replacement by more lucrative activities. Yet, for such to occur requires bureaucratic, commercial and planning procedures which facilitate change.

It has been recognised for many years that land and property consolidation provide the key to efficient urban renewal in Hong Kong (Bristow, 1984, 218–42; Fong, 1985; Adams, 1987). The Hong Kong government first intervened actively in this sphere in 1965, but unwillingness to commit major financial resources produced minimal results until the setting up of the Land Development Corporation (LDC) in 1987. The LDC has been empowered to buy up obsolescent properties, consolidate sites, and sell-on to the private sector for redevelopment. However, even though almost all land in Hong Kong is leased from the government, small lots, multiple-ownership of buildings, and the expense of buying out existing private interests make major urban renewal in existing urban-core areas ruinously expensive, whether for public or private organisations. The result has been a consolidation of private-sector participation in the hands of major property companies commanding large amounts of investment capital, and a search by them for 'new' sites where development or redevelopment can most easily be undertaken. A further important influence on this process is that, as in other Far Eastern countries, property investment and speculation in Hong Kong have played a dominant part in fuelling stock-market cycles, which led to spectacular crashes in the 1960s and 1980s. Consequently, successful property development and land production are seen as being crucial, not just to waterfront redevelopment, but to the well-being of Hong Kong as a whole by both the private and public sectors.

As Figure 10.1 depicts, waterfront change in Hong Kong involves a number of distinctive processes, but the major component remains land reclamation. For the urban core this represents the sole remaining source of substantial new land and development sites, and as a bonus provides additional 'mainland' sites on the platforms left after excavating fill materials from nearby hillsides. Given the difficulties of modifying the existing urban infrastructure, planners and government have increasingly come to regard new reclamations as overspill sites for the amelioration of existing problems, as well as opportunities for open space development, civic amenities, and commercial or housing expansion. Such ideas and schemes are not new, particularly in the central business district – roads parallel to the present waterfront represent former shorelines, to which have been added over this century successive stages of reclamation, new facilities and building of ever-increasing intensity. Plans for the 1990s (Government Information Services, 1985) are already committed to yet further major extensions of this programme, particularly in the Western Harbour. These will provide new areas for housing expansion, extensions to the central business district, and for specific requirements such as expansion of the Hung Hom railway terminal, exhibition and cultural sites and, of course, expansion of the port itself.

The dominance of the reclamation programme in the process of change in the core areas points up a crucial factor behind any understanding of the dynamics of change in the territory – the key role of government. Land and its control has always been at the centre of the colonial government's concerns – perhaps not surprisingly, given that in good years recently around one-third of the government's income has come from land revenues. Land supply and development have involved key government committees over the years (Bristow, 1984, 171–2), and annual land-sales programmes by government are an important ingredient of the development dynamics. However, the use of a relatively simple zoning system within the government's land-use planning mechanisms means that choice on the use of potential sites by developers is often wide and easy to influence.

The result is that, in the terminology of professional planners, the role of government is clearly that of facilitator. Its function is to enable the local economy to prosper, to allow the aims and objectives of capital to be achieved and, particularly, to facilitate property investment. To do this it provides land, sites and services, makes transport and infrastructure as efficient and effective as possible, and provides sufficient housing and social services to satisfy a growing workforce of increasing wealth and expectations. It thereby maintains security and stability for the long-term enhancement of capital production and wealth accumulation in the territory. It is a set of objectives that seems unlikely to change much in 1997 when the transition to Chinese rule takes place, although the possibility that new political imperatives may then intervene cannot be totally discounted.

Hong Kong, therefore, represents attempts to create an environment where private capital can seek out the best opportunities, and be allowed to pursue them, with assistance rather than hindrance from government. Even where government does promote schemes of its own, such as public housing, transport investments, or even prestigious cultural facilities on the waterfront, they are perceived as contributions to the general welfare of Hong Kong – a welfare that is centred around the best interests of business and capital, the engine of its economic growth and prosperity.

This approach has not been without criticism. It has been suggested that the role of the planning system in Hong Kong might be termed 'planning by demand' (Bristow, 1981). 'Much of the government's action until very recently has been piecemeal in nature – *reactive* planning in response to external demands or crises, rather than forward (or *proactive*) planning aimed at implementing a longer-term vision of the territory's future development pattern' (Taylor, 1987, 26). As we shall see, this has been as true of waterfront redevelopment as of other areas of planning concern. In particular, the government has been forced to react to a programme of private initiatives which were presented to it as *faits accomplis*. This has produced a series of seemingly *ad hoc* decisions which have significantly shifted the direction of the territory's development, and difficulties in promoting public planning objectives which do not demonstrate clear private benefits.

Waterfront components of change

The basic motivation for waterfront change in Hong Kong is not dissimilar to that elsewhere. At its simplest it can be seen merely as the replacement of obsolescent uses by those that can use sites more efficiently – with efficiency largely measured in terms of economic returns to private entrepreneurs. Only in speed, magnitude and specific activities displaced is Hong Kong in any way unique. Within the displacement process – and with the exception of change in the central business district – only rarely has like been replaced by like. Obviously, the reclamation programme – by definition – displaces land uses that require a waterfront. More generally though, for reclamation to remain profitable, land must be sold to the highest bidder. As a result, some displaced industrial uses once located at the edge of the urban areas have been forced to relocate to new peripheral sites, sometimes more than once. As an example, the shipbreaking industry, which began at Cheung Sha Wan in the 1950s, moved first to Gin Drinkers Bay (now Kwai Chung) in the north-west, then to Junk Bay in the north-east in the 1960s, and finally, in the 1980s, with the development of Junk Bay New Town (on the same site), to extinction.

This model of evolution, however, does not apply everywhere. In the case of the original deep-water wharves, and the early commercial dockyards (first built at the turn of the century), obsolescence in the 1970s led to a lucrative search for other uses of the same site. Those wharves nearest to the urban core were largely turned over to commercial activities, while the dockyards became residential estates. Other land uses – like the original railway terminus at Kowloon Point – outgrew their locations and transferred elsewhere, releasing their old sites for profitable redevelopment. Similar transformations have occurred as technical change or changing markets have affected other activities, such as the obsolescent power-station site on Ap Lei Chau, now replaced by new capacity built in the early 1980s on nearby Lamma Island (Figs. 10.1–10.3).

The Hong Kong prototype for such redevelopment initiatives dates from the early 1960s and was begun on a site to the far west of New Kowloon. In

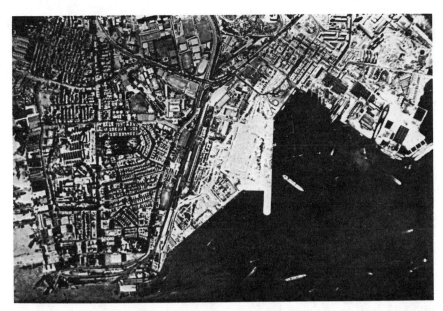

Figure 10.2 *Hong Kong: Tsim Sha Tsui waterfront in the 1960s. The former rail terminal and wharves can be seen lower left, with the new reclamation for commercial expansion in the centre. Hung Hom Dockyard, redeveloped in the 1980s, is at the far right. (Courtesy: Hong Kong Government, ref. 5/5596)*

the 1930s, with the growth of oil bunkering for the expanding steamship trades, the international oil companies established Hong Kong as one of their major bunkering stations. The need for safe sites away from the then urban core led to the selection of Lai Chi Kok by the Standard Oil Company (Mobil) of the United States, while other companies located near Tsuen Wan and Aberdeen, and at a site in Kwun Tong. All were to become engulfed by expansion of the urban area after the 1940s war, but Standard Oil was the first company to unlock the unused potential of their original site by redevelopment (*Asian Architect and Builder*, 1974). In partnership with local developers, during the period 1963–76, they invested over HK$ 560 million to transform their 16-hectare tank farm into a new comprehensively planned housing and commercial complex for 90,000 people in 100 high-rise cruciform towers. Mei Foo Sun Chuen was the first major private-sector self-contained scheme in the territory. 'Included in the 40-acre estate – more appropriately termed a city within a city – will be some 400,000 square feet of commercial space, more than 165,000 square feet of schools and playgrounds, and landscaped areas for recreation and relaxation' (*Asian Architect and Builder*, 1974, 1). The integration of ancillary uses on the site provided a planning model which was to be copied and improved upon in subsequent schemes, both public and private.

In the second major initiative, Swire Properties' 1972 scheme for the redevelopment of their 1908 dockyard at Taikoo Shing (*Building Journal*,

Figure 10.3 *Hong Kong: Tsim Sha Tsui waterfront in the 1980s. The former railway and dock areas have been replaced by an international hotel, plus a major exhibition and arts complex. Completed commercial development at Tsim Sha Tsui East can be seen in the right foreground. In the background, commercial and office buildings have replaced the former warehouses of Kowloon Wharf. Only the Ocean Terminal remains to show the area's maritime past*

1976) set yet more advanced standards, and proved influential in setting up its developers as a major force in the Hong Kong property world of the 1980s (Fig. 10.4). Not being affected by the same height restrictions as in Kowloon (caused by the flightpaths into and out of the international airport at Kai Tak), the designers this time were able to space out their towers more widely; and by aiming at a higher-status segment of the flat market were able to incorporate higher standards of environmental design, building finishes and ancillary services than were possible at Mei Foo. By the 1980s, the new scheme's commercial centre had become a dominant shopping focus for the whole of the eastern end of Hong Kong Island.

Subsequent major commercial and housing complexes have been introduced in the 1980s on the sites of the Hung Hom Dockyard in East

Figure 10.4 *Taikoo Shing private housing estate, Hong Kong, 1980. Remnants of the old dockyard buildings are rapidly being engulfed by the residential towers of the new development. To the right, the old sugar refinery has been replaced by new multi-storey factory buildings. Since 1980, further reclamation has taken place in the foreground. (Courtesy: Swire Properties, and Wong Tung and Partners, Hong Kong).*

Kowloon and the Caltex (Texaco) tank farm site adjacent to Tsuen Wan New Town (Table 10.1). Looking ahead, 1988 saw the announcement of the largest scheme yet by a consortium formed from some of the largest private property companies in Hong Kong. This involves a complex reorganisation of sites, whereby part of the current site of the Hong Kong Dockyard complex on Tsing Yi Island is to be taken for oil storage by Shell Petroleum, thus freeing their two existing sites in Kwun Tong and Ap Lei Chau (near Aberdeen) for subsequent redevelopment (Fig. 10.1). At Ap Lei Chau the redevelopment area also includes the old Hong Kong Electric power station (owned by one of the participant developers) which is redundant following the building of the larger, more modern, plant on nearby Lamma Island. The value of the two sites to be developed is estimated at about HK\$ 8 billion at 1988 prices, with a profit on completion in 1995 estimated at some HK\$ 4 billion (*Far Eastern Economic Review*, 1988a). Property-development returns in Hong Kong can be great if the market is right and the high capital costs of setting up projects can be found.

The ability to finance such massive private investments – and the Hopewell Holdings proposed airport–seaport scheme off Peng Chau

Table 10.1 Representative   statistics   for   selected   private   waterfront-
redevelopment schemes in Hong Kong

Scheme	Mei Foo Sun Cheun	Taikoo Shing	Hung Hom	Texaco, Tsuen Wan	Shell, Kwun Tong/ Ap Lei Chau
Date planned	1963–65	1971–72	1983–84	1982	1987–88
Date constructed	1965–76	1975–86	1986–91	1985–90	1990–95
Cost (HK$ million)	560	na	4,000	3,000	8,000
Site area (ha)	16	21	21	6	19[a]
Target population	90,000	45,000	40,000	24,000	na
No of towers	100	54	94	20	na
No of flats	13,000	10,000	11,200	6,000	na
Residential area (000 sq m)	900	800	710	217	440[b] 731[c]
Commercial area (000 sq m)	37	200	160	8	15[b] 29[c]

na: not available
[a] Tsing Yi (replacement industrial) only
[b] Kwun Tong
[c] Ap Lei Chau

would dwarf them all at some HK $25 billion (about £2 billion) – leads one
to ask whether or not there are special circumstances in Hong Kong which
give rise to the successful undertaking of such major projects. Two
ingredients would seem essential: an appropriate organisational framework and business confidence.

The first of these – an organisational framework – involves both public
and private agencies. Although private financing of major reclamations has
been suggested in the past, most recently within government in the early
1980s, experience since the 1920s has caused government to retain such
schemes wholly within the public domain. An important principle that has
influenced such activity is that revenues from sales of the sites should repay
or provide a profit over the capital costs of each scheme. There is therefore
an incentive for government to maximise its land-sales revenues, which
leads private developers to go for the most lucrative land uses and
developments. This situation inevitably creates the potential for conflict
between private objectives and public requirements, particularly where
those requirements do not provide revenue-earning opportunities. But in
fact, only in recent years have public uses of the Hong Kong waterfront
been seen as an important ingredient in the strategic replanning of waterside frontages within the harbour area.

Part of the explanation for this relates again to the role of the planning system. While internal strategic planning documents were produced in 1948, 1970, 1979 and 1984, land use of individual sites has always been largely determined by local district zoning plans. It was not until 1987 that detailed comprehensive strategic planning for the whole harbour area was publicly considered, and not until the mid-1980s that full coverage of the whole urban area by formal statutory plans was actually achieved. According to Wilson (1987, 30):

the reclamations now being planned at Hung Hom, Western Kowloon, Central District and Kennedy Town will provide a real opportunity to plan a restructuring of the harbour area so as to reduce some of the present excessive building density. With this aim in mind, a special team is being set up under the Lands and Works Branch to produce a comprehensive master plan for the whole Metropolitan Area.

Viewing past achievements, it is perhaps surprising that so much has been accomplished without formal statutory planning methods. Although it would be wrong to conclude that there has been no planning – non-statutory departmental planning has a long history in Hong Kong – the result has been that, to date, each private or public redevelopment scheme has been designed, considered and approved on an individual basis with little consideration of its wider context. Indeed, the early schemes like Mei Foo or Taikoo Shing had no public plan with which to conform, and were situated on lots with old leases which contained few restrictive conditions. Thus, when the developers' proposals first appeared before the government, it was difficult for the latter to impose conditions from a non-existent or ill-prepared public negotiating position. The placing of major private initiatives within a planning context at district level proved difficult, and the consequences of each scheme in terms of effects on nearby areas had to be accepted rather than changed, since powers to alter them were then so limited.

It was only with the agreement to allow redevelopment of the Hung Hom Dockyard in East Kowloon in 1985 (*Building Journal*, 1985, 1986; *Asian Architect and Contractor*, 1986) that real co-ordination of private and public requirements was accomplished. Prior to the 1984 Sino–British Agreement on the territory's future, confidence dropped and the property market was weak. Consequently the developers of Hung Hom were able to negotiate a lower-than-usual premium payment to the government of just HK$ 390 million to change the land use specified on their original lease, since the government wished to encourage the scheme as a symbol of confidence. In addition, however, they were also persuaded to pay a further HK$ 200 million to finance the construction of the new and improved road access to the main site in the adjacent urban area – a significant planning gain for the local community despite the extra road traffic generated. Furthermore, the developer is also providing schools, a public transport terminal, open space, and community and indoor recreation facilities for general neighbourhood use.

With the precedent established, the most recent schemes for redevelopment in Hong Kong have involved more sophisticated bargaining and negotiation between private-interest and public-planning objectives than before. Nevertheless, the initial impetus for such schemes has remained firmly within the domain of the private sector, and government has remained primarily a reactive rather than a formative agency for land-use change on the harbour waterfront.

Yet, despite the organisational qualities of the private sector, with its ability to conceptualise and capitalise schemes, despite the benign benevolence of government and its planning system towards them, and despite the practical skills of the contemporary Hong Kong construction sector (now regarded as one of the most efficient in the world), all would be for nothing without a second crucial ingredient. Property investment in Hong Kong thrives, as elsewhere, only on confidence. Lack of it in the early 1980s led to the greatest property crash seen in the territory, with bankruptcies, retrenchment and bank failures as outward manifestations of the problems. While none directly affected the waterfront redevelopment schemes, their effects remain as a warning about the fragility of that phenomenon known as business confidence.

The first requirement for confidence in property development is an expectation, as in all property markets, of satisfactory future rates of return, and forecasts of favourable supply–demand balances within relevant sub-sectors of the market. In Hong Kong, while high-rent accommodation has often depended on a volatile expatriate market, the bedrock of the prosperity for property companies has been the steady and, in recent years, seemingly insatiable demand for smaller units of residential accommodation for purchase by local Chinese displaying rising wealth and expectations. This has not only proved sufficient to sustain pre-sale of residential buildings before construction commences – a characteristic feature of the Hong Kong market which guarantees early financial returns to developers – but it has also allowed commitment to increasingly large-scale projects in the knowledge that demand will be sufficient to take up supply. Moreover, the fact that the role of the private sector is considered, allowed for and explicitly supported in the government's own housing plans (see, for example, Hong Kong Housing Authority, 1987) provides additional stability to a largely guaranteed demand.

It is, therefore, not at all surprising that large-scale private residential development has been the principal outcome of waterfront redevelopment schemes in Hong Kong. Public housing has gone to cheaper sites elsewhere, increasingly of late in the eight new towns outside the metropolitan core, while only in a few specialised sites near the core have other combinations of land uses proved attractive or viable, and then often only with major public-sector involvement.

Change for the twenty-first century

Mention of the hiccup in investment confidence in the early 1980s emphasises a concern which has always affected the property cycle in Hong Kong: the perception of long-term security for the territory itself. Maintenance or enhancement of this has always been seen as a fundamental purpose of the territory's government, and past actions and interventions in the property market (such as the favourable terms given to the Hung Hom Dockyard developers) are but one small manifestation of this all-pervading policy imperative. Moreover, one current view of the late 1980s and the lead-up to the 1997 handover to China is that at present Hong Kongers are hedging their bets. Individual families send out their children to favoured countries like Canada or Australia to set up alternative residence status, while the emigration of bright young professionals is accelerating.

Yet, for the majority of the population emigration remains a distant dream, and for the developers time is still left to make a killing before 1997 finally comes; in Hong Kong the pay-back on property investment is nearly always assumed to be less than ten years. Economic growth and personal wealth accumulation thus continue to proceed apace, at least for the moment, and it is these that fuel the new waterfront redevelopments that already have a life well into the next century. Profit levels remain sufficiently high to justify taking the risk of possible major downturns in the market. Moreover, current economic integration with China, especially with the Shenzhen Special Economic Zone across the northern frontier, already suggests to Hong Kong's major entrepreneurs that overall prosperity will be maintained after 1997 because it will remain in China's best interests. Indeed, as future political changes become clearer, the maintenance of power by existing business interests in Hong Kong seems more rather than less likely as 1997 draws nearer, providing yet another boost to the confidence upon which the property sector clearly depends.

Gazing into the crystal ball of the twenty-first century, what specific future developments seem likely? There do still remain a few industrial and other sites where obsolescence or rising land values may yet cause conversion to other uses. The wish to remove the incinerator plant at Kennedy Town on the north-western tip of Hong Kong Island or the tank farm at Nga Ying Chan on Tsing Yi Island are possible examples that might be cited. But none of these prospective sites approaches in scale those that have gone before; the opportunities for major units of land-use change on the waterfront have now already gone – all, that is, bar one.

The greatest opportunity of all perhaps still remains – the possible replacement of Hong Kong's international airport at Kai Tak. Its future lies within the government's present investigations into the viability and necessity of the various Western Harbour reclamation schemes, and the reassessment of the early-1980s scheme to relocate the airport off north Lantau Island near Chek Lap Kok. Should it occur, not only would it result in a major planning gain and development opportunity for much of North Kowloon, but it would bring on to the market the largest single redevelopment site yet made available, and would lead to a reversion to a land-use pattern first foreseen by Sir Patrick Abercrombie in 1948 (Abercrombie, 1949) and Chinese developers in the 1920s.

That possibility aside, it remains clear that housing demand and increasing pressures to improve conditions in the existing metropolitan area will maintain the momentum of further reclamation projects. The costs of urban renewal, the strategic decision to run down the existing new town programme in the 1990s (Bristow, 1988) and the ongoing demand for new housing for sale (Hong Kong Housing Authority, 1987) seem certain to bring further removal of existing waterfront activities. They will be replaced by further high-rise, multi-purpose urban construction, both private and public, along the lines of those schemes already described. Only in the business and tourist core of southern Kowloon and the central business district across the harbour will older uses continue to be displaced by major office building and public facilities as reclamation and new construction continue apace. The main differences from the past will be the competition for space for housing between private and public sectors, the new towns having been completed, and the scarcity of opportunities for the relocation of industry and port users.

Some conclusions

The central theme of waterfront redevelopment in Hong Kong remains that of institutional confidence and the ability to seize initiatives when they become apparent. Hong Kong has been likened to Mammon's home town, but to live up to such a title requires government to provide an environment where profit-taking, entrepreneurial freedom, and low levels of intervention and regulation are accepted as the norm. The exception is that the mechanisms of capital formation and investment depend on the provision of public support in the form of infrastructure and services. All of these conditions exist in Hong Kong, and a dominant role for the planning function in the territory is as a major facilitator for private entrepreneurial enterprise in the development field. The provision of major road and public transport networks, utilities and industrial land and premises are all part of the same facilitating of private capital formation and growth by the state. Additionally, the state abhorrence of subsidies means that the incentive for private capital to move quickly out of less-profitable uses (such as under-utilised waterfront sites) is encouraged. The combination of these circumstances leads to a land use–activity system where rapid change is endemic, the lives of buildings are often short, and the property cycle volatile.

Such rapidity of change, and its dependence upon myriad private decisions great and small, does however give rise to problems, particularly in the planning and environment field. The reliance upon site-by-site consideration and control, and individual private decisions, adds up to rather less than a whole when considered at the urban or city scale. Schemes do not always relate particularly well to their neighbours in design, activity or even functional terms. There is, as yet, no sense of the grand design in Hong Kong, not even on the waterfront. Yet one finds it hard to deny that the place has an aura of success, which is obviously partly derived from the visual impact of its waterfront, which so dominates the very being of Hong Kong as a city and an urban experience for businessman and tourist alike, as much as for its inhabitants.

Perhaps this is the lesson that we all might learn from Hong Kong when considering waterfront redevelopment as a process. It is not so much the problems of the detail that matter, as the ambience of the whole. The lesson is that success breeds success: investment flows where benefit can be demonstrated and where capital has confidence and the means. However, even though private initiative predominates in Hong Kong, it could not prosper without the enabling protection and assistance provided by the public sector. Waterfront redevelopment in the territory exemplifies, therefore, a successful marriage of public and private interest. The projects now providing an ever-improving lifestyle for thousands of contemporary Hong Kongers are a monument to the ways of Chinese business and the order of British bureaucracy. While the design solutions in recent waterfront change in Hong Kong may not always appeal, they nevertheless represent an important outcome of the dynamism for which the city has become renowned, and present a challenge to the ways of other cities where renewal of obsolete waterside frontages is currently awaiting entrepreneurial initiative.

References

Abercrombie, Sir Patrick (1949), *Hong Kong: preliminary planning report* (Hong Kong: Government Printer).

Adams, C.D. (1987), 'The Land Development Corporation in Hong Kong', *Planning Practice and Research*, 3, 13–6.

Asian Architect and Builder (1974), 'City within a city', *Asian Architect and Builder 3(2), 1—11.*

Asian Architect and Contractor (1986), 'Whampoa Garden development – from dockyard to housing estate', *Asian Architect and Contractor*, 15(10), 26–30.

Bristow, M.R. (1981), 'Planning by demand – a hypothesis about town planning in Hong Kong', *The Hong Kong (Asian) Journal of Public Administration*, 3(2), 192–223.

—— (1984), *Land-use planning in Hong Kong – history, policies and procedures* (Hong Kong: Oxford University Press).

—— (1988), 'The role and place of strategic planning in Hong Kong', *Planning and Development – Journal of the Hong Kong Institute of Planners*, 4(1), 14–20.

Building Journal Hong Kong (1976), 'Taikoo Shing – urban housing on 53 acres', *Building Journal Hong Kong*, August, 18–26.

—— (1985), 'Project news: Whampoa Garden – an urban area "new town"', *Building Journal Hong Kong*, January, 20–1.

—— (1986), 'Building feature: Whampoa Garden – the urban area's newest township', *Building Journal Hong Kong*, January, 66–71.

Chiu, T.N. (1973), *The port of Hong Kong – a survey of its development* (Hong Kong: University of Hong Kong Press).

Container Committee (1966), *Report of the container committee* (Hong Kong: Government Printer).

—— (1967), *Second report of the container committee* (Hong Kong: Government Printer).

Far Eastern Economic Review (1987a), 'Transport: dredging up the future – a Hong Kong consortium airs sweeping plans for a new airport', *Far Eastern Economic Review*, 135(5), 46–7.

—— (1987b), 'Projects: the Hong Kong quartet – the government starts to look seriously at infrastructure proposals', *Far Eastern Economic Review*, 135(12), 114–6.

—— (1988a), 'Property: a vote of confidence – a massive Hong Kong development project is announced', *Far Eastern Economic Review*, 139(6), 50–1.

—— (1988b), 'Shipping: boxed in for space – developers bid high for new Hong Kong container port', *Far Eastern Economic Review*, 140(16), 60–1.

Fong, P.K.W. (1985), 'Issues in urban redevelopment', *Built Environment*, 11(4), 283–93.

Government Information Services (1985), *Planning for growth* (Hong Kong: Government Printer).

Hong Kong Housing Authority (1987), *Long term housing strategy – a policy statement* (Hong Kong: Government Printer).

Lau, E. and Westlake, M. (1987), 'Projects: heading for the islands – a Hong Kong group floats a proposal for a new airport', *Far Eastern Economic Review*, 135(3), 49.

Marine Department (1986), *Port development strategy study – final report* (Hong Kong: Government Printer).

Pun, K.S. (1986), 'Urban planning', in T.N. Chiu and S.L. So (eds), *A geography of Hong Kong* (Hong Kong: Oxford University Press).

Taylor, B. (1987), 'Rethinking the territorial development strategy planning process in Hong Kong', *The Asian Journal of Public Administration*, 9(1), 25–55.

Wilson, Sir David (1987), Speech to the Legislative Council, 7 October, *Hong Kong Hansard*, 27.

Wong, D.O.Y. (1986), 'Planning for the expansion of the port of Hong Kong', *Planning and Development, Journal of the Hong Kong Institute of Planners*, 2(2), 60–4.

Part III: Strategic planning issues

11 Waterfront redevelopment, economic restructuring and social impact

Iain Tweedale

Introduction

Previous chapters have confirmed that the redevelopment of decaying urban docklands and waterfronts is occurring in advanced capitalist countries through the world. Many of these programmes have two important characteristics in common. Firstly, they share a common form of redevelopment, usually involving houses for sale, shops, offices, leisure facilities, as can be seen in cities as diverse as London, Baltimore, Philadelphia, Vancouver and Melbourne (see, for example, Chapters 5, 9 and 12). Secondly, the issue of waterfront redevelopment is linked to debate on the 'inner-city problem' and its solution. This problem is characterised by high unemployment, poor housing, depopulation, poverty, high proportions of ethnic-minority residents, high crime rates, strained relations with the police, deindustrialisation and environmental decay (Hall, 1981). However, such characteristics, although useful in defining the elements of the problem, tend to obscure the distinction between causes and symptoms. Without a clear view of the processes which have created the problem, it is impossible to assess whether the type of response typified by dockland redevelopment actually represents a potential solution.

This chapter aims to define the inner-city problem and to trace the processes which have led to its development. It then goes on to suggest that dockland and waterfront redevelopment, rather than being a model solution to the problem in its entirety, addresses only half the problem, and that the changes occurring actually represent the urban spatial outcome of wider international processes of economic restructuring. Using evidence from Britain, it is argued that linking dockland redevelopment with the inner-city problem is in fact an (expedient political response) to the high level of public concern over the issue, and its effect has been to lay the ground for massive public-sector subsidisation of the restructuring process.

The inner-city problem is made up of two inter-related components which have been created by the normal historical processes of capitalism, rather than something specific to the last twenty years during which time the term 'inner-city problem' has come to prominence. The first is the existence of an-inner-urban area population exhibiting characteristics of multiple deprivation; the second is the existence of an industrial wasteland characterised by the loss of traditional staple industries. These components are discussed individually below.

Creation of an 'inner-city' population

Any assessment of the creation of the inner-city population must commence with consideration of the nature of capital. At the basic level there are two forms of capital: variable and fixed. Variable capital is investment in labour power. Fixed capital, notes Harvey (1985), comprises capital enclosed within the production process, and that which functions as a physical framework for production such as machinery and factories. Marx (1954), in his general theory of capitalist accumulation suggests that, in order to maintain rates of profit, levels of variable capital will be progressively reduced in favour of fixed capital. A number of measures have been adopted to facilitate this transformation, but in the process they have also led to a restructuring of the economy and have been major contributory factors in the creation of what has become known as the inner-city problem.

Measures adopted in this context generally aim to reduce investment in variable capital by increasing the productivity of labour. Particularly important has been the introduction of cheap labour into the domestic economy. This has had major implications for the composition of the inner-city population since this labour has historically been drawn from colonial and neo-colonial countries and has led to the formation of multi-ethnic residential concentrations. The continued existence of these concentrations highlights two factors of capitalist accumulation which are crucial to the development of the inner-city problem. Firstly, there is an historical tendency to produce labour that is surplus to the needs of the production process, the existence of which becomes particularly apparent during trade downturns. Secondly, this surplus becomes differentiated so that sections remain redundant even when trade revives. Thus, the surplus population can be divided into the 'ordinary unemployed' who are likely to regain employment with relatively good pay and conditions once the economy revives, and the 'labour reserve' which comprises those unemployed workers who are likely to remain permanently unemployed or employed in badly paid jobs with poor conditions.

Unemployment, rather than being the result of the personal characteristics of the individual or of market forces over which we have no control, may be seen as a consequence of the way in which employment is organised within and between societies (Ashton, 1986). A reserve pool of permanently unemployed or underemployed workers is useful for capital in that it is available for work when labour is in short supply during economic booms and wars, and its existence reduces the chances of labour organising itself since certain sections of the labour force see themselves as being qualitatively different from others.

A number of social processes have developed to ensure that this population remains a labour reserve. These include discrimination in employment; unequal access to the right to collective bargaining over wages; unequal access to education; and unequal access to housing (Rex, 1986). The net effect of these processes is inner-city ghettoisation as described by Blaut (1983). He asserts that ghettos exist to maintain the labour reserve rather than to facilitate social and economic integration into wider society. He illustrates his arguments with the experience of Puerto Rican, Mexican and rural black migrants in the industrial conurbations of the United States – and the same is certainly true of migrants from the West Indies and Indian sub-continent in Britain. The long history of some of these ethnic-minority concentrations reflects the normal workings of capitalism which are not specific to the last twenty years over which the inner-city problem is said to have developed.

Deindustrialisation of the inner city

Recent recognition of the inner-city problem can be attributed to the dramatic urban effects of two other measures adopted by capital in an effort to increase productivity of labour: the use of new technologies in the production process and the internationalisation of production. They have led to large-scale economic restructuring (Newby *et al*, 1985), and to deindustrialisation of the inner urban areas, creating the classic inner-city industrial wastelands. The introduction of new technologies into the production process enabled labour to become considerably more productive through automation. On the other hand, employers failing to invest in new machinery – or responding to new technology too slowly – soon found their production process becoming uncompetitive and obsolete. The over-dependence on older heavy industries, combined with other political and economic factors, meant that this is what happened in the inner-city areas, resulting in accelerated closure rates.

At the same time, industrial capital was increasingly being invested abroad where it could take advantage of cheaper wage-rates, local markets and fewer pollution restrictions. With over £6 billion of British capital invested in industry abroad between 1979 and 1986, the development of a new international division of labour has accentuated the deindustrialisation of heavy engineering and manufacturing at home. National employment in manufacturing fell by 25 per cent from 7.1 million to 5.3 million between 1976 and 1986. The inner cities were hit particularly hard, and by 1976 their manufacturing workforce had fallen to almost half of its 1951 level (Cambridge Economic Policy Group, 1982).

In Britain, the inter-relation of the measures adopted by capital can be seen in the effects of deindustrialisation on unemployment rates in the inner cities in general, and among the labour reserve in particular. Between 1971 and 1981, unemployment in Britain rose from 2.4 to 10.9 per cent. Male unemployment in the English inner-city Partnership districts in 1981 varied from 15.5 per cent to 26 per cent (Hamnett, 1983). The ethnic-minority labour reserve was the first to be made unemployed and those who entered the labour market found it harder to find employment. One study found 60 per cent of black and 40 per cent of Asian teenagers to be unemployed (Commission for Racial Equality, 1982). Deindustrialisation has also transformed the nature of the employment which remained in the inner city. The exploitability of the labour reserve allowed remaining firms to offer the poorest of wages and conditions, thus maintaining the cycle of poverty and deprivation (Rees and Lambert, 1985).

The recent economic recession has accelerated the process of deindustrialisation, and the rise of monetarist policies has led to decreased public expenditure on housing, education, health and social services. As a result, the problems faced by the inner-city labour reserve have been accentuated, forcing it into a position of dependence on the state for subsistence, a situation that can easily lead to other problems. Young people with time on their hands and little prospect of a job in the foreseeable future may well come into contact with a criminal sub-culture (Roberts, 1984). Inevitably, this leads to contact with the police and eventually to strained relations between whole districts and the police. The urban riots in Britain between 1980 and 1985 were the most graphic outcome of this process. They brought the inner-city problem into popular focus, and to the forefront of the political agenda for the Conservative government's third term of office in 1987. Although it has been claimed that the direct cause of the riots was police action (Kettle and Hodges, 1982), they were the indirect consequence of social and economic processes which have led to the creation of an inner-city labour reserve faced with long-term unemployment in a deindustrialised and derelict environment.

Dockland redevelopment as a response to the inner-city problem

Urban redevelopment, typified by dockland redevelopment schemes, is the conventional response of many capitalist governments to the inner-city problem. However, rather than moving straight into an assessment of the constituents of such schemes, it is first necessary to ask why the response is one of physical redevelopment rather than one which aims to address the social processes which have created the problem in the first place. The answer to this can be found by considering how the process of urbanisation reflects the normal workings of capitalist accumulation. Addressing the social processes which have created the inner-city problem is not in the interests of capital, but the restructuring of the urban environment in specific forms clearly facilitates capital accumulation.

The previous section described how a major trend within the restructuring process has been the internationalisation of industrial capital. The demand from individual capitalists who wish to invest away from their own production maintains the existence of a well-developed system of financial institutions. However, the recent expansion of these institutions is indicative of a major transformation whereby finance capital has become dominant over industrial capital in domestic economies. The activities of these organisations involve the movement of capital from what can be called the primary circuit of capital to the secondary circuit (Harvey, 1974). The primary circuit comprises capital flows in the production process. The secondary circuit, on the other hand, involves the capital which flows into fixed assets in the built environment and into the consumption fund. The consumption fund is made up of commodities which function as aids to consumption, such as consumer durables, and it also provides the means for collective consumption, through parks and footpaths, for example. The difference between fixed capital and the consumption fund is based on the use of commodities, not on their material mode of being. Therefore, a warehouse acts as fixed capital if it has an industrial function, but becomes part of the consumption fund upon refurbishment into an apartment block (Harvey, 1982).

It has been suggested (Harvey, 1974) that this shift from the primary circuit of capital – in which questions of industrial growth are paramount – to the secondary circuit, where investment in the built environment becomes dominant, is encouraged by a number of conditions which arise periodically within the primary circuit. These include overproduction; falling rates of industrial profit; surplus capital in the form of money which lacks investment opportunities; and a surplus of labour (Harvey, 1985). These factors lead to 'over-accumulation', when too much capital is produced relative to the available opportunities to employ it. Financial institutions seeking to invest their considerable pools of capital in projects with the highest returns, invest more readily under conditions of over-accumulation in the built environment. Dockland redevelopment is one such lucrative form of investment – and property speculation, as witnessed recently in many docklands sites, further increases potential profits.

The transfer of capital between primary and secondary circuits via the financial institutions is also dependent on mediation by the state. The risk involved in such ventures is usually underwritten by the state – in the form of grants covering unprofitable aspects of schemes – and through co-ordination of activities between the different agencies involved, by means of specific corporations and the town-planning system in general. The public–private partnerships involved in most dockland redevelopment schemes in advanced capitalist countries are excellent examples of this relationship. The state 'primes the pump' by putting forward grants to cover aspects of the schemes which are unprofitable, enabling derelict industrial land to be cleared and serviced. Private developers then invest the remainder of the capital to develop the site. This helps to explain the similarity in land use between different schemes across international boundaries, since only the most profitable developments are constructed. Obviously, local factors such as the ability of local authorities and community groups to persuade developers to include community facilities and cheaper housing may alter some of the details of individual schemes but, in general, these represent planning gains, and in many cases are actually funded by local authorities themselves. The overall result of these development pressures and compromises is the typical dockland redevelopment comprising – with some local variation – new houses for sale, warehouses converted into luxury apartments, retail units, offices, factory units, and leisure facilities.

The Cardiff docklands redevelopment

The cityport of Cardiff in south Wales provides an excellent setting within which to illustrate and examine these points in more detail. The city has undergone a dramatic deindustrialisation from the 'coal metropolis of the world' to the capital city of Wales with all its associated administrative and service functions. The old docklands are now the site of the largest redevelopment in Britain outside London, and this site is directly adjacent to the inner-city ghetto district of Butetown whose history as 'Tiger Bay' is described by Hilling (Chapter 2).

The Cardiff docklands redevelopment was conceived in 1983. The Labour-controlled county council awarded the contract to Tarmac plc and work began in 1985. Plans for the scheme were subsequently extended to cover the whole of Cardiff Bay and, in 1987, the Cardiff Bay Development Corporation was established with the consent of the county council to co-ordinate a two-stage regeneration programme (Fig. 11.1). As the second stage of the scheme – involving a barrage across the mouth of the rivers Taff and Ely, and subsequent development around Cardiff Bay – is still only on paper, analysis is restricted to the first stage, known as the Atlantic Wharf development (Fig. 11.2). This involves the clearance and redevelopment of thirty-six hectares of wasteland adjacent to the derelict Bute East Dock, which closed nearly twenty years ago after coal exports from Cardiff ceased. The development has ingredients similar to many schemes across international boundaries, namely: the refurbishment of three warehouses, the construction of over 700 new housing units, together with a retail centre, a 'technology campus', mixed commercial development, leisure facilities, and a new county hall. Indeed, parallels have been drawn between Cardiff and Baltimore with fact-finding visits being made

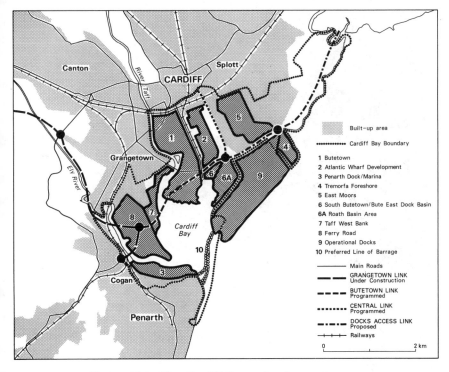

Figure 11.1 *The Cardiff Bay redevelopment area*

by local politicians and state officials to that city. The post-war decline of Baltimore, its subsequent economic revival and displacement of its inner-city population are described elsewhere (Harvey, 1974; Smith and Williams, 1986; Law, Chapter 9).

The funding arrangements for the Atlantic Wharf scheme are crucial to the argument that follows and are therefore considered here in some detail. The relative profitability of different components of the scheme is of vital importance to the developers. Naturally, they aimed to maximise land use given over to the most profitable aspects of the redevelopment. However, the county council sought to ensure that the scheme would benefit the local inner-city population in terms of jobs, housing and community facilities. Negotiations with Tarmac were said to be quite difficult at times, but it is slowly becoming apparent who were the winners and who were the losers. Table 11.1 illustrates Tarmac's costings for the Atlantic Wharf development. By far the most profitable land use is retailing, and this helps to explain why Tarmac wanted to develop a major superstore on the site, against the wishes of the county council. Eventually, a compromise was reached and a district shopping centre will be constructed.

Housing is the second most profitable land use. However, projected profits are not as great as in many other redevelopments due to the county

Figure 11.2 *Artist's impression of the Atlantic Wharf redevelopment, Cardiff*

council's condition that a substantial proportion of the units must be low-cost starter-homes. The figures in Table 11.1 only refer to the 720 new homes that are to be built. Old warehouses converted into luxury apartments yield much greater profits, but in Cardiff the county council originally wanted the largest warehouse to be converted into workshops to encourage small businesses into the area. In the end, this plan was dropped, and the warehouse will now be converted into expensive apartments, thus increasing Tarmac's profits from the housing component of the scheme.

The poor returns from investment in industry compared with those from housing help to explain the fate of industrial units. Originally, small factory units were planned for occupation by local businesses. However, the numbers of units have since been reduced and only 'hi-tech' users will be actively encouraged into what has become known as the 'technology campus'. This is despite the fact that existing dockland industry has been adversely affected by the scheme. A public inquiry rejected the objections of dockland employers to the compulsory purchase and demolition of their premises, resulting in the loss of between 250 and 300 jobs.

Land clearance and site preparation remain the most unprofitable operations for the developer, and have led to the most direct form of state subsidy. A £9 million Urban Development Grant was eventually made to Tarmac, justified on the grounds that it was a 'pump-priming' exercise,

Table 11.1 Tarmac's costings for the Atlantic Wharf scheme, Cardiff

Description	Cost (£m)	Income (£m)	Profit (%)
Site preparation	12.50	0.00	−100.0
Warehouse conversions	3.95	3.83	− 3.0
Flats	4.90	5.60	+ 14.3
Houses	11.23	13.21	+ 17.6
Mixed commercial	3.15	3.31	+ 4.7
Technology campus	3.13	2.45	− 21.7
Retail	2.72	4.65	+ 71.0
Leisure facilities	1.09	1.12	+ 2.8
Total income		34.16	
Urban Development Grant		8.51	
Total cost	42.67		

Source: Tarmac plc, 1985

whereby a small amount of public money would encourage greater investment by the private sector. Evidence from Table 11.1 suggests that this has been the case, with a respectable ratio of £4 of private money forthcoming for every £1 of public money. According to many observers, this is an excellent example of successful partnership between public and private sectors in an attempt to solve the inner-city problem. However, the real level of public-sector investment is much greater than the Urban Development Grant. Table 11.2 illustrates that the Atlantic Wharf development is actually costing in excess of £100 million, more than two-thirds of which is public-sector funded. The disparity between the two sets of public-sector investment figures can be explained by the exclusion

Table 11.2 Division of costs between public and private sectors for the Atlantic Wharf scheme, Cardiff, 1985

	Private sector (£m)	Public sector (£m)
Tarmac plc	34.2	
Roads		37.0
County hall		24.0
Urban Development Grant		9.0
Total	34.2	70.0

Figures for the public sector are approximate.
Sources: Tarmac plc and South Glamorgan County Council

from the first set of costings of the new county hall and the road network serving the site. Both of these elements are essential for the success of the project. The county hall was the first new building to be constructed, and represented both an act of faith by the county council and a catalyst to attract further investment into the scheme. The roads will provide essential access from the site to the city centre and to the M4 to the north.

A reassessment of the ratio of private to public money, taking these costings into account, shows that the private sector is investing only £1 for every £2 of public money. With this in mind, it is hard to claim that redevelopment is being led by the private sector. It would be more realistic to say that the public sector is massively subsidising the private sector's efforts to transfer capital from the primary to the secondary circuit of capital. The redevelopment does not, therefore, represent an attempt to solve the inner-city problem. Rather, it is an attempt to restructure the spatial form of the city in line with the restructuring of its economy, enabling new land uses to match the new economic functions of the city (cf. Carter, 1986). This interpretation of the redevelopment, which places it firmly within the realm of national economic restructuring, leads one to ask whether the social component of the inner-city problem – the labour reserve – will benefit from the scheme. Will the redevelopment alleviate the social processes which have produced and maintained the labour reserve? In other words, does it address inequality of opportunity in the fields of employment, housing, and education?

In terms of employment it is hoped that the project will create temporary construction jobs and permanent jobs in offices, shops and industrial workshops. Before work began, great emphasis was placed on the promise that local people would be employed in constructing the new docklands. However, the nature of the construction industry is such that Tarmac – the main contractors – only employ a very small number of staff. It is more cost-effective for them to sub-contract most of the work to smaller companies who invariably bring in their own workforce – and main contractors prefer to work with sub-contractors with whom they have worked before (Bresnen *et al*, 1985). The Atlantic Wharf scheme has been no exception, and very few local people have been employed. Discriminatory recruitment procedures have continued and no binding agreements were signed to compel construction companies to employ specific numbers of local workers. Indeed, contract compliance – which would oblige employers to take a certain proportion of local workers – is still illegal in Britain.

It is hoped that more than 2,000 permanent jobs will be created once the project is complete. But the reduction in the industrial workshop component of the scheme means that the vast majority of these new jobs will be in offices, shops and leisure activities, and will provide few opportunities for the local workforce. A recent survey found that only 3.5 per cent of local people employed in the docklands (excluding the working docks) were in non-manual jobs, and, although the booming commercial district of the docklands employed 697 people, only 19 came from the local population. The predicted number of office jobs to be created by the redevelopment is also rather misleading, in that many will be relocations of jobs that already exist elsewhere. Ironically, the best example of this is the new county hall.

It follows that the jobs created by the redevelopment will be of little long-term benefit to the local population as they are unsuited to local skills, and will go mainly to people from outside the area. Undoubtedly, some jobs will be created for the local population, but they will be largely unskilled and low paid. In short, the employment created as a result of the redevelopment will be of marginal importance to the dockland population because there has been no attempt to tackle the processes of employment discrimination which have ensured that this population remains as a labour reserve.

Inequality in access to housing is another of the main mechanisms that leads to the creation of a ghettoised labour force. Will the massive public funding of Atlantic Wharf alter this situation? Negotiations between the county council and Tarmac led to an agreement whereby low-cost housing would form a major part of the redevelopment, in an effort to ensure that local people could afford to buy the new houses. Advanced publicity claimed that property in Atlantic Wharf would not be restricted to the rich, since houses would be available at prices from £25,000. However, with still only a handful of houses complete, speculation (arising partly from the activities of property developers) has inflated the asking prices for a two-bedroom house to £55,000. This is well beyond the reach of the dockland population, and indeed the majority of people in Cardiff. Even if prices had remained at the lower figure, few dockland residents would have been able to afford it with one in two workers being unemployed. Furthermore, those in employment also face racial and spatial discrimination which have made it historically difficult for local people to obtain mortgages (Bloom, 1971).

Redevelopment will not, therefore, provide a general improvement in housing opportunities for the existing dockland population. If they wish to remain in the area, they will be faced with the grim reality of long waiting lists to gain access to a badly designed and poorly maintained 900-unit high-rise council estate starved of funds by government expenditure cutbacks. New council houses are needed, but none will be incorporated into the redevelopment, despite massive public-sector investment in the scheme. In 1985, a City Housing Department report expressed concern about local reaction to the Atlantic Wharf redevelopment in the light of the poor state of housing elsewhere in the area. Since the report was received, the council estate has been designated a Priority Estates Project – an action seen by some as 'gilding the ghetto', as it entails an attempt to improve the management of the estate without a significant increase in funding.

Education has been of crucial importance to the creation of an inner-city population. In a certificated society, lack of qualifications ensures confinement to the labour reserve and confinement to housing in the depressed state sector. Why inner-city children fail to obtain qualifications is an important question in itself, but discussion here is confined to assessing the effects of the redevelopment on education. In short, it cannot be expected to have any effect as it simply does not address social issues such as education. This is probably the most striking illustration of the purely physical emphasis of this type of inner-city policy. Discussion on educational issues within the redevelopment agenda has been confined to how much land should be earmarked for the construction of a primary school to ensure that the children of the new docklands population will not have to go to the schools on the other side of the dock wall.

The inevitable conclusion one must draw is that the redevelopment will be of little benefit to the existing dockland population, and do little to reverse the systematic and historical denial of equality of accessibility to employment, housing and education. The people themselves have largely acquiesced to the change in the face of overwhelming enthusiasm for the project within Cardiff. Indeed, their collective voice of opposition was heard only briefly in protest against one of the new roads scheduled to split their residential district and run alongside one of its schools. However, their lack of political power and knowledge of the 'system' condemned their protest to failure and few concessions were gained.

Conclusion

In Britain, dockland and waterfront redevelopment is closely tied into the debate on the inner-city problem. Most British politicians believe that such redevelopment is a model solution to the problem, involving the physical redevelopment of the industrial wasteland into areas of private housing, commercial and retail uses. However, this response, backed by massive public subsidy, only addresses the physical half of the problem and ignores totally the social processes which have created and maintained the inner-city labour reserve in its unfavourable economic and social position.

That land-use patterns similar to those emerging in Cardiff can now be found in cities throughout the advanced capitalist world, reflects the fact that Britain is far from being unique in applying a physical rather than a social response to this problem. Moreover, the ubiquity of such a pattern is a further indication that what we are seeing is part of a much wider process of long-term restructuring within the urban environment in line with new economic functions. Illustrations of projects in Baltimore, Philadelphia, Vancouver and Melbourne bear this out (Smith and Williams, 1986). Increased investment in the physical form of cities tends to be non-industrial, representing a shift from the primary circuit of capital to the secondary circuit. This shift is dependent on the increased role of financial capital within the domestic economy and illustrates the changing role of money. Once money loses its relation to the industrial product it becomes a thing in itself, separate from producers (Marx, 1973). Although this results in capital being made available for investment in the built environment, it also allows for speculation leading to prices unrelated to the real value of buildings. This accounts for the high prices of (and profits from) houses within dockland redevelopments; the exclusion of local people from the purchase of these houses; and the vulnerability of the property market to fluctuations in financial markets.

Although it has been shown that it is incorrect to consider dockland and waterfront redevelopment as a solution to the whole inner-city problem, physical redevelopment as typified by projects such as Atlantic Wharf in Cardiff appear to make the problems disappear, apparently justifying the public-sector investment involved. This impression comes from a fundamental misunderstanding of the nature of the inner-city problem. It is a social process problem, not a spatial problem. This is well-illustrated by the fact that, as the inner city is being redeveloped, it is being transformed into a space which houses those executives, public servants and professionals who service the newly restructured economy. Their recolonisation of the inner-urban areas has the effect of displacing the existing 'problem' population. But reducing the concentration of this population does not mean that the problem, or the processes which created it, have been eliminated. The effect of dockland redevelopment is only to transfer the 'inner-city problem' to the outer city, where its dispersed nature can be more easily ignored. It is, perhaps, more useful to consider the 'inner-city problem' as a 'capitalism problem'. Dockland and waterfront redevelopment serves to accentuate the capitalism problem, not solve it.

References

Ashton, D.N. (1986), *Unemployment under capitalism* (Brighton: Wheatsheaf).

Blaut, J.M. (1983), 'Assimilation versus ghettoization', *Antipode*, 15(1), 35–41.

Bloom, L. (1971), *The psychology of race relations* (London: Allen and Unwin).

Bresnen, M.J., Wray, K., Bryman, A., Beardsworth, A.D., Ford, J.R., and Keil, E.T. (1985), 'The flexibility of recruitment in the construction industry; formalisation or re-casualisation?', *Sociology*, 19(1), 108–24.

Cambridge Economic Policy Group (1982), *Economic Policy Review No. 8* (Aldershot: Gower).

Carter, H. (1986), 'Cardiff: local, regional and national capital', in G. Gordon (ed.), *Regional cities in the UK, 1890–1980* (London: Harper and Row) 171–90.

Commission for Racial Equality (1982), *Young people and the job market* (London: CRE).

Hall, P. (ed.) (1981), *The inner city in context* (Aldershot: Gower).

Hamnett, C. (1983), 'The condition of England's inner cities on the eve of the 1981 riots', *Area*, 15(1), 7–13.

Harvey, D. (1974), 'Class-monopoly rent, finance capital and the urban revolution', *Regional Studies*, 8, 239–55.

—— (1982), *Limits to capital* (Oxford: Blackwell).

—— (1985), *The urbanization of capital* (Oxford: Blackwell).

Kettle, M. and Hodges, L. (1982), *Uprising: the police, the people and the riots in Britain's cities* (London: Pan).

Marx, K. (1954), *Capital (Volume 1)* (London: Lawrence and Wishart).

—— (1973), *The Grundrisse* (Harmondsworth: Penguin).

Newby, H., Bujra, J., Littlewood, P., Rees, G. and Rees, T.L. (eds) (1985), *Restructuring capital: recession and reorganization in industrial society* (London: Macmillan).

Rees, G. and Lambert, J. (1985), *Cities in crisis* (London: Arnold).

Rex, J. (1986), *Race and ethnicity* (Milton Keynes: Open University).

Roberts, K. (1984), 'Youth unemployment and urban unrest', in J. Benyo, (ed.), *Scarman and after* (Oxford: Pergamon), 175–83.

Smith, N. and Williams, P. (eds) (1986), *Gentrification of the city* (Boston: Allen and Unwin).

12 Demand-led planning, the inner-city crisis and the labour market: London Docklands evaluated

Andrew Church

The contemporary international phenomenon of waterfront redevelopment, wherever it occurs and whatever form it takes, nearly always involves some form of public expenditure by local, regional or central government. In fact, the internationally prescribed model for waterfront redevelopment used in Australia, the United States, Canada, the United Kingdom and other European countries is for public-sector money to be used as a stimulus for private-sector investment. As is evident from other chapters in this book, only in very rare cases is the redevelopment process totally financed by private-sector organisations. Since waterfront redevelopment schemes are frequently located in depressed inner-urban areas, the justification for using public funds is that redevelopment will contribute significantly to the economic and physical regeneration of the surrounding inner-city areas. This is well exemplified within the UK, where Liverpool, London, Cardiff and Manchester have all experienced the overlapping economic and social problems that are collectively referred to as 'the inner-city problem'. In all four, the regeneration of derelict dock and waterfront areas is designed to tackle the problems of the neighbouring areas whilst also being beneficial to the regional and national economies.

Of all the waterfront redevelopment schemes in the UK that are also intended to act as local neighbourhood-revitalisation programmes, the one receiving by far the most public money is that in the former Dockland's area of East London. In 1981 the Conservative government established the London Docklands Development Corporation (LDDC), an organisation with a remit not just to encourage new physical development, but also to enable the social and economic regeneration of this very depressed area. Although the LDDC has a substantial budget, its prime aim is to encourage high levels of private-sector investment in London Docklands, an approach to inner-city problems that is consistent with the government's national policies. The scale and speed of recent physical change in London Docklands means that the policies and effects of the LDDC have received much attention from politicians, academics and the media. In 1987 *The Times* argued that 'the regeneration of London's Docklands will undoubtedly be seen as one of the greatest successes in urban renewal anywhere in the world' (*The Times*, 19 February 1987, 26). Conservative politicians indicated their approval in 1987 by establishing five new Urban Development Corporations, similar in character to the LDDC, elsewhere in Britain.

Government policy is, of course, just one of many factors affecting the economic fortunes of a particular area and altering the geography of uneven development. Rapid change in dockland and waterfront areas is an international phenomenon resulting from the interaction of various economic, social and political forces operating on a variety of spatial scales. Consequently, explaining change and assessing the impact of policy is extremely problematical. Through a number of locality studies (cf. Cooke, 1986) the influence of such different processes on urban centres has been examined. These studies, focused on change in local economies and labour markets, reveal how the global processes of restructuring have interacted with local economic and class structures. The study of waterfront or dockland localities subsumed within larger urban areas is less straightforward. Nevertheless, in an area of intense policy initiatives an investigation of the changing economy and labour market can be fruitfully used: firstly, to determine the nature and scale of the changes that have occurred; secondly, to assess the impact of policy initiatives on local development and, thirdly, to identify which other 'external' forces have been responsible for bringing change about or have affected the outcome of policy expenditure. Given that economic decline and labour-market problems are two of the key issues currently facing policy-makers in inner-urban areas, there is a clear need to assess the impact of waterfront redevelopment and accompanying public expenditure on these pressing problems. This chapter, therefore, critically examines the economic and employment changes that have occurred in London Docklands since the LDDC's formation in 1981.

Docklands in decline

The term 'London Docklands' refers to that part of East London which borders the river Thames and contains a number of distinct communities including Wapping, Rotherhithe, the Isle of Dogs, Silvertown and North Woolwich. For present purposes the area is defined by the administrative boundary of the LDDC, which encloses the riverside portions of three London Boroughs – Tower Hamlets, Newham and Southwark – and covers a total area of 20 square kilometres (Figs. 12.1 and 12.2). The East London area, which has over one million inhabitants, has experienced the recent economic and social malaise typical of many inner-urban areas in Britain. Its population fell by 12.5 per cent between 1971 and 1981, while employment contracted by 10.1 per cent, both rates being significantly

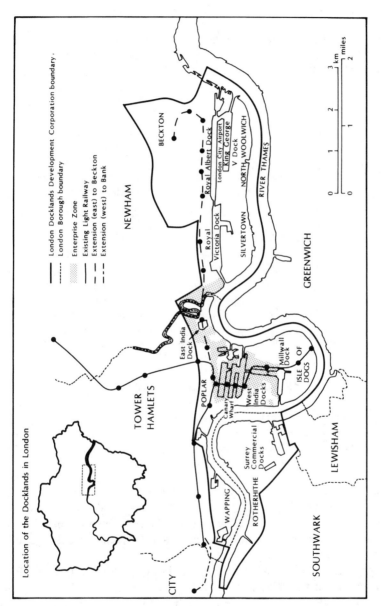

Figure 12.1 *London Docklands and the LDDC area*

Table 12.1   Indicators of change in the London Docklands (LDDC) area

Total employment	1978	37,261	
	1981	27,213	41% manufacturing; 52% services
	1985	28,123	24% manufacturing; 70% services
Employment growth	1981–85	5,677	1,690 banking, finance, insurance, leasing 2,165 distribution, hotels, catering, repairs
	1981–86	7,897	5,059 transfers; 2,838 new jobs
	1981–87	10,000	LDDC estimate
Employment loss	1981–87	3,335	Only includes notified redundancies
Population	1981	39,429	Census of population figure
	1986	44,700	LDDC estimate
	1991	86,000	LDDC estimate
Housing	1982	13,000	LDDC target to 1991
	1987	25,000	Revised LDDC target to 1991
	1987	11,975	Dwellings completed or under construction
LDDC land bank	1981	2,048 ha	Area over which LDDC given authority
	1981–87	790 ha	Acquired by LDDC
	1987	270 ha	Disposed of by LDDC
	1987	520 ha	Still owned by LDDC
LDDC expenditure	1981–87	317 £m	

Sources: Church, 1988; LDDC, 1987a; LDDC, 1987b; *Hansard* 9 April 1987

greater than for Greater London as a whole (Ham, 1983). Economic decline, however, was even more marked in the smaller Docklands area where jobs were lost in the docks, dock-related industries and the local manufacturing sector. In a three-year period, total employment here fell by 27 per cent (Table 12.1).

The decline of the Docklands economy has been studied in some detail. Overprovision in the Victorian period created future problems of profitability for the docks which were exacerbated by changing trade patterns and transport technology (Hardy, 1983). The gradual closure of the dock system between 1967 and 1981 has also been attributed to dock-labour militancy (Oram, 1970) and short-sighted management by the Port of London Authority (GLC, 1985). The loss of the docks also led to the

closure of many other dock-dependent companies. But a substantial proportion of the local job losses also resulted from large multinational
employers restructuring their operations and disinvesting in Docklands
(Church and Hall, 1986). Clearly, the rapid contraction of employment
was not the outcome of some precise process, but rather a combination of
international, national and local factors resulting in rapid deindustrialisation.

Concern for the area's plight in the 1970s led to a number of political
initiatives. The London Dockland Study Team, set up in 1971, was
commissioned by the then Conservative government to assess strategically
the area's problems and development potential. The following Labour
administration funded a specially constituted strategic-planning authority.
The Docklands Joint Committee (DJC), established in 1974, was made up
of representatives from central, metropolitan and local government as well
as the local community, and it successfully completed a comprehensive,
land-use, needs-oriented plan for the area, the London Docklands
Strategic Plan. This was primarily concerned with using the land of
Docklands and public finance to meet the economic, social and environmental needs of the residents of East London. However, public-sector expenditure cuts, a lack of power for acquiring land and political in-fighting
meant that the DJC's operational programme was soon behind schedule
and plans remained just that. The establishment of the LDDC in 1981,
after the Conservative election victory of 1979, marked the start of a very
different era of waterfront and dockland redevelopment in East London.

LDDC: the strategy

The LDDC was designated the managing body of the Docklands Urban
Development Area by the Secretary of State for the Environment using the
powers contained in the Local Government Planning and Land Act 1980.
The Corporation is broadly directed to promote physical, economic and
social regeneration in the area and, after a series of briefs and directives
from the Secretary of State for the Environment, it was able to define a
number of broad objectives (LDDC, 1987a). The LDDC was equipped
with a strong combination of power, incentives and money, but its strategy
gives a leading role in the regeneration process to the private sector. The
intention is to use public-sector investment, a less bureaucratic planning
system and a number of incentives to attract large-scale private-sector
investment. With a planned public:private leverage ratio of 1:5, this
strategy was intended to revive the local property market and economy and
bring in new residents and jobs (LDDC, 1982).

The LDDC has very useful powers with respect to land acquisition. Since
1981 vesting orders, compulsory purchase orders and purchase by agreement have allowed it to build up a substantial land bank in an area of

large-scale dereliction (Table 12.1). The LDDC was also granted powers of planning approval for the area, although it is not the statutory plan-making authority. The LDDC Chief Executive claims it has used its powers to become an 'unbureaucratic, fast-moving organisation . . . with a flexible development plan' (Ward, 1986). The LDDC's control over the planning process is strengthened by the fact that it has a non-elected board appointed by, and accountable to, the Secretary of State for the Environment and in practice, therefore, has been able to ignore both statutory local plans and locally elected councillors.

The flexible planning regime is one of the main incentives the LDDC has to offer potential investors. Others result from the designation of an Enterprise Zone in part of the Isle of Dogs (Fig. 12.1). In 1987 there were 17 Enterprise Zones in England (DoE/DE, 1987), each offering exemption from local-authority rates, development land tax, and industrial training levies; plus 100 per cent tax allowance for construction costs, and a relaxation of certain planning controls and government demands for statistics. These incentives, which are attractive to businesses in general but particularly to developers (Catalano, 1983), have made the Isle of Dogs the focus of commercial and industrial redevelopment, while elsewhere the majority of available sites has been used for the construction of private housing for sale.

The LDDC's powers and incentives have been backed by considerable sums of money made available by the Treasury (Table 12.1). This has allowed it to implement its strategy, which is largely based on land acquisition and disposal, marketing and infrastructure provision. Thus, between 1981 and 1986, the LDDC spent 77 per cent of its budget on land acquisition, reclamation and treatment (LDDC, 1986: this figure excludes the cost of one large transport infrastructure project), and also spent heavily on infrastructure and image-promotion. The completion of the Docklands Light Railway (DLR) in 1987 at a cost of £77 million provided a once-inaccessible part of East London with its own rapid-transport system and linked it to the rest of the capital's public transport network (Fig. 12.1). But the DLR has a symbolic as well as a practical function. It connects Docklands directly to the City of London and allows the LDDC to claim that the DLR 'proves the psychological point, consolidating Docklands' position in relation to the City and the rest of London . . . As such the railway will play a vital role ensuring the commercial success of the new business community' (LDDC, 1987b). Promoting the advantages of the DLR has been part of a much larger marketing project that is designed to change perceptions of the area and, in the words of the Chief Executive, give the impression that Docklands is 'a most accessible place – a hub, at the *centre* of things' (Ward, 1986).

The central emphasis of LDDC policy on land assembly and providing services to attract new businesses and residents has meant that other objectives have often been far less clearly defined. For instance, each year

Figure 12.2 *London Docklands from the west. Beyond Rotherhithe and the Surrey Docks lies the Isle of Dogs, now an Enterprise Zone.*

since 1984 the LDDC has published a Corporate Plan which sets out in the opening pages eight broad objectives, none of which contains any mention of economic or job-creation goals. Economic aims are set out later in these documents, and indicate that 'the task of reviving the Docklands economy is central to regeneration' (LDDC, 1984) and is to be achieved, as already stated, by using incentives and marketing to attract businesses in what it refers to as the 'growth sectors' (LDDC, 1987b) – including telecommunications, banking and financial services, media activities, high technology, and tourism. The LDDC is also able to use powers under the Inner Areas Act 1978 to provide assistance to existing firms in Docklands who wish to expand or modernise their activities.

This approach to the local economy is supported by 'initiatives aimed at making job search and appropriate training accessible to local residents . . . to ensure that local people are able to take advantage of job opportunities being created in Docklands' (LDDC, 1987a). In reality, labour-market initiatives funded partly or wholly by the LDDC have mainly taken the form of training schemes for young people that complement either national schemes or locally based further education provision. For example, the LDDC sponsored the building of a training centre that provided accommodation in Docklands for one of the several Information Technology Centres established in Britain. It has also provided £1.04 million over five years for Skillnet, a major training initiative designed to promote vocational training for young people aged 16–25 and resident in the Docklands boroughs, by acting as a 'broker' collaborating with existing providers in the Inner London Education Authority and the Borough of Newham. It should be noted, however, that Skillnet has also received substantial funds from the European Community (EC) and the Manpower Services Commission (MSC). Also in conjunction with the MSC, the LDDC has provided low-cost business accommodation in a Youth Enterprise Centre for young people on the government's Enterprise Allowance scheme. These various initiatives have the broader aim, in keeping with the personal-betterment policies advocated by Conservative ministers, of 'encouraging local people to broaden their aspirations within Docklands' (LDDC, 1987b).

The type of strategy adopted by the LDDC has been referred to variously as 'demand-led planning', 'leverage planning' and 'pump-priming'. It has been argued that, while the LDDC's approach was 'an extremely flexible one . . . it has all the elements of traditional planning: a strong transportation infrastructure . . . strongly differentiated activity areas, functional land uses, a strong sense of townscape . . . even a mix of housing' (Hall, 1988). Whichever way the LDDC's approach is characterised, it undoubtedly has strong political motivations that reflect the ideology of the current Conservative government. A study of Docklands (Ambrose, 1986) suggests that 'it is necessary to keep this ideological dimension in mind when analysing events'. Other studies of the emergence of the LDDC have argued that such an organisation is part of the wider attempt by central government to reduce the power of local government (Duncan and Goodwin, 1985; Lawless, 1986). Indeed, the Secretary of State for the Environment felt it necessary to justify the undemocratic nature of the LDDC by claiming that 'this transformation from decline to renewal . . . can only be achieved by a level of expenditure that only the Treasury can afford. London Docklands can only be successfully regenerated by a single-minded development agency' (LDDC, 1987a). At the time of its inception, there was strong opposition to the LDDC because of its lack of local accountability (Colenutt and Lowe, 1981) and criticism focused on this issue is still strong. These studies of the political economy of the LDDC, therefore, have convincingly shown it to be a product of national government ideology which clashes with the interests of a local social and political structure. Consequently, the political role of the LDDC is well understood.

Criticism has also been directed at the likely economic consequences of this strategy. Urban Development Corporations (Cooke, 1983) were intended to 'recycle the redundant inner-city labour force back into productive activity through a mixture of notoriously exploitative service employment . . . and the ubiquitous small business'. Goldsmith (1982) presents a similar view when discussing Enterprise Zones in the US and UK, arguing that they were a useful 'weapon for business in the struggle with labour over production costs'. There have, however, been few substantive evaluations of this aspect of the LDDC's work. It is pertinent to ask, therefore, what sort of economy is emerging in London Docklands, and whether the academic predictions have become reality.

LDDC: the record of achievement

Private investment and land management

The LDDC's approach according to *some* of its own broad objectives has been a major success, as Figures 12.3 to 12.7 illustrate. The rapid rate of land development in general, and of housing construction in particular, have allowed the LDDC to revise upwards the targets initially set in 1981 (Table 12.1). From its land bank, the LDDC has successfully disposed of 270 hectares. Eighty thousand square metres of office and industrial floorspace have been constructed, the majority of this in the Enterprise Zone (LDDC, 1987a). Large 'catalyst' projects – major developments that attract further investment – are acknowledged to have played an important role in this process. The recently opened London City Airport in the Royal Docks, and the advanced telecommunications facilities available in the area, are perceived to have been particularly important, and are likely to continue to influence future investments (Ward, 1986).

The scale and pace of development have resulted in the LDDC's achieving its leverage targets. The £1.2 billion of private-sector money invested in the area between 1981 and 1986 gave the LDDC a public:private leverage ratio of 1:6.4 (LDDC, 1986), a figure subsequently revised upwards to 1:9 by basing the public-sector investment figure on net LDDC expenditure (LDDC investment minus receipts from land disposals: LDDC, 1987b). These calculations, however, exclude very large-scale expenditure by other areas of government such as the Department of Transport which will have to fund the major road improvements necessary to serve the area.

The undoubted success of the LDDC in making Docklands an attractive location for private-sector investment is indicated by the enormous size of proposed future developments. Olympia and York, a Canadian property company, are proposing to construct a one-million-square-metre development of mainly office space at Canary Wharf on the Isle of Dogs (Fig. 12.1). This proposal is believed to have created a 'bow-wave of momentum' (LDDC, 1987b) that has resulted in four proposals being put forward by developers for the Royal Docks. These adjoining schemes, if implemented, would result in the construction of nearly 0.9 million square metres of space that would include office, high technology, retail and leisure land uses.

Economic change

The Docklands economy and labour market have undergone significant change since 1981. In 1985 the LDDC estimated that firms which had opened in, or relocated to, Docklands accounted for 5,677 jobs (Table 12.1). A large proportion of these were in the sectors that the LDDC was trying to attract to the area. For instance, 30 per cent were in banking, finance, insurance, business services and leasing, many of which were located in the World Trade Centre in St Katharine's Dock on the edge of the City of London. But 40 per cent were in distribution, hotels, catering and repairs. This is mainly because between 1981 and 1985 two Asda retail superstores opened, each employing a large number of part-time workers. Since 1985 other large retail units have started trading in the area and three national newspaper printing works – *The Daily Telegraph*, News International (*The Times* and *The Sun*), and *The Guardian* – have relocated there from the Fleet Street area of London. The LDDC suggests that by 1987 the figure for jobs was approaching 10,000 (Table 12.1).

At first glance these figures suggest a substantial expansion of employment and, clearly, the LDDC initiatives have played a key role in bringing about these changes. But to appreciate fully the restructuring that has

Figure 12.4 *New residential development at Stave Mill. The view underlies the proximity of Docklands to the City of London.*

Figure 12.3 *Oliver's Wharf, Wapping. This former warehouse has now been converted into apartments.*

taken place, it is necessary to ask two additional questions. Firstly, are these really *new* jobs or are they relocations from elsewhere in the UK space economy? The most accurate figures on this issue suggest that, between 1981 and 1986, 64 per cent of jobs that came to Docklands were transfers from outside the area and 36 per cent were newly created (Table 12.1). The number of non-transfer jobs created by the redevelopment to date is, therefore, quite small. Moreover, since 1986, the number of transferred jobs will have increased significantly due to the relocation to Docklands of the three print works, a process that resulted in a net job loss to the London economy.

Secondly, what has happened to the substantial number of businesses that were already in Docklands prior to 1981? In fact it appears that through natural wastage, notified and un-notified redundancies there have been widespread and rapid job losses. Between 1981 and 1985 these almost offset the number of 'new' jobs, so that total employment rose by only 910. But the nature of the economy of Docklands has altered significantly with far more jobs now being in the service sector (Table 12.1).

Proponents of the LDDC approach would argue that it is too early to assess the employment effects of Dockland redevelopment. Indeed, the LDDC optimistically suggest that by 1991 the number of jobs new to the area will have risen to 50,000 (LDDC, 1987a). Furthermore, although rapidly increasing land prices may result in a large number of jobs leaving Docklands in the near future, even greater job increases are predicted as a result of the massive developments proposed for Canary Wharf and the Royal Docks. Consultants vary in their estimates, but one report on Canary Wharf predicted 45,270 jobs in the development and another 19,340 multiplier jobs. The corresponding figures in another forecast were 40,000 and 20,000, although this second report also argued that 18,000 would be transfers from the City (Church, 1988). The only impact study of the Royal Docks proposals suggested that three of the redevelopment schemes would between them create 32,000 jobs directly and 16,000 multiplier jobs (LDDC, 1987b).

Of course, both schemes – but especially Canary Wharf – depend on continued high levels of demand in the London property market. Yet the initial development consortium for Canary Wharf collapsed when the two main bank partners, Credit Suisse First Boston and Morgan Stanley, pulled out because of delays and the cost of infrastructure improvements contained within the development contract. In July 1987 Olympia and York took over, but by then the demand for office space in central London, fuelled originally by the influx of foreign investment after the 1986 deregulation of London's Stock Exchange, seemed to be lessening, and the stock-market crash on 19 October 1987 is certain to have accelerated this trend. The *Architects' Journal* published excerpts from a confidential LDDC report that displayed worries about declining office demand in

Figure 12.5 *New homes at Clippers Quay, Isle of Dogs.*

Figure 12.6 *South Quay Plaza in the Isle of Dogs Enterprise Zone. The 100,000 square metre office development is served by both the Docklands Light Railway and the Docklands Clipper bus route.*

London (*Architects' Journal*, 4 November 1987, 9) and just after the crash on 'Black Monday', Michael Cassidy, the chairman of the City of London planning committee, claimed that the slowdown in planning applications in the City of London indicated that London's office boom was over (*Chartered Surveyor Weekly*, 14 January 1988, 30). But opinions of the impact of the stock-market fall are divided. One report by a firm of property consultants that surveyed seventy-six of the largest City office establishments claims that many firms envisaged future expansion, but that the West End of London was far more attractive as an alternative location to the City than Docklands to the east (*Chartered Surveyor Weekly*, 28 January 1988, 6). The project manager of the Canary Wharf development, Mr Michael Dennis, counters pessimism with the claim that space in the development will be of a high quality with extensive supporting facilities and will attract companies not just from the City of London but from all areas of south-east England (Anon., 1988, 71). Nevertheless, these recent changes in the nature of London's property market suggest that the future Canary Wharf and Royal Docks developments may be slightly less grandiose than the original proposals.

Accounting for employment change

Job growth

Debates over the role of policy in local economic change can all too easily degenerate into hair-splitting discussions. In the Docklands context, for example, it may be possible for political reasons to argue that, since the Asda superstore was being constructed before the LDDC was established, the credit for bringing those jobs to Docklands does not lie with the LDDC. But such arguments do not really explain the causes of local economic growth. LDDC incentives have played a major role in attracting firms. A survey of 241 firms which had moved to the Isle of Dogs since 1981 found that for 19 per cent financial incentives were the main reason for moving there, while another 18 per cent cited the availability of premises (Roger Tym and Partners, 1987). But it is important to examine whether other forces are attracting or driving firms to Docklands. In the key sectors of financial services, retailing and newspaper publishing, which provide the largest group of 'new' jobs, any explanation must take account of the extensive restructuring and deindustrialisation affecting Britain as a whole (Massey and Meegan, 1982; Urry, 1987). Many of the private-sector companies that have relocated to, or opened in, Docklands are participating in this restructuring process in response to alterations in the competitive conditions of the global economy. This fact has been recognised by the LDDC which has quite deliberately and opportunistically

Figure 12.7 *The Tower Hotel, St Katharine's Dock, Wapping.*

harnessed the spatial outcomes of these forces to bring a number of businesses to the area.

The increase in the number of jobs in financial services is a good example of this process in operation. Daniels (1987) shows how the producer-services sector has undergone increasing 'concentration, diversification and internationalisation', partly in response to ever-improving information and communication technology. This process has a distinct spatial outcome, as Daniels goes on to explain:

A relatively small number of key cities, most notably London, New York and Tokyo are the principal beneficiaries of this process. London, and in particular the City, continues to be transformed by the internationalisation of services . . . . Deregulation (the so-called Big Bang) has stimulated further rapid change and placed new demands upon the City and its environs . . . there has been a major upswing in demand for office space . . . which has rejuvenated the economic prospects of east London Docklands.

Of course the Docklands area has not been a passive respondent to the internationalisation of the financial sector. A significant number of related jobs had already been attracted there by 1985, and the LDDC has continued to respond to, and exploit, the changes that have occurred since then. The Chief Executive claimed that 'the City is entering into a major phase of evolution and expansion which coincides with Docklands' ability to offer uniquely convenient and appropriate space for that expansion' (Ward, 1986).

As has been indicated, another growth sector has been distribution, hotels, catering and repairs, due mainly to the increase in the number of retail outlets. The expansion may be partly attributed to the demand created by the growing population of the area, but undoubtedly also reflects a national growth and restructuring in retailing. Wrigley (1987) reports that the concentration of retail capital in a number of major corporations has brought increased competition for key sites as the corporations expand from their traditional areas, and he also predicts a continuation of existing policies of diversification into more rapidly growing and more profitable sub-sectors. With these developments, total employment has expanded, but increasingly the jobs provided are only part-time.

In this context, the growth of retailing in London Docklands is hardly surprising. Sites in Docklands are surrounded by a large urban catchment and have space for car parks. Nearby high-street shopping centres are often run down and provide limited competition. The sites are now recognised as good potential retail locations, especially in the increasingly profitable household goods and do-it-yourself (DIY) markets. Therefore, alongside the Asda superstore in Beckton are to be found large Currys (hi-fi goods) and Texas Homecare (DIY) warehouses; Tesco are constructing a 28,000 square metre unit in the Surrey Docks, where there will also be large British Home Stores and W H Smith outlets; and the redevelopment proposals for the Royal Docks contain a staggering 230,000 square metres of retail space. Tesco have chosen the Surrey Docks location for major investment since it is calculated to be within twenty minutes' drive from the homes of 900,000 Londoners (*Chartered Surveyor Weekly*, 3 December 1987). Naturally, the growth of the retail sector has been actively encouraged by the LDDC, who commissioned studies of the area's shopping potential to provide marketing data to attract companies. The LDDC also recognise the importance of shopping facilities as a magnet to attract new residents to the area and thus maintain the housing market. Here again, therefore, LDDC policy has harnessed the momentum of commercial restructuring to bring about economic change.

The other industry that has become a major part of the Docklands economy is newspaper printing. Several print works are already in production and in the future they will be joined by the *Financial Times*, Reuters and Associated Newspapers (printers of the *Daily Mail*). The restructuring of Fleet Street's print industry has been well researched (Melvern, 1986) and needs little further explanation here. Suffice to say that the pressure for rationalisation, technological change, reductions in manning levels and alterations in union and management relations had been increasing in Fleet Street throughout the 1970s. Change would allow many newspapers to alter radically their profit levels, and the extensive reorganisation needed could be achieved most easily by a change in the geographical location of printing capacity. *The Daily Telegraph* and *The Sunday Telegraph* were moved to Docklands after negotiation with print unions, and in the process nearly 500 jobs were shed (*The Times*, 24 March 1983). News International, on the other hand, moved to Wapping without consulting the print unions and dismissed 5,500 workers. Docklands provided the sites and convenient location near central London that allowed the print industry to be reorganised, but its relocation there may also be seen as an outcome of the global and national economic processes that have affected London's Fleet Street.

Job losses

The same combination of global industrial restructuring and local policy has also determined job losses. Despite the influx of new industries, some of the area's largest employers are still manufacturing firms. Nearly all these firms are part of larger multinational corporations that have embarked on major rearrangements of their UK operations. For instance, Crosse and Blackwell, a subsidiary of the Swiss multinational Nestlé, faced with a declining market in canned and packet soup, chose to rationalise by closing their plant at Silvertown in Docklands and intensifying production at their two plants in Scotland. The outcome for London Docklands was the loss of 450 jobs in 1986. A further 420 jobs were shed by natural wastage at the Tate and Lyle sugar refinery, the largest private-sector employer in Docklands, as the parent company faced profitability problems in its UK refining activities due to a shrinking market and EC cane import quotas (Church, 1988). More recently, Tate and Lyle announced the likely future closure of their packaging plant with the loss of 586 jobs (*Financial Times*, 4 December 1987). Like so many local economic development agencies elsewhere in the UK, the LDDC is unable to prevent job losses caused by company restructuring, and interventions by LDDC board members did not prevent the closure of the Crosse and Blackwell plant. This does not mean, however, that the LDDC does not have any influence over existing firms. The Inner Urban Areas Act allows it to provide assistance to firms outside the Enterprise Zone, and it claims that under this act £2.4 million worth of grants have led to the creation of 1,590 jobs and the retention of a further 1,527 (LDDC, 1987b).

At the same time, the processes set in motion by LDDC policy have led to actual job losses. Compulsory purchase orders, or at least the threat of them, have forced some firms to leave; others have simply taken advantage of the rapidly rising land prices and either closed down or relocated, selling valuable sites in the process. Individual examples of jobs lost in this way are many. A transport company employing 420 was forced to move from Greenland Dock in the Surrey Docks area to make way for housing. The company found alternative premises in Thurrock, Essex, which was too far away to allow some local residents to remain employees. An LDDC internal report states that, between 1981 and 1987, eighty-five firms were relocated by the LDDC outside Docklands and a further 100 were being assisted with relocation (Docklands Consultative Committee, 1988). The same report also suggests that, although a high proportion relocate within a reasonable travel-to-work distance, a small proportion are relocating a substantial distance away, resulting in a loss of employment opportunities from the area.

Change in the local labour market

It is through the local labour market that the effects of economic restructuring and policy initiatives have an influence on the lives of inner-city residents. In April 1981, the male unemployment rate in the LDDC area was 21.7 per cent and the female 7.9 per cent. By 1983, the male rate had risen to just under 30 per cent and the female nearly doubled to 15.1 per cent. Partly as a result of changes in recording unemployment rates, the figures had dropped by January 1987 to 27.5 and 13.9 respectively (LDDC, 1987a). These high levels of unemployment are only partly a result of local job losses. Equally important are the fall in labour demand throughout London and the housing-market processes which concentrate disadvantaged labour-market groups in Inner London areas (Buck *et al*

1986). The effect of LDDC policy initiatives and local economic change on these labour-market problems is partly determined by the location of Docklands within the wider London labour market. Buck *et al* suggest that adjustments within that wider labour market play a very important role in determining the impact of local employment growth on local unemployment rates. Alterations in commuting patterns and changes in levels of concealed female unemployment mean that new employment opportunities in an area that is 75 per cent open to commuting are dispersed throughout the surrounding labour market and have very little effect on local unemployment rates.

The level of in-commuting by employees in jobs new to Docklands suggests that this is exactly what has occurred there. The LDDC's own monitoring indicates that only 28 per cent of Enterprise Zone jobs are filled by residents of the three Dockland boroughs (LDDC, 1986). A later survey (Roger Tym and Partners, 1987) found that 29 per cent of employees in Isle of Dogs' firms established after 1981 were from the surrounding Borough of Tower Hamlets, although for firms established before 1981 the figure was 60 per cent. The same report concludes that three-fifths of workers on the Isle of Dogs now come from outside the wider East London area. Looking to the future, an analysis of unemployment in London (Gordon, 1986) has been used by a consultancy study to predict the impact of Canary Wharf on local unemployment rates if no special labour-market initiatives are established (Hall and Church, 1986). This study found that, if a proportion of Canary Wharf jobs were 'transferred' rather than new, the number of unemployed people in the surrounding London Borough of Tower Hamlets, which stood at 16,000 in October 1986, would fall by only 2,900 by 1996. The LDDC's own consultants predicted that transfers and in-commuting would mean that Canary Wharf would provide only 1,800 menial jobs for local residents (*The Independent*, 7 October 1986).

These findings imply that even if the LDDC is able to create substantial numbers of new jobs – which it has yet to do – the impact of any new employment opportunities on the local labour market and local residents may be quite limited. So, here again, the impact of dockland redevelopment on the local labour market is being determined by wider processes operating in the urban space economy.

Further analysis of the local labour market, however, has revealed other forces that are perhaps exerting a more crucial influence on the employment experiences of local residents. In 1986 a very detailed survey was undertaken of 150 young adults aged between 17 and 21 who had been pupils at the only secondary school actually in the LDDC area. The results of this survey have been reported in more detail elsewhere (Church, 1987; Church and Ainley, 1987) but its broad findings indicate the impact of dockland redevelopment on the labour-market experiences of young people. The survey was partly longitudinal, with sixty-nine of the 150 respondents having been interviewed previously in 1984. Inner East

London has notoriously low levels of educational attainment and this group was no exception: 36 per cent of the sample had no educational qualifications and a further 24 per cent had three CSEs or fewer (none at grade 1). At the time of interview 55 per cent were in paid employment, 28 per cent were unemployed, 15 per cent were in training and 2 per cent were not in paid work but not unemployed.

Detailed data on individual careers since leaving school highlighted some important segmentations within the group which reflected those that are emerging in the UK youth labour market. Some respondents, usually the better-qualified, had obtained well-paid, secure jobs with prospects. The careers of other respondents, however, had been far from satisfactory. The survey did not reveal some permanently unemployed sub-class: only two respondents had been permanently unemployed since leaving school. Rather there was a distinct sub-group which, although not permanently unemployed, had experienced regular and lengthy periods without work. One-quarter of the sample had been unemployed for over a third of the time. This group are referred to as the 'lower quartile' and their labour-market histories might test be described as disjointed. They had worked on and off since leaving school: 50 per cent had been on a training scheme and they had all experienced long periods of unemployment. None of the lower quartile admitted to choosing to follow such a career pattern and the incidence of work in the informal economy by this group was small.

The disjointed work histories of the lower quartile resulted from the type of jobs they had obtained. Their longest periods of employment were not concentrated in any particular occupational sector. The jobs they obtained were less well-paid than those held by the rest of the sample and provided no training, unlike 30 per cent of those done by non-lower-quartile respondents. Poor conditions, temporary appointments and a lack of prospects were also features of their posts. Larger-scale studies have revealed the recent growth of such jobs throughout the British economy, arguably reflecting a desire amongst companies for occupational and employment flexibility (*Labour and Society*, 1987). Similar changes occurring in the youth labour market have been described as 're-creating the dead-end youth jobs that became infamous before the Second World War' (Roberts *et al*, 1987).

The evidence suggests, therefore, that the labour-market experiences of young adults in general, and the lower quartile in particular, cannot be solely attributed to the changes occurring as a result of redevelopment. Rather, they are the outcome of the combination of these changes with adjustments taking place in the national labour-market. Nevertheless, these findings have worrying implications for dockland redevelopment policies that are designed to alleviate inner-urban labour-market problems. Even if regeneration is successful in bringing jobs back to declining dockland areas, and even if local unemployed residents can be placed in those jobs, the 'dead-end' nature of those jobs may still prevent the least qualified from establishing stable work histories. At any point in time, therefore, there would always be a substantial number of umemployed people in the area. The LDDC is hoping that the Skillnet training initiative mentioned earlier may tackle some of these problems. But many Skillnet courses are quite short, and the effectiveness of short courses in tackling entrenched labour-market disadvantage and skill deficiencies has been questioned (Church and Ainley, 1986). Whether these training initiatives will really alter the labour-market experiences of groups such as the lower quartile remains to be seen. A drop-out rate for the first round of Skillnet courses of over 50 per cent suggests that many trainees doubt the useful-ness of these courses. Skillnet is currently being reorganised to increase collaboration with local educational providers and the community, and to improve the standard of courses. But six years after its designation it is still doubtful whether the LDDC has a coherent strategy for dealing with the labour-market problems of London Docklands.

Conclusion

This study has attempted to explain the rapid economic and labour-market changes that have occurred in London Docklands since the inception of a demand-led planning regime in 1981. The conclusions provide a number of insights from an international perspective concerning the causes and outcomes of waterfront and dockland redevelopment wherever it occurs. Successive writers have shown the diverse political motives that led to the establishment of the LDDC in 1981, and the same central-government political ideology affected the type of dockland redevelopment that has occurred in London. Political structures are an obvious influence on both the agencies and outcomes of waterfront redevelopment throughout the world.

But, however much it would like to take credit for them, recent alter-ations in the economic structure of London Docklands are not solely due to the politically-motivated policies of the LDDC. Certainly it has facilitated change, and incentives have been important in attracting firms to the area. More importantly, though, the LDDC has benefited from, and been able to exploit, the spatial consequences of the restructuring process presently occurring in a number of industries. In particular, the global restructuring of financial services and the national restructuring of the British retail and newspaper-printing industries have determined the nature of recent job growth. Similarly, job losses since 1981 are the consequence of both local policy and the more general deindustrialisation process. LDDC policy and rising land-prices have seen a number of firms leave the area, while the competitive environment facing large manufacturing firms has led to job losses and plant closures. The outcome of these various processes, leading to both job growth and loss, is only a limited expansion in the numbers of jobs in the Docklands economy. In advanced capitalist countries such as Britain, therefore, this continual process of global and national industrial restructuring plays a key part in redefining the role in the space economy of derelict and declining urban zones such as old dockland and waterfront areas.

The impact of these economic changes on the local labour-market has been subject to the adjustment mechanisms of the London labour market and the changing nature of work in the British economy. This means that, to date, the physical redevelopment of Docklands has made very little impact on the labour-market problems of the local area. Whether existing labour-market initiatives or large-scale future developments will alter this situation is open to doubt. Broader forces alongside policy are determining the direction of economic change in London Docklands, but these same forces may also prevent dockland redevelopment, despite the hopes of policy-makers, becoming a solution to Britain's inner-city problems. In fact, if waterfront or dockland redevelopment is to play a major role in tackling the social and economic problems of urban areas, the experience of London indicates that it must be more than just a large-scale physical redevelopment process.

References

Ambrose, P. (1986), *Whatever happened to planning?* (London: Methuen).

Anon (1988), 'London Docklands: where derelict land is a greenfield site', *The Economist*, 13 February, 71–7.

Buck, N., Gordon, I.R. and Young, K. (1986), *The London employment problem* (Oxford: Oxford University Press).

Catalano, A. (1983), *A review of UK Enterprise Zones*, Research Paper 17 (London: Centre for Environmental Studies).

Church, A. (1987), *Young adults in a rapidly changing labour market*, Programme of research into youth labour markets report 7, Department of Economics, Queen Mary College, London University.

—— (1988), 'Urban regeneration in London Docklands: a five-year policy review', *Environment and Planning C: Government and Policy*, 6, 2, 187–208.

Church, A. and Ainley, P. (1986), 'Education after the Big Bang', *Times Educational Supplement*, 21 November, 4.

—— and Ainley, P. (1987), 'Inner city decline and regeneration: young people and the labour market in London Docklands', in Brown, P. and Ashton, D.N. (eds), *Education, unemployment and labour markets*, (London: Falmer), 71–92.

Church, A. and Hall, J.M. (1986), 'Restructuring and current research in the London Borough of Newham', in Cooke, P. (ed.), Global restructuring: local *response* (London: ESRC), 226–35.

Colenutt, B. and Lowe, J. (1981), 'Does London need the Docklands urban development corporation?', *London Journal*, 7(2), 235–8.

Cooke, P. (1983), *Theories of planning and spatial development* (London: Hutchinson).

—— (ed.) (1986), *Global restructuring: local response* (London: ESRC).

Daniels, P. (1987), 'The geography of services', *Progress in Human Geography*, 11(3), 433–47.

Docklands Consultative Committee (1988), *Urban Development Corporations: six years in London's Docklands* (London: DCC).

DoE/DE (1987), *Action for cities: building on initiative* (London: HMSO).

Duncan, S. and Goodwin, M. (1985), 'The local state and local economic policy', *Policy and Politics*, 13(3), 227–53.

Greater London Council (1985), *The London industrial strategy* (London: GLC).

Goldsmith, W.W. (1982), 'Enterprise Zones: if they work, we're in trouble', *International Journal of Urban and Regional Research*, 6(3), 435–42.

Gordon, I.R. (1986), *Unemployment in London*, Working paper London project, Urban and Regional Studies Unit, Kent University.

Hall, J.M. and Church, A. (1986), *The regional impact of Canary Wharf: a report to the London Docklands Development Corporation*, Department of Geography, Queen Mary College, London University.

Hall, P. (1988), 'The coming revival of planning', *Town and Country Planning*, 57(2), 40–5.

Ham, B. (1983), *Economic review of the five Docklands Boroughs* (London, GLC).

Hardy, D. (1983), *Making sense of London Docklands: processes of change*, Geography and Planning paper 9, (Enfield: Middlesex Polytechnic).

Labour and Society (1987), 'Labour market flexibility', 12(1).

Lawless, P. (1986), *The evolution of spatial policy* (London: Pion).

LDDC (1982), *London Docklands Development Corporation. Annual report 1982* (London: LDDC).

—— (1984), *London Docklands Development Corporation. Corporate plan 1984* (London: LDDC).

—— (1986), *London Docklands Development Corporation. Annual report 1986*, (London: LDDC).

—— (1987a), *London Docklands Development Corporation. Corporate plan 1987* (London: LDDC).

—— (1987b), *London Docklands Development Corporation. Annual report 1987* (London: LDDC).

Massey, D and Meegan, R. (1982), *The anatomy of job loss* (London: Methuen).

Melvern, L. (1986), *The end of the street* (London: Methuen).

Oram, R.B. (1970), *The dockers' tragedy* (London: Hutchinson).

Roberts, K., Dench, S. and Richardson, D. (1987), 'Youth rates of pay and employment', in Brown, P. and Ashton, D.N. (eds), *Education, unemployment and labour markets*, (London: Falmer), 198–217.

Roger Tym and Partners (1987), *The economy of the Isle of Dogs* (London: London Borough of Tower Hamlets).

Urry, J. (1987), 'Some social and spatial aspects of services', *Environment and Planning D: Society and Space*, 5, 5–26.

Ward, R. (1986), 'London: the emerging Docklands city', *Built Environment*, 12, 117–27.

Wrigley, N. (1987), 'Guest editorial: the concentration of capital in UK grocery retailing', *Environment and Planning A*, 19, 1283–8.

13 The need for a more critical approach to dockland renewal

Michael Clark

Dynamic contention

The last few years have seen dockland redevelopment shift from academic obscurity and professional wishful thinking, to be an important focus of political attention and commercial profit. Political interest is heightened by the unfortunate juxtaposition of some speculative waterside development schemes and areas of inner-city deprivation. Such extremes may be unacceptable, particularly where waterside renewal harms the interests and opportunities of established residents while providing public subsidy for the extravagant lifestyle of an élite. On the other hand, vast amounts of private – as well as public – capital are now being invested on land that was, until recently, little-used or derelict, and from which the public was generally excluded.

Cases of rapid change often make for extreme disagreement. Much recent speculative development in docklands can be attacked as irrelevant or harmful to local people and existing jobs. It is tempting to attempt explanation in terms of 'class war' confrontation between distinct social categories: yuppies, workers, dockers, dockland residents, etc. (Smith, 1987). Blame for docklands' wasted assets and the vulnerability of associated industry may be put on complacent or incompetent port management, on outdated and uncompetitive working practices, and on the excessive influence of dockers and port unions. Alternatively deindustrialisation, deskilling and economic marginalisation may be seen as symptoms of necessary change for local economies based on manual dock work and an uncompetitive mix of industrial processes. Change, it may be argued, will integrate economies in 'hub' locations with the high-technology 'knowledge-based', global marketplace and, elsewhere, will achieve closer linkage with the new growth activities such as services and leisure.

Without consensus about its goals or implications, planning policy for these redevelopment areas requires a more critical approach than is currently adopted. This chapter helps us towards this by exploring control shifts underlying disagreement, by considering the problem of performance

assessment, and by being cautiously realistic about the difficulties facing
any attempt at evaluation.

Control shifts and developers' clichés

The limits on alternative land uses experienced in docklands in many
advanced countries correspond with changes in effective control. In general, strictly port-related administration has given way to local-authority
and public-sector initiatives, and these in turn have been superseded by
commercial ambitions. In Britain this most recent phase has been orchestrated by central government, and is arguably dependent on government
for practical and financial support. It contrasts with the traditional port-
administration phase, which tended to safeguard operational land for good
practical reasons. These included the difficulty of acquiring new real estate
to meet the heavy land demands of mechanised berths, and the view that
unused sites on dock estates should be used to attract traffic and firms
which would generate significant increases in income and employment
(Takel, 1974).

Politicians and bureaucrats can easily be caught by the vast scale of
opportunity perceived to exist in dockland areas. Wastelands both challenge and threaten. It is unacceptable that scarce resources should lie idle
in so public a way. Yet the resource-management imperative entails
control, and the hidden agenda may contain strong resistance to any
measures which would destroy the now artificial great estates that occupy
former dock areas. Many municipal takeovers of dock land, and the
subsequent preparation of plans for port redevelopment by urban uses,
have shown a general wish to meet local needs. Severe land shortage and
associated housing problems in port neighbourhoods have been reflected
in extensive proposals for public-sector housing, as Pinder and Rosing
(Chapter 7) demonstrate with respect to Rotterdam. Similarly, industrial
estates have generally been suggested to help compensate for the massive
and localised job losses associated with mechanised cargo-handling and
with new patterns and forms of trade. Other goals have included radically
improved accessibility for these congested districts – a target that has
usually led to grandiose road proposals.

More recently, local authority initiatives have frequently envisaged the
creation of an eclectic mix of activities that are attracted to, or can be
steered towards, dock premises and sites. These often include museums,
art and media studios, craft workshops, small firms, community associations and voluntary agencies, yacht storage and repair, water sports and
leisure centres. This – sometimes accidental – creation of recreational and
tourist complexes has led to 'maritime village' developments that have, at
best, done far more than rehabilitate an old dock neighbourhood. What
must be emphasised is that the shift towards such schemes, and away from

more carefully-orchestrated developments, is often a necessary expedient. In the 1980s, a decade in which the curbing of public expenditure has been pursued in many countries, elected local authorities have found it increasingly difficult to finance the implementation of plans. Commercial viability has replaced public-sector identification of need as the main control on development proposals.

What is built once proposals have been formulated reflects a much broader political process which, some would argue, weighs all impacts before making a decision. However, before this long-established system of environmental and social impact assessment can be carried out, an initiative is required. Drastic restraint on public-sector finance, and a political environment that is often increasingly hostile, mean that relatively few initiatives now come from local authorities and other non-profit-making organisations. Most proposals have a commercial motivation. Investment appraisal within business, and the interests and fears of corporate leaders and money managers, therefore determine the composition of much of what is proposed for dockland and waterside sites — even if the opportunities are packaged and promoted by local authorities or development corporations, and the outcome conforms to an approved plan.

Where local authorities have been unwilling to compromise with commercial investors, or where sites or planning policies have been unattractive to the private sector, land has often remained derelict and unused. In the UK the experience has been that, increasingly, this land has been 'freed' by central government removing planning powers from the local council and establishing a development corporation to act as a planning authority and exercise special powers for land assembly and infrastructural expenditure. This body is appointed by the minister for a fixed term with the specific task of 'turning round' a difficult site. Despite their administrative similarity to Britain's New Town Development Corporations, those authorities responsible for redevelopment in selected docklands and other inner-urban areas have been dominated by market consideration, (Church, 1987). Site assembly, preparation and promotion is aimed primarily at the achievement of good 'leverage ratios' (the proportion of private capital to public spending). Maximisation of land values and commercial activity appear as overriding virtues, from which all other benefits flow.

Important consequences of the coupling of municipal control with commercial interests – and of the creation of organisations such as development corporations – have been, firstly, the emergence of a somewhat arbitrary view of the sorts of land use that are desirable or feasible in former dock estates and, secondly, a great reluctance on the part of the authorities to sacrifice their quite exceptional control over very large areas of development land (Clark, 1980, 1985). These consequences combine to produce a restrictive set of developers' clichés which deny opportunities that do not fit an accepted or anticipated package, timescale, areal unit, type of activity or built form. Where future uses or occupants are identified from the outset, the mix tends to be wide ranging but conventional: office and retail development, hotel and conference facilities, a marina with associated accommodation, shops and tourist facilities and a fairly generous supply of carparking space. More remote dockland sites are frequently promoted for industrial use, or for activities which occupy industrial-type premises (retail warehouses, car showrooms, private sports clubs, etc). 'High-tech' business premises and futuristic leisure facilities are relatively new additions to this standard mix. Museums, cultural and community facilities and other public assets may be promoted as proof of 'planning gain', and also as a way of attracting extra customers towards commercial ventures.

Other clichés associated with waterfront revitalisation arise from architectural and design fashions. In Britain, for example, schemes have been dominated by pseudo-vernacular warehouses, red brick roads, 'high-tech' commercial buildings and the retention of water areas. It is, of course, essential that design is given thorough consideration, but it is also important to appreciate that decisions in this sphere may feed through to influence the perception of 'appropriate' land uses. This perception may lead to the displacement of established uses, perhaps at considerable social cost, and it is highly likely that it will restrict the variety of incoming activities considered suitable. Those in power seem to dislike temporary and low-status land uses, so redevelopment projects become a crusade to drive out the pariahs and short-lease tenancies, and realise site potential in terms of land values and social status.

Performance

The commonplace terms used to judge dockland schemes are summarised in Figure 13.1. It is notable that both popular and professional evaluations tend to fix on either the good or the bad points. There are also subtle but ideologically important differences between the two, polarising, perspectives.

'Success' is claimed in terms of concrete achievements: the amount of land reclaimed and put to profitable use, the rise in land values, the creation of new jobs and new business opportunities, the attraction of new types of residents and customers, and the construction of new houses, flats and leisure facilities. Retention of docklands' considerable maritime and architectural heritage may also be claimed as a favourable result of recent policy, especially when it is 'packaged' for tourist, retail or recreational advantage.

It is essential to recognise, however, that this line of argument equates change with success and largely avoids the challenge of evaluation. This may be partly because evaluation in the planning discipline is too weakly developed – and too closely linked to individual projects and to choice

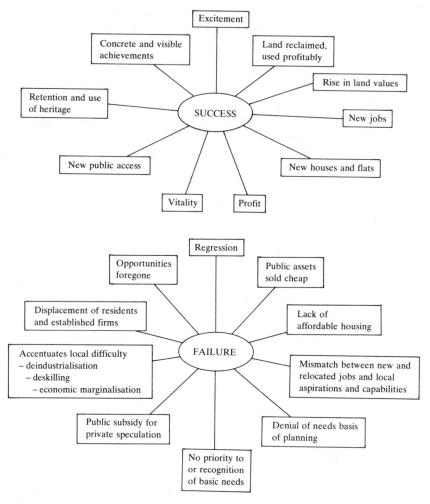

Figure 13.1 *Rival grounds for the assessment of waterfront revitalisation*

between highly constrained options – to provide much of a theoretical framework. The outcome is, however, that pragmatism often rules. A good scheme is one that 'works'. This immediately faces the penalty of discarding all better, but now hypothetical, options in the name of realism. The flightdeck adage of a good landing being one you can walk away from has a certain attraction when coping with difficulty. Particularly when there have been long delays in stimulating redevelopment, anything built and operated successfully is an achievement.

The implication of this analysis is that the evaluation of change must examine opportunities foregone. Have public assets been sold cheap, to the benefit of private speculators and to the permanent disadvantage of local people (Spearing, 1978, Docklands Consultative Committee, 1985)? Has there been a failure to give priority to local basic needs? Is there a lack of appropriate and affordable housing? And has a mismatch been created between new or relocated jobs and the needs and capabilities of the local labour force and unemployed? This line of argument may be extended to judge redevelopment schemes by what they lack. When this is done, the 'urban frontier' may appear very tame. New ideas and opportunities for risk-taking and innovation may be suggested by some of the architecture, but where are the experiments? There are no alternative communities attempting a more satisfying and self-sufficient lifestyle. New ways of linking work and home may be implied by satellite aerials and high-technology firms, but there is little evidence of the telecommunications revolution reorganising domestic or occupational built form. There is much reference to watersport opportunities and leisure potential, but permanent yacht occupation and houseboats seem to be as unacceptable as caravan sites or the sale of individual plots of land to single small firms or families. Most development is in some form of estate, standardised unit or high-density complex. Despite this dominance, however, the opportunity to relocate multi-site inner-area universities, polytechnics, colleges and hospitals onto new campuses seems to have been lost. Often there is little parkland and, in most cases, landscaping is therefore 'hard'. Changed attitudes towards nature have not found their obvious potential in the greater use of informal public open space or temporary parkland as an intermediate state between dereliction and active reoccupation, though some progress has been made at a small scale (Peters, 1979). Ecology has temporary status as a convenient, low-cost land use which avoids many of the problems of human occupation. However, the idea of creating permanent wilderness remains revolutionary: all must be swept away eventually, or tamed, as part of the restoration of land values (Nicholson, 1987).

It is, of course, argued that the old order was incapable of turning round zones of dereliction, and that the quality of waterside development now beginning to be realised – and reflected in rising land values – vindicates short-term pragmatism and an attack on anti-market ideologies (*The Economist*, 13.2.88). However, from an overall view, everything that is legal has a right to exist somewhere. Old docks were a convenient, if short-term, location for many activities that are not especially popular neighbours (Pearce, 1976). Adjacent districts similarly accommodated many people with limited access to housing – generally because of their poverty, disability or minority-group membership (Laska *et al*, 1982). To realise the market potential of these areas has generally involved displacement of the previous inhabitants. This may be acceptable if there is positive provision elsewhere to accommodate the nuisance of pariah firms and overcome the unacceptable living conditions of inner-city slums. However, as a property development exercise, 'urban renewal' can amount to little more than regressive social engineering.

Here the developers' clichés discussed above are highly relevant because, as has been indicated, the market which develops serves a far narrower range of possible uses – and has more restrictions on site acquisition or ownership – than is generally the case elsewhere. Although planning continues to have considerable influence (Cope, 1987), the status of welfare objectives is far less than implied by the 'needs' basis of its comprehensive approach. In effect, short-term political considerations and pragmatism can easily overrule the medium- to long-term consensus element of planning. The promise of future action enables a comprehensive development package to stop smaller-scale, or more immediate, projects from trespassing on its territory. It may also block local commercial initiatives and push 'social' objectives such as the provision of affordable housing or new public facilities into a bolt-on 'planning gain' category. Such objectives then become a bribe to the local community in return for exclusive rights to the site, rather than a prime objective.

Towards a more rigorous approach and realistic criteria

The argument that we should not equate a project's commercial success with the wider public good – or assume that it will justify opportunities foregone – makes it necessary to be as explicit as possible in the treatment of the criteria by which planning processes and their outcomes are to be assessed. While this may do little to counter those who disagree with the ideological basis for assessment, it should improve the quality of argument by identifying areas of disagreement (Wenger, 1987). It should also help avoid the intellectual corruption which goes with factional politics, as where consultants are only appointed, or evidence is only collected, if the outcome can be guaranteed to conform to a sponsor's wishes. This intellectual corruption is readily understandable: a great deal may be at stake, while the politics of planning are adversarial and contain much disagreement between incompatible interests and ideologies. But, from the public's viewpoint, it is also highly undesirable. In similar vein, circumstances in which public-relations 'hype' and the conviction politics of objectors confront each other should be clarified by greater objectivity. Such confrontations are not infrequent, and they create an undoubted need for dispassionate and rigorous investigation and evaluation. A further advantage is that, through *post hoc* evaluation of plans and projects, it may be possible to learn from recent mistakes and, indeed, limit their damage. Lastly, improved approaches should help overcome the general difficulty of coping with something as intangible as 'what might have been'. Hypothetical situations are notoriously worthless, yet planning has – and should not relinquish – the institutional function of providing an informed framework for choice between alternative futures.

Appreciation of the need for explicit criteria to test the performance of individual proposals and of the wider planning system must, however, be tempered with recognition of the dangers inherent in evaluation. Any routine system of tests will tend to emphasise those factors that can be easily and reliably measured or observed. Thus testing may become a political mechanism for the assertion of particular (conveniently-measurable) criteria or goals. As in education, commitment to testing may elevate the status of identifiable and reliable indices of progress, and so demote other important but obscure aspects of attainment (Hayward, 1979, 20).

Checklists of impacts and objectives may help political and professional judgement, but any complex or contentious issue will result in disagreement about the factors to be included, their relative importance and the reliability of information. It may be more sensible to attempt to achieve agreement of a qualitative nature. For instance, it may be argued that good schemes and plans are just and socially acceptable in their allocation of costs and benefits, respectful of the interests and aspirations of the people they affect, and not arbitrary in their exclusion of certain groups (Clark, 1988). While such criteria are so vague and self-evidently virtuous as to appear uncontentious, much disagreement in planning is associated with charges of injustice, and with failure to agree on 'legitimate' interests or priorities.

Maximisation of potential is more obviously a contentious criterion for assessment, though it is a useful general concept. In the example of land values it can be argued that maximisation optimises site use, has a tendency to minimise transport costs and helps the whole urban system operate as efficiently as possible. Even the benefit to landowners can be expressed in terms of the public good: value derived from a site's special advantages is a secure basis for investment, and anything less than optimal use imposes a Pareto cost by depriving society of wealth which would otherwise be created. However, an approach dominated by property values may be adversely affected by speculation, may impose harsh penalties on existing occupants and activities and may damage other interests or potential. It can also be inappropriate when markets are constrained by planning controls and other arbitrary interventions which create monopoly value or amount to public subsidy (Klausner, 1987). This makes land-value maximisation suspect as a basis for assessing waterfront redevelopment.

Similar risks are associated with economic potential. Priorities such as job creation, income levels, investment activity and business expansion may conflict with such criteria as respect for social relationships, local identity, 'heritage' and environmental diversity. An effective planning system must be able to cope with these contradictions – and the hazard that success, in terms of any particular set of objectives, is likely to bring penalties elsewhere. Here multi-objective planning and policy integration have lost credibility in recent years, partly because of the growing influence of rival, market-based and ostensibly less-interventionist approaches. But this setback should not halt the search for effective alternatives.

Conclusions

This chapter has explored the control shifts that have typified many waterfront development sites, and has sought to demonstrate the links between these shifts and the emergence of very limited definitions of successful revitalisation strategies. The re-establishment of value in abandoned dockland areas may be achieved at considerable concealed cost to society as a result of the influence which capital is often able to exert in decision-making processes. At its worst, planning machinery intended to represent need has become a vehicle for speculation, and has been stripped of much of its capacity to co-ordinate land use and transportation. This is not to argue that commercially inspired change on the waterfront is invariably bad; such a conclusion would be just as erroneous as the all-too-popular view that needs-based planning is fundamentally flawed. What is argued, however, is that the over-valuation of rapid change and short-term profit entails many risks. The benefits are unlikely to solve the socio-economic problems of disadvantaged groups which, by force of circumstance, have often been channelled into the maritime quarters of cities. Equally, there is no guarantee that short-term policies will produce new physical environments that will be applauded in a hundred years' time. Planning, after all, was created as a reaction to dissatisfaction with the environment spawned by market forces. There remains, therefore, a clear need for planning approaches capable of engineering change *and* of ameliorating these socio-economic and physical planning difficulties. As the previous section has emphasised, the formulation of these approaches is likely to be fraught with difficulty. But is this a valid excuse for failing to rise to the challenge?

References

Church, A. (1987), 'Urban regeneration in London's Docklands: a five year policy review', *Environment and Planning C, Government and Policy*, 6(2), 187–208.

Clark, M. (1980), *Planning processes and ports*, unpublished PhD thesis (Cardiff : University of Wales, Institute of Science and Technology).

—— (1985), 'Fallow land in old docks: why such a slow take up of Britain's waterside redevelopment opportunities?', *Maritime Policy and Management*, 12(2), 157–67.

—— (1988), 'Towards criteria for planning: Britain and the spirit of the EIA', in P.T. Kivell and G. Ashworth (eds) *Land, water and sky: European environ-*

mental planning (Groningen: Institute of British Geographers and the Rijksuniversiteit Groningen).

Cope, P. (1987), 'Chief officers missed out in bay renewal', *Planning*, 742, 6–7.

Docklands Consultative Committee (1985), *Four year review of the LDDC* (London: Greater London Council).

Hayward, C. (1979), *A fair assessment* (London: Central Council for Education and Training in Social Work).

Klausner, D. (1987), 'Infrastructure investment and political ends: the case of London's Docklands', *Local Economy* 1(4), 47–59.

Laska, S.B., Seaman, J.M. and McSeveney, D.R. (1982), 'Inner-city reinvestment: neighbourhood characteristics and spatial patterns over time', *Urban Studies*, 19, 155–65.

Nicholson, M. (1987), 'Greening the city: a personal view of the problems of our inner cities and the contribution nature can make towards a solution', *Landscape*, November (2), 58–61.

Pearce, F. (1976), *On the waterfront, Bristol City Docks in pictures* (Bristol: PBG Publications).

Peters, H. (1979), *Docklandscape* (London: Watkins).

Smith, N. (1987), 'Of yuppies and housing: gentrification, social restructuring, and the urban dream', *Environment and Planning D: Society and Space*, 5, 151–72.

Spearing, N. (1978), 'London docks: up or down the river?' *London Journal*, 4(2), 231–44.

Takel, R.E. (1974), *Industrial port development* (Bristol: Scientechnicia).

The Economist (13 February 1988), 'London's docklands', 306, (7537), 71–7.

Wenger, G.C. (1987), *The research relationship*, (London: Allen and Unwin).

14 Deindustrialisation and forgotten fallow: lessons from Western European oil refining

David Pinder and Sohail Husain

Introduction

Earlier contributors have focused on the decline and revitalisation of old port zones – naturally enough, since it is in these areas that strategies to deal with the challenge of redundant space have been most widely applied. As Riley and Shurmer-Smith (Chapter 3) have underlined, however, the impact of forces causing land redundancy in advanced countries is not confined to the older parts of ports. Since the early 1970s, the combination of intensified global competition and deep economic recession has placed industries associated with newer port areas under severe pressure. Shipbuilding, steel, oil refining and chemicals are among the major activities to come under attack and, while they have withstood the onslaught with varying degrees of resilience, all have increased the redundant-space problem. This has come about partly through failure to invest in prepared sites, and partly through closure or contraction of established plants.

The contention of this chapter is that the study of change on the waterfront must not focus on highly publicised revitalisation schemes in old port zones – important though they are – to the exclusion of this alternative type of fallow. To do so is to ignore major new forms of redundant space which have distinctive characteristics, problems and constraints, and which may require policy approaches quite different to those appropriate in 'typical' revitalisation areas. Moreover, as revitalisation of typical areas continues apace, and redundant space is increasingly viewed as an asset rather than a liability, the disused-land problem in these more peripheral zones may now provide a more difficult challenge to planning and port authorities. To demonstrate the nature and scale of the problems caused by recent deindustrialisation, and to indicate the challenges it poses, this chapter offers an analysis of Western European oil refining – one of the prime generators of redundant space in the 1980s. The implicit argument, however, is that the land-use consequences of oil-refining restructuring – impressive though they have been – are but an illustration of a considerably wider challenge facing industrial port areas.

Oil refining, port growth and crisis

As is well known, in the post-1945 growth era a symbiotic relationship developed between the refining industry and the seaport system. Port expansion was essential for the provision of trans-shipment facilities, refinery sites and tank farms storing crude oil. Conversely, ports were heavily dependent on industrialisation for the maintenance of growth, and the oil-refining and petrochemical industries dominated the expansion of industrial demand. In this way the interests of ports and the refining industry ran parallel for more than two decades.

After the first oil-price shock in 1973–74, however, refining companies rapidly abandoned the policy of capacity expansion – other than to complete new projects too advanced to cancel. Planning for growth gave way to planning for stability, as companies waited to discover how strong any recovery would be (Bachetta, 1978; Commission of the EC, 1985; Odell, 1986, 136–40; Pinder, 1986a; Pinder and Husain, 1987b). Soon after 1979 it became apparent that the second oil crisis had transformed a weak recovery into a demand slump. European oil consumption in 1981 was 16 per cent lower than in 1979 and was still falling. The most obvious problem to emerge in these new circumstances was a large refining-capacity surplus. In 1981, refinery throughput was down to 58 per cent of capacity – well below the 80 per cent considered adequate in the industry. Less obvious, but also pressing, was the rapid growth of a fuel-oil 'lake', caused by a particularly steep fall in demand for this product. Together, these difficulties created a crisis which forced industry planners to reject stability and opt instead for large-scale restructuring, over which port authorities could exert little influence. A wedge had begun to be driven between the planning systems of ports and those of oil companies.

Crisis responses, the seaport system and redundant space

Earlier investigations (Molle and Wever, 1984a and 1984b; Pinder, 1986a; Pinder and Husain, 1987a and 1987b) have established that three distinct restructuring strategies have been pursued by companies. Only one has generated redundant space but, as all three have a bearing on whether such space is created, a brief review of each is appropriate.

Somewhat paradoxically, but very importantly, many ports have bene-fited from heavy *investment* programmes in the crisis period. These pro-grammes have been undertaken to improve the efficiency of refineries and, above all, to 'upgrade' their ability to convert surplus fuel oil into lighter products for which demand is strong. Clearly, the greater this investment the more confident port authorities can be that companies intend to maintain their operations. The most outstanding concentration of invest-ment has been in Rotterdam (Pinder, 1986b; Pinder and Husain, 1987b)

Table 14.1　The expansion of fuel-oil conversion processes in coastal refineries, 1979–87

Process	Process expansion	Process initiation	Capacity 1979	Capacity 1987	Capacity expansion
	(Number of refineries)		(% bpd)		(%)
Vacuum distillation	31	11	2040	2634	+29
Thermal conversion	8	27	447	1209	+170
Catalytic cracking	17	14	722	1167	+62
Catalytic hydro-cracking	2	3	93	156	+68
Total refineries with at least one form of process expansion or initiation = 59					

Source:　Southampton University Oil Refinery Database

but upgrading has been a Europe-wide phenomenon. It has been pursued in 59 of the 105 coastal refineries operating in 1979, and the capacities of all the major technologies which convert fuel oil have been rapidly expanded (Table 14.1).

The second strategy has been *disinvestment* achieved by the contraction or 'downrating' of refineries. This has entailed decommissioning crude-oil distillation units, the aim being to improve efficiency by the elimination of surplus plant. Typically, between two and five million tonnes of capacity have been scrapped during downrating programmes. Forty-one coastal refineries have lost more than 5 per cent of their capacity and, altogether, the process has reduced European coastal refining capacity by 18 per cent since 1979. The immediate implication of downrating for port authorities is that substantial increases in oil imports – which would justify retaining refineries intact – are not anticipated by the refiners. Lost port revenue is therefore likely to remain lost. Downrating does, however, offer port authorities some short-term assurance that companies wish to maintain their operations. This is particularly true if downrating is combined with investment to upgrade installations, as has happened in thirty-five instances.

While it can be argued that prompt company action to upgrade and/or downrate refineries may have helped to improve the long-term economic prospects of ports, this is not true of the third restructuring strategy – refinery closure. Closures began in earnest in the late 1970s, and by 1987 shutdowns had taken place at twenty-four sites around the European seaboard (Fig. 14.1). From one viewpoint this reversal should not be over-emphasised: the probability of a coastal refinery closing in this period was only half of that for an inland refinery site. Nonetheless, the cumulative effects of coastal closures were impressive: one refinery in five was eliminated. Shutdowns reduced coastal refining capacity by 15 per cent – almost as much as the loss caused by downrating. And even though some companies opted to 'mothball' rather than dismantle installations, few port authorities could envisage the reopening of such sites. There was, of

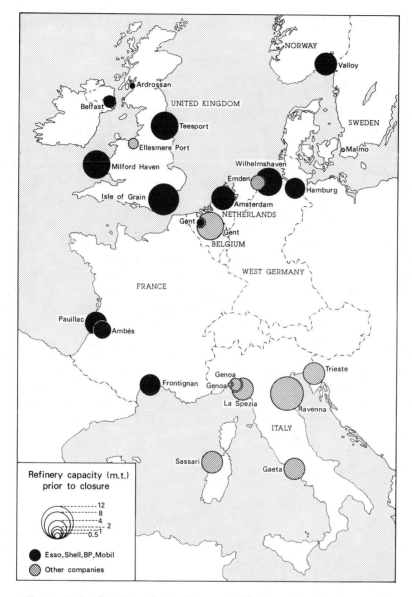

Figure 14.1 *Coastal refinery closures in Western Europe, 1979–87*

course, an immediate and permanent impact on port traffic as closures were implemented, but they also generated the new and totally unexpected redundant space problem that is the focus of this paper. Three issues arising from this challenge will be considered. What is the scale of the problem? What strategies are being employed for its solution, and might others also be appropriate? Last – but not least – can port authorities be alerted to the types of refinery likely to be at risk as restructuring continues?

The scale of land release

So far as scale is concerned, it is necessary to distinguish between gross and net land release. Gross release is the total area occupied by closed refineries. Its scale naturally varies considerably from one locality to another, and there is, of course, a loose correlation between refinery capacity and areal extent. At one extreme a major closure may lead to the release of several square kilometres of land, not least because of the extensive tank farms normally associated with large refineries. A case in point is BP's Isle of Grain refinery on the Thames estuary: immediately prior to closure, this covered 5.45 square kilometres. In contrast, several refineries with an annual capacity of less than a million tonnes per year have been shut down and have naturally created a much smaller land-release problem. At Shell Ardrossan (annual capacity only 0.3 million tonnes) the affected zone is less than 0.2 square kilometres. But between these extremes the typical extent of closed refineries is in the range 1.5 to 3 square kilometres, with an average approaching 2 square kilometres. Altogether the twenty-four closures around the European seaboard cover between 40 and 45 square kilometres – roughly twice the area for which the much-publicised London Docklands Development Corporation is responsible. At the local scale, it is quite likely that the redundant space potential of any particular closure may be as extensive as, for example, the entire central business district of a major city.

Company strategies, however, have in some instances meant that the gross area that is potentially redundant has not been fully abandoned; where this has happened, land redundancy must be seen in terms of net release. In most cases land has been held back by companies for one of two reasons. Firstly, as was indicated earlier, some installations have been 'mothballed' rather than dismantled for sale, for transfer to another refinery, or for scrap. This strategy entails no immediate release of land and is particularly associated with Mobil, which at one point had 19 million tonnes of mothballed capacity at Amsterdam, Wilhelmshaven and Frontignan (Fig. 14.1). Secondly, while companies may opt to cease refining at a location, they may also wish to maintain it as a distribution centre for products refined elsewhere. Because this strategy necessitates the use of product storage tanks, a substantial proportion of a refinery site might well remain in use after closure – as has happened at Shell Pauillac and Mobil Amsterdam. Detailed assessment of the difference between gross and net land redundancy is desirable, but requires local investigations beyond the scope of this chapter. However, data gathered for a sample of eleven of the closures suggests that the net redundant area is between half and three-quarters of the gross area. Land retention by companies has not, therefore, reduced redundant space in the industry to negligible levels. Moreover, the net redundancy figure may rise as mothballed installations are re-evaluated. Two major motivations for mothballing are that an upturn in the market will justify the resumption of refining, and that opportunities may arise to sell installations to other companies. Yet, while a few sales have occurred, and while the fall in oil prices has led to limited market recovery, neither trend is strong (Pinder, 1986a and 1986b; Pinder and Husain, 1987a). This could well incline firms towards the complete closure of mothballed plant and further release of land.

The implications of this type of redundant space for a port authority vary markedly with location and ownership. When it occurs *within* port areas – such as at Gent, Teesport, Genoa and Hamburg – port authorities are clearly involved in the problem, especially when the redundant site is owned by the port and leased to the company. But closures have also affected free-standing sites developed by companies *outside* port areas, often in response to land availability and navigational imperatives. Sites of this type may be adjacent to urban areas, as is the case at Ellesmere Port on Merseyside and Frontignan (sandwiched between Sète and Frontignan on the Languedoc coast). However, greenfield sites – such as BP Isle of Grain (an outlier of the UK's Medway Ports), Shell Pauillac and Esso Milford Haven – are more typical. Because ownership of a free-standing site is likely to lie with the refining company, the local port is relieved of an immediate space problem. In addition, local planning authorities become more heavily involved than would be the case if the redundant site lay within a traditional port area. As the following discussion indicates, however, certain strategies for the rejuvenation of free-standing sites could be highly relevant to the development of nearby local ports.

Redevelopment strategies

As the closure movement progressed in the 1980s, it was not matched by the formulation of detailed redevelopment strategies. Most port and local authorities lacked the experience to plan the rejuvenation of these areas, and future use was a remote consideration for refining companies pre-occupied with immediate reduction of financial losses. Failure to make progress partly reflects the fact that this type of redundant space is new, but it is also an indicator that the land-fallow problem in newer port areas may be significantly different from that in other localities. Some sites (such as BP Hamburg) are in close proximity to continuing industrial activity, making them relatively unattractive for residential use. Others (Esso Milford Haven, for example) are in greenfield locations with extremely attractive surroundings, but here further development may be opposed on environmental grounds. Sites remote from central business districts are not likely to be in demand as expansion zones for business or commercial activities, as has been the case in London. Perhaps most significantly, because such sites are not closely linked to the inner-city problem, pump-priming public investment is not likely to be forthcoming. Thus the conventional models of rejuvenation are unlikely to be appropriate or feasible for decision-makers to apply to this type of redundant space. In the late 1980s, therefore, clear responses are still emerging, and any discussion of appropriate strategies must necessarily be speculative. This is underlined by employment data relating to the sample of eleven sites referred to above. Prior to closure, employment totalled 6,100; continuing oil-related employment supports more than 500 workers; but new initiatives have generated fewer than 200 jobs.

The strategy that is crystallising most clearly is perhaps the most obvious option: site conversion for light industry, warehousing and other storage that will typically be unrelated to port activity. It is arguable that this response may not appeal to many port authorities, since they may be reluctant to convert zones that are still relatively new to non-port activities. But for companies owning redundant free-standing sites, several attractions may be identified. Once the site is cleared, physical conversion to alternative industrial uses is likely to be technically straightforward. It is unlikely that planning authorities will impede the transition from refining to other industrial or commercial uses. Damage to a company's local image can be minimised by presenting redevelopment as an opportunity to introduce activities which may be more labour intensive than the original refinery. Last but not least, if job creation appears a realistic prospect, local authorities may enter into partnerships with companies, or may even assume complete responsibility for projects. At Pauillac, Shell and local authorities are co-operating closely to regenerate, as an initial goal, the 300 jobs lost by closure. At Ellesmere Port, Burmah-Castrol has been responsible for site clearance, but marketing of the resulting 280-hectare industrial–commercial estate is the responsibility of the local authority which has now become the owner.

While conversion to industrial sites may be appropriate in some instances, this should not preclude consideration of other strategies. Many variants could be proposed, and the available options will be constrained by local circumstances. However, three broad approaches merit discussion.

Firstly, where sites lie within port areas it is only realistic to recognise that the prospects of redevelopment based on heavy industrialisation are, in today's economic climate, extremely poor. Also, the general setting of these sites, in active port areas, is likely to be inimical to strategies based on leisure and tourism – the models so frequently employed in older port areas. Conversely, however, sites of this type could well be promoted as relocation zones for buoyant activities whose expansion is impeded in older and more congested parts of a port. The implication underlying this option is, of course, that the process of port migration would be accelerated, but this argument does not justify outright rejection of the strategy. Port authorities wish to ensure that, wherever possible, port users have access to infrastructure that will contribute to their efficient development. Indeed it is arguable that, by providing this infrastructure, ports could make a significant contribution not just to the *expansion*, but to the *survival* of activities that would otherwise be threatened by inefficiencies imposed by the structure of older docklands. Moreover, this relocation strategy would in effect transfer the problem of redundant space to the traditional port–city interface, the zone for which successful planning responses to the redundant-space problem have been formulated.

Most closures have depressed port traffic significantly, except where – as at Amsterdam and Gent – the refineries in question have been fuelled by pipeline from more accessible ports. This traffic downturn leads directly to the second strategy that may be proposed for abandoned refinery sites. Port authorities affected by closures are understandably anxious to generate substitute port traffic and, while this may be partially achieved by intensifying throughput at some facilities, it may also be encouraged by the provision of additional berths, equipment and cargo-storage space. Clearly the conversion of a disused site could make a substantial contribution to the pursuit of this policy. What must be recognised, however, is that diversification into compensating cargoes is in many instances a slow process, as a survey conducted in nineteen ports demonstrates. There were, it is true, some instances of growth in oil-related traffic being outstripped by the expansion of non-oil cargoes (Table 14.2). But in most of the sample – and generally in ports where dependence on oil traffic was high – substantial falls in this commodity were only partially offset by increased trade in other goods. In these ports the ratio of tonnage lost to tonnage gained was 4.5:1. If Rotterdam – an exceptional port – is excluded from the calculations, the loss:gain ratio rises to 6.3:1. This strategy therefore requires the adoption of a long-term planning horizon. And, as with the strategy of converting redundant sites into relocation zones, it is most likely to be beneficial when ports have no competing redundant space.

The discussion so far has concentrated on the problem of redundant space *within* port zones. Arguably, however, the strategies outlined above could be extended to *free-standing* refinery sites. If ports possess inadequate restructuring space, yet are appropriately close to a vacant site, the possibility of a partial or complete port takeover should certainly be investigated. In some instances this option might prove impracticable – for example, if topography were unsuitable, or if there were local political obstacles. But elsewhere the strategy could offer attractive opportunities which could be quickly exploited, and probably at low cost. A further point, which also applies to redundant sites within ports, is that the option would provide restructuring space without consuming previously undeveloped land. Environmental conflicts, which must still be anticipated despite the effects of recession, could therefore be minimised.

Table 14.2   Net change in annual traffic at selected West European Ports, 1973–4 to 1985–6

	Oil traffic (m.t.)	Non-oil traffic (m.t.)	Oil-traffic dependence (% 1973–4)
Net traffic gains			
Antwerp	+3.6	+10.6	22
Malmoe	−0.7	+2.0	52
Tees and Hartlepool	+0.6	+4.2	60
Gent	+0.2	+10.0	23
Lisbon	−0.9	+1.2	42
Porvoo	+4.4	0.0	100
Amsterdam	+6.8	+3.2	28
La Coruna	+1.5	+1.2	80
Total	+15.5	+32.4	
Net traffic losses			
Milford Haven	−26.5	+0.2	100
Medway Ports	− 20.3	+4.9	91
Wilhelmshaven	−12.1	+1.6	97
Rotterdam	−79.5	+26.5	63
Brunsbuttel	−1.5	+0.5	90
Le Havre	−42.5	+5.0	88
Huelva	−0.8	+0.8	56
Bordeaux	−5.0	+0.9	75
Total	−188.2	+40.4	

Sources: Direct communications

Thirdly, it is appropriate to question whether approaches to the redundant-space problem need invariably focus on industry and port-based solutions. This issue is particularly relevant to free-standing sites, where constraints are not imposed by adjacent port activities. Arguably these localities could exploit the expansion of demand for leisure, recreation and tourist facilities, but in a rather different form to that typical of older port areas. This exploitation might take various patterns. At one extreme, investment-intensive commercial ventures – which would otherwise consume undeveloped land – can be envisaged. One option is the 'theme park' model, which could be especially appropriate where populous regions provide a reliable 'baseload' market. Commercial exploitation for leisure purposes could also be considered in southern Europe, where space and climate provide a particularly attractive combination of resources. At Frontignan, for example, the mothballed Mobil site – now undergoing clearance – lies immediately inland of the beach and is adjacent to the old town of Sète. Conversely, it is unlikely that sites in sparsely populated areas could support such ventures. Indeed, if valued landscapes are involved – as at Esso Milford Haven where a national-park boundary bisects the site – commercial exploitation could be presumed undesirable. But is not conversion to low-density, informal recreation a viable option in such cases – particularly if sites, or parts of sites, are released to public authorities for development?

Risk factors and the future

While it is necessary to consider responses that are appropriate for existing open space, the possibility that closures may continue should not be ignored. Although there are signs that the pace of restructuring is slackening because of lower oil prices, most industry observers do not believe that the process is complete. Port authorities may therefore find it advantageous to assess whether local refineries are at risk. Forewarned is forearmed.

One approach to prediction is to extrapolate from past experiences. Decisions concerning the closure of specific refineries naturally reflect individual company circumstances and perceptions of the market. However, earlier work (Pinder and Husain, 1987a) can be developed to identify general risk factors which fostered closures up to the mid-1980s. One such factor is *refinery scale*. Economies of scale improve rapidly with capacity (Molle and Wever, 1984a, 52–5), with the result that closures to date have been biased towards relatively small refineries. Those with capacities of less than 2.5 million tonnes have been culled particularly severely: in 1979 19 per cent of all coastal installations were in this size category, yet they provided 37.5 per cent of subsequent closures. *Technological influences* have been even more marked. As was indicated earlier, changes in the structure of demand during the crisis have underlined the viability of refineries possessing so-called conversion technologies. The specific advantage of these technologies – primarily thermal cracking, catalytic cracking and catalytic hydro-cracking – is that they allow low-value heavy products created by initial refining processes to be split into lighter, more valuable, fractions for which demand is strong. Figure 14.2 demonstrates that the contrast between technologically simple and complex refineries has been fundamental to the identification of plant for closure. In the industry as a whole, 27 per cent of all coastal refineries had no downstream conversion technologies in 1979, yet plant in this category accounted for 54 per cent of closures. Moreover, a further 30 per cent possessed only vacuum distallation – a weak process – for conversion purposes. Conversely, 91 per cent of refineries possessing thermal conversion facilities, or more advanced processes, survived the crisis.

Refinery size and technological considerations have been important individually, but they have also interacted to create a compound risk

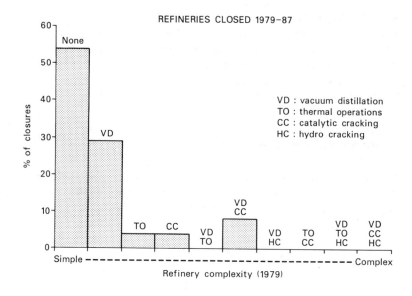

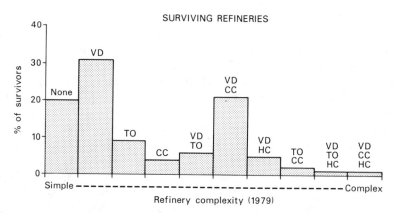

Figure 14.2   *Technology contrasts of closed and surviving Western European coastal refineries*

(Fig. 14.3). In 1979, 45 per cent of all refineries had less than 7.5 million tonnes capacity and lacked technologies more advanced than vacuum distillation. Yet this group accounted for 70 per cent of all closures and had a closure rate of 34 per cent. For plant with the same technologies, but less than five million tonnes capacity, the 'death' rate was 39 per cent; and below the 2.5 million tonne level it was 53 per cent.

One final factor which must be noted is *ownership*. Here the important distinction to be made is between companies owning a number of coastal refineries and those with more restricted investments. Analysis of owner-

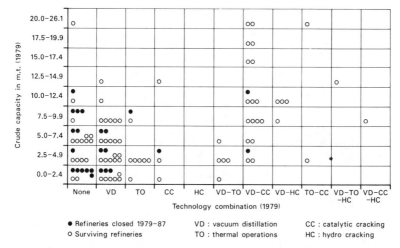

Figure 14.3 *Closed and surviving coastal refineries in Western Europe: technology–size relationships*

ship data demonstrates that the more heavily committed companies were prepared to implement much more severe closure programmes than their smaller counterparts. For example, four companies – Esso, Shell, BP and Mobil – were the only ones operating more than four coastal refineries in 1979. In the subsequent restructuring period the closure rate for installations belonging to these corporations was 36 per cent, compared with a rate of only 15 per cent for other companies. What is also significant is that this incisive approach to restructuring contributed to the industry's general tendency to close small and technologically unsophisticated installations. The companies in question owned only 26 per cent of all coastal refineries with (1) less than 5 million tonnes capacity and (2) technologies no more complex than vacuum distillation; yet they were responsible for 58 per cent of all closures in this group.

Refinery capacity, technology and ownership have been central to past closure decisions, but one issue remains. Despite the recent restructuring, are there still installations which may be considered at risk according to these criteria? So far as capacity and technology are concerned, the picture appears clear. From Figure 14.4 it is evident that the technological characteristics of coastal refineries have changed radically in the 1980s. This has happened partly because of the closure of simple refineries, but also because the conversion-technology investment programmes noted earlier have upgraded simple installations into more complex plant. Yet, despite this upgrading, 28 per cent of the eighty-one surviving refineries have either no conversion technologies or are simply equipped with vacuum distillation. When technology is related to scale, 22 per cent of the installations are shown to have (1) less than five million tonnes capacity and (2) processes no more powerful than vacuum distillation. In addition,

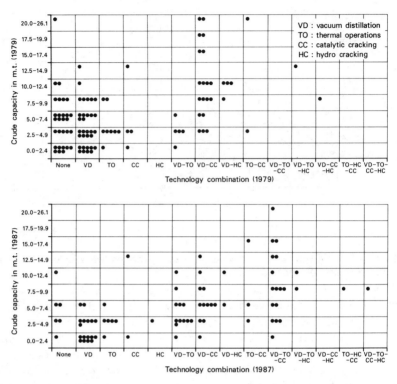

Figure 14.4 *Technology profiles of Western European coastal refineries, 1979 and 1987*

in 43 per cent of the simple refineries, capacity is less than 2.5 million tonnes. On past experience, these results would suggest that at a significant number of sites – perhaps one in four or five – the industry's future may be far from secure.

When ownership is brought into the equation, however, the validity of this conclusion is called into question. The four leading companies identified above now control only four refineries in the small, simple category, which is therefore dominated by the less prominent companies and these, as was emphasised above, have been far more reluctant than the majors to close plant. Now that the collapse in oil prices has relieved pressure on the industry, it is unlikely that this reluctance will weaken. In the late 1980s, therefore, predictions based on a scale–technology formula could prove less reliable than at the start of the decade. Given this uncertainty, port and local authorities may well wish to consider a range of possible outcomes. We conclude with a brief outline of two possible, but contrasting, scenarios.

The first envisages no rapid return to high oil prices, but continuing reconstruction by major companies aiming for improved profitability. In these circumstances the refineries of leading companies could still be most at risk and, since few simple refineries remain in their ownership, sites with substantial conversion capacity might not be immune from closure. But, if investment is associated with commitment, the most vulnerable locations could prove to be those where major expansions of upgrading capacity have not been made. Also, sites with ageing installations, where expensive overhauls of upgrading facilities are due, might then be at risk. Secondly, given the volatility of the oil market, a scenario entailing the return of high oil prices must also be considered. If this were to occur, the likely outcome would be renewed crisis in the industry and a re-acceleration of closures. Major companies might again opt to shut installations in which little upgrading investment had taken place in the 1980s, but their remaining complex refineries would in most instances be highly efficient. This efficiency would intensify pressure on small companies, significantly weakening their earlier ability to resist disinvestment. In these circumstances the probability of closure amongst small, simple refineries – largely owned by the smaller companies – could well escalate once more.

Conclusion

Redundant space caused by restructuring in the oil-refining industry is now common around the European seaboard. Using only a limited number of variables – refinery scale, technologies and ownership – insights can be gained into factors that were central to decisions on which refineries should close and, therefore, which localities should bear the main burden of restructuring. The outcome of these decisions has been that redundant industrial space is now found in a range of environments: post-war port zones, free-standing sites in highly developed regions and greenfield sites in lightly developed areas. For this reason, no single strategy can provide a satisfactory prescription for the regeneration of this type of fallow. What is also evident is that progress towards the formulation of a range of alternative strategies has been limited. It is not claimed that those sketched above will simply fill this vacuum, but debate of this issue is needed, and the suggestions are offered as a stimulant to discussion.

What must also be borne in mind is that, while oil refining provides an excellent example of port deindustrialisation, it is no more than a prominent representative of a set of activities that has generated the forgotten fallow of newer port areas since the early 1970s. Further investigation and debate must focus on these other activities, since each will produce its own constraints and opportunities which may be quite distinct from those caused by the decline of other industries. In addition, the extent of the debate required, and the problems of formulating suitable redevelopment strategies, point to the desirability of identifying industrial plants that are at risk of closure in a locality. Anticipation of risk could well assist port and local authorities to formulate strategies that would smooth the transition from one form of productive land use to another. Such forecasting is, of course, a major challenge, as the investigation of oil refining has indicated. But, as with other challenges posed by forgotten fallow, this is no argument for neglect.

References

Bachetta, M. (1978), 'The crisis of oil refining in the European Community', *Journal of Common Market Studies*, 17, 87–119.

Commission of the European Communities (1985), *The situation in the oil refining industry and the impact of petroleum products imports from third countries*, COM Document (85) 32 Final (Brussels: Commission of the European Communities).

Molle, W. and Wever, E. (1984a), *Oil refineries and petrochemical industries in Western Europe: buoyant past, uncertain future* (Aldershot: Gower).

—— (1984b), 'Oil refineries and petrochemical industries in Europe', *GeoJournal*, 9, 421–30.

Odell, P.R. (1986), *Oil and World Power*, eighth edition (Harmondsworth: Penguin).

Pinder, D.A. (1986a), 'Crisis and survival in Western European oil refining', *Journal of Geography*, 85, 12–20.

—— (1986b), 'Oil refining in the Netherlands and Belgium: growth, crisis and restructuring', *Dutch Crossing*, 30, 54–75.

Pinder, D.A. and Husain, M.S. (1987a), 'Innovation, adaptation and survival in the West European oil refining industry', in K. Chapman and G. Humphrys (eds) *Technical Change and Industrial Policy* (Oxford: Blackwell), 100–20.

—— (1987b), 'Oil industry restructuring in the Netherlands in its European context', *Geography*, 72, 300–8.

15 Retreat, redundancy and revitalisation: forces, trends and a research agenda

David Pinder, Brian Hoyle and Sohail Husain

Waterfront revitalisation is a major challenge facing cityport planning systems in the late twentieth century. The problems of redundant older port areas and associated inner-city decline were clearly identified in North America by the early 1960s. Some cities, especially those with major ports, began to face this challenge and to seize new development opportunities, so that a waterfront revitalisation movement became well established in the USA and Canada during the 1970s (Tunbridge, Chapter 5). In Western Europe the need to resolve the dilemmas of derelict docklands and neighbouring maritime quarters became widely appreciated in the 1970s, and in the 1980s awareness of the need for, and the potential of, revitalisation has rapidly increased. On both sides of the Atlantic, however, as the waterfront-redevelopment movement gathered pace, it became apparent that revitalisation processes could contain seeds of conflict and doubt – as well as of harmony and progress – with respect to appropriate goals and their related outcomes.

Redevelopment has now been adopted as a major policy in many cityport localities. This proliferation has involved not only large seaport cities but also, increasingly, the emergence of smaller coastal and interior ports as actors on this particular stage (Clark *et al*, 1979). Lakeshore and riverside locations have not been slow to join the trend, and in North America it has been claimed that virtually every urban settlement with water access has made some recent changes in the revitalisation sphere, even where the history of commercial waterfront activity is minimal. In the UK and elsewhere in Western Europe, although the uptake of opportunities has been rather later and slower than in North America, there has been a conscious emphasis on the timing – as well as on the character and layout – of redevelopment schemes. Increasingly the aim has been to create new urban waterfront environments for the twenty-first century and, perhaps above all, to re-unite ports and cities that have drifted apart.

This explosion of revitalisation activity presents opportunities not only for planners and developers but also for researchers in port transformation and urban change. The growth of the waterfront redevelopment movement – no longer confined to the North Atlantic sphere but increasingly evident in Australia and parts of the developing world, such as Hong Kong – has produced an increasing number of cases for investigation, comparison and evaluation. Proliferation, however, also poses a problem: as the movement grows, there is increasing difficulty in distinguishing the wood from the trees. Yet, because revitalisation has become such a widespread phenomenon, it is now essential that the forces, issues and outcomes that are of general significance should be distinguished from features which – despite their intrinsic interest – are essentially locality-specific. In this chapter we adopt a model-based approach to this general analysis of the revitalisation scene.

Change on the waterfront may be interpreted in terms of the product life-cycle model (Richardson, 1986), and earlier chapters in this volume have also presented models outlining the essential forces at work. Hoyle (Chapter 1) has focused on factors moulding the waterfront interaction process; Hayuth (Chapter 4) has analysed the ecological, socio-economic, and technological contexts within which these factors operate; and Riley and Shurmer-Smith (Chapter 3), although they have not proposed a formal model, have stressed the conceptual importance of scale-related perspectives on the processes observed. The model outlined here builds on this work, and incorporates many of the trends and features identified in other chapters. While drawing on these earlier contributions, however, it offers a different perspective in that it is intended to serve as a general framework for future-oriented studies of port-land redundancy and revitalisation. What must be emphasised is that the model is not considered definitive. Nevertheless, it provides an initial and very necessary step towards the clarification of this increasingly complex field of research and development activity.

Retreat

The processes underlying port retreat – and therefore the emergence of redundant space – are now clear. The period since the mid-1940s has been characterised by basic intense technological changes in shipping and cargo-handling methods, the key to these developments being an emphasis on scale and scale economies (Fig. 15.1). Traditional port areas have in many instances proved incapable of accommodating new types and generations of shipping and new types of trade while, on the landward side, a mismatch has developed between the need for, and the provision of, handling facilities (Gilman and Burn, 1983; Slack, 1980). To a great extent this mismatch derives from the technological, commercial and other changes that have made possible the proliferation of containerisation and bulk cargo-handling methods.

Reactions to these well-understood forms of technological change have been widespread, and inevitably varied, among port users and port

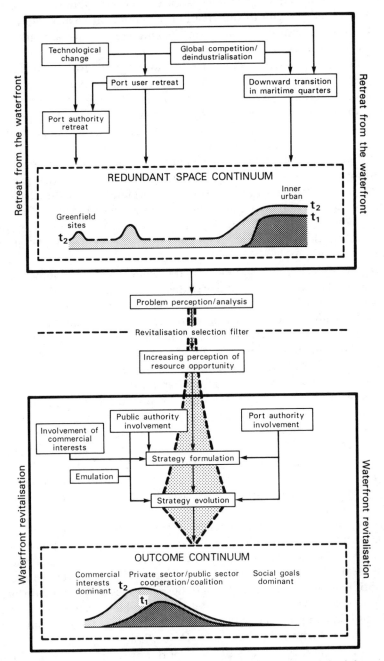

Figure 15.1 *Retreat, redundancy and revitalisation: a model of forces and trends*

authorities. Three principal strategies have been available to port users, and all have led directly to the creation of redundant space. The first is outright closure, associated with firms lacking the resources, markets or initiative to restructure successfully *in situ* or elsewhere. The second is migration to deeper water and more spacious handling areas within the same port. The third is migration between ports in response to effective interport competition. Both within-port and external migration are closely related to the strategies adopted by ports as they respond to the new technological environment. Clearly an aggressive port, pursuing a strategy of heavy investment for the provision of new facilities, may be strongly placed to capture customers seeking an improved operational environment and willing to look outside their existing port. Equally, the pace of downstream migration within a port may accelerate as a direct consequence of the port authority's investment in new facilities. Thus a planning strategy which safeguards – and perhaps enhances – a port's existing activities and throughput can simultaneously enlarge the scale of the redundant space problem.

A further aspect of port strategy is that it is natural for port authorities to focus their attention on areas and activities which remain healthy and have obvious potential for ensuring economic viability, now and in the future. Organisationally, these authorities are structured to provide land that is in demand by port users, not to deal with the problems of discarded space. This does not mean that ports give no attention to resuscitating docklands which are at risk of abandonment. As Pinder and Rosing (Chapter 7) indicate, Rotterdam provides an example of restructuring in early-twentieth-century areas to pre-empt the downward spiral. Similarly, in the 1980s the vehicle and grain trades have been successfully developed in the late-nineteenth-century general-cargo area at Southampton, a port that has experienced successive functional and physical transformations throughout its history and continues to do so today (Hoyle, 1986). Yet, in general, the perception of port authorities has been that their older port zones have become exhausted assets from which it is best that they, like port users, should retreat.

The impact of technological change, expressed through the decisions of port users and port authorities, is not, however, solely confined to the port area. One of the major recurrent themes of earlier chapters in this book is that of the damage done to port–city socio-economic linkages by the decline of traditional port functions. Although these linkages may extend through-out a cityport, there has normally been a discernible bias towards districts developed in conjunction with the port function – Hilling's maritime quarters or 'sailortowns' (Chapter 2). Here whole communities grew and prospered for a time on the basis of port and maritime employment, typically interspersed with a liberal sprinkling of port-related businesses. Both employment and business have been undermined by the collapse of traditional port activities and the growth of new trades and cargo-handling

methods, triggering downward transition and fragmentation in these formerly socially cohesive, but nowadays generally far-from-prosperous neighbourhoods.

Port and shipping technologies have therefore been fundamental forces
producing retreat from traditional waterfronts and maritime-quarter
decline. The vacuum of abandonment may be intensified by a range of
other 'top-down' forces, but any model would be seriously incomplete if
deindustrialisation were omitted. As Figure 15.1 indicates, this factor is, of
course, related to the maritime technological forces discussed above.
Innumerable industrial concerns in older port-areas have closed or
migrated as a result of pressures exerted by the modernisation of transportation and cargo-handling systems. But deindustrialisation has two other
major facets. Firstly, port industrial decline – in many cities at least – is
inextricably linked with the general pressures on inner-urban manufacturing. Indeed, many port-related industries were located in the inner-city
residential areas rather than in the port itself. Whether inside or outside
the port zone, however, the pressures have been similar: outmoded infrastructures, urban congestion, factory dilapidation, and the difficulties of
effective *in situ* restructuring. Secondly, industrial decline is a response to
global economic forces which have intensified competition and have
exacerbated sharp recessional influences.

Recognition of these distinctions is necessary to highlight the differing
consequences of port deindustrialisation. Clearly, closure or migration
generated by technological considerations or inner-urban pressures may
intensify the redundant space problem within port areas, but there is also a
strong possibility that the sites vacated may lie in adjacent maritime
quarters. If so, a further twist is likely to be given to these quarters'
downward environmental spiral. In any case, the maritime quarter communities are likely to be disproportionately affected by direct job loss and,
perhaps, by the demise of linked activities. Global pressures, meanwhile,
may similarly affect inner-urban activities, but their potential spatial
impact is far wider because of the nature of the industries affected. The
demise of shipbuilding in western countries, for example, has affected yards
of all ages, creating major redundant spaces in twentieth-century port
zones. Moreover, the impact of maritime industrial restructuring may
extend to the abandonment of port outliers beyond a conurbation. Also,
the cessation of growth by major port industries since the 1970s has
created yet another form of redundant space: port areas prepared in
anticipation of growth but never colonised.

These observations on the role of global forces highlight the fact that, in
conceptualising redundant port-related space, it is easy to over-generalise
by focusing simply on the abandonment of old port land areas. Such areas
are certainly numerous, and they are also important because of their
relationships with, and proximity to, declining inner-urban maritime quarters. Yet the rapid emergence of new types of unused port land must not be

overlooked. Also, water spaces associated with port lands, old or new, must be considered. The model therefore emphasises that opportunities exist for redundant space to occur along a continuum extending from inner-urban locations to ex-urban sites. Historically (t_1) the inner-urban dimension of this problem has been dominant, and at t_2 (the present) it is still of great importance. By this stage, however, the inner-urban peak has been augmented by the extension of retreat, albeit in a discontinuous manner, to new port areas and greenfield locations, any one of which may be as large as – or even larger than – 'traditional' areas of port abandonment on which the spotlight of publicity normally falls.

Transition – from problem recognition to intervention

As the experience of many cityports testifies, action to revitalise abandoned waterfronts does not follow naturally from the emergence of redundant space. Normally a transition phase – sometimes brief but possibly very protracted – has been necessary for port retreat to be perceived as a problem requiring urgent attention and offering the prospect of significant response. Very frequently two factors have been central to the eventual recognition of the problem: the contribution made by port retreat to the growth of urban dereliction, and employment decline resulting from large-scale redundancies among the port and industrial labour forces. Both factors have been particularly catalytic for local authorities, who are responsible for the cityport's urban fabric, and who see rising redundancies as a threat to the urban economic base. What must be recognised is that the lead in problem recognition has not always been taken by public authorities. In Baltimore (Chapter 9), pressure for action came from downtown traders fearful of the impact of dereliction on their businesses. Also, as Desfor *et al* show in the case of Toronto (Chapter 6), problem recognition can sometimes best be attributed to the continuing politico-economic interaction between authorities in a locality, rather than to any specific organisation. But cityport authorities have normally been in the forefront, although it is arguable that the urgency they have felt has varied with the nature and location of activities lost. Much more concern has normally been caused by major redundancies and large-scale dereliction on the doorstep of the central business district than by the abandonment of downstream sites. Thus the model envisages that problem recognition in this transition phase has been a selective process that has filtered redundant space and ensured that older port zones normally dominate the list of areas considered ripe for revitalisation. Moreover, this selectivity has been reinforced by observation of revitalisation in practice elsewhere. It is safer and far quicker for a city authority to embark on revitalisation in the type of port area that has been transformed in other ports, than it is to pioneer new approaches to the problem. We return to this point below.

Revitalisation

While the creation of redundant space is primarily a consequence of 'top-down' technological and industrial forces, revitalisation is much more a question of interplay between local actors, and between those actors and external forces. In addition, the model proposes that this interplay possesses a significant time-dynamic that is important both in individual ports and in revitalisation schemes in general.

As with problem recognition, early action has typically been dependent on cityport authorities. Several factors have underpinned this situation. As was indicated above, port authorities have emphasised their primary role as commercial port developers; frequently, therefore, they have been unwilling to become involved in revitalisation not based on port traffic. Secondly, the fact that the impact of retreat has spread beyond the port boundary to the maritime quarters has done much to place port decline firmly on the agendas of city authorities. This is particularly true of the physical consequences of decline. Thirdly, particularly in the era of early experimentation with revitalisation, both in North America and in Western Europe, commercial interests frequently shared the port authorities' view that abandoned docklands were exhaused assets. Lastly – but by no means insignificantly – in many ports the scale of the dereliction problem, coupled with a lack of commercial enthusiasm, demanded the early involvement of interests for whom the profit motive was not a dominant factor.

Largely for these reasons, it has been common for cityport authorities to act as prime movers in several senses. In purely practical terms they have done much – often with the assistance of provincial or central government grants – to tackle the immediate problems of derelict land clearance. In this context the rationale has been that dereliction is the legacy of past prosperity, and that it is reasonable that the society which benefited from that prosperity should invest in clearance as a prelude to another era of productive use. Public authorities have also frequently been instrumental in initiating the search for appropriate revitalisation strategies. Typically, this role has entailed fostering a local dialogue between potential actors in the revitalisation process, as suggested earlier – a learning process based on the emergent strategies of other (sometimes foreign) cityports. There is no shortage of reports by delegations despatched to investigate other cities' strategies, and it is argued that emulation derived from this learning process has been a powerful force in strategy formulation, particularly in a trans-Atlantic context. Organisations faced with major, pressing challenges which they are ill-equipped to meet are likely to shun solutions perceived to entail high risk and delay; conversely commonly adopted approaches that appear to offer relative security and early progress may well be viewed favourably (Pinder and Husain, 1987, 101, 103).

Lastly, public authorities have frequently taken their financial commitment beyond site clearance and preparation to include catalytic investment in new developments such as historic-building preservation and conversion, or the familiar provision of maritime museums. Here two sequentially related aspects of strategic thinking can be identified. Public investment has been seen as an end in itself, one which preserves heritage, converts it to a resource, attracts a significant section of the public and, thereby, contributes to the goal of port–city reintegration. Beyond this, successful investment in such public goods has been seen as one method of converting commercial interests to the view that abandoned port areas are not exhausted assets but offer profitable long-term investment prospects.

While it is argued that cityport authorities have frequently played a central role in the initiation of revitalisation, the model does not propose that these authorities have typically produced and implemented blueprint strategies. The evidence offered by many studies in this book is that the role of public authorities is very variable from case to case, but that dominance is unusual. A better generalisation is that the early strategy-formulation role of the authorities has been to construct a broad framework for change, a framework which – even at this stage – may incorporate a commercial-sector input and perhaps some port-authority influence. The planning assumption is that this early framework is essentially a starting point to be revised and developed in the light of changing circumstances, such as rising commercial interest, assessments of past achievements and changes in the supply of unused waterfront land. In practice, therefore, many revitalisation schemes are to a great extent exercises in flexible 'incremental' planning, as opposed to the 'rational-comprehensive' approach (Healey *et al*, 1982; Lindblom, 1973). This is not to argue, however, that waterfront revitalisation has from its earliest days necessarily been a demand-led exercise subservient to commercial interests. At each step in incremental planning, the opportunity should exist to measure new proposals against planning goals and, if necessary, initiate negotiations with developers to achieve closer correspondence between commercial and planning objectives.

What is now evident, however, is that – despite opportunities for negotiation presented by incremental planning – the revitalisation model must reflect a strong tendency for the influence of commercial interests to increase with the passage of time. Once again a number of factors have contributed to this trend. Prominent among them is the private sector's growing realisation that some types of abandoned waterfront, at least, present lucrative investment opportunities. Law's discussion of Baltimore and Salford (Chapter 9) proposes that private investment takes on a new momentum once publicly subsidised redevelopment reaches a critical threshold. This interpretation, useful in the context of individual ports, can be extended to revitalisation schemes in general. The results of early rejuvenation programmes have highlighted the potential profitability of redevelopment so that developers have lost their original perception

barriers and – far from shunning old port areas – may now seek out
localities ripe for investment. This rising interest is closely connected with
the spread of waterfront redevelopment – noted earlier – to lower and
lower levels in the urban–port hierarchy. For many urban authorities,
therefore, the problems and costs of establishing sustained revitalisation
have lessened significantly. Indeed, it is now quite likely that the initiative
for a revitalisation project will come from a developer rather than a local
authority. North American experience certainly underpins this point, but it
is increasingly relevant to European and other areas.

Growing commercial interest also reflects structural change among
private-sector developers. Here the key factor has been the emergence of
companies either specialising in waterfront renewal or including it in their
general redevelopment activities. In this connection, emulation has once
more been important: successful firms have encouraged others to enter the
field, and projects proposed by new firms have frequently been based on
schemes already launched by more experienced competitors. In addition, it
now appears that the shift towards revitalisation in which the pace is set by
investors has been strengthened by the changing attitudes of port
authorities. As commercial interest has risen, port managements have
begun to appreciate that they now control assets that can be profitably
realised as they retreat from unwanted port areas.

Theoretically, growing private-sector demand to be involved in revitalisation should strengthen the power of cityport authorities in the planning
process. Clark (Chapter 13) emphasises, however, that a feature of the
1980s – especially in the UK, but also elsewhere – has been growing
disquiet at what is perceived in planning circles to be a significant decrease
in the influence exerted by planning authorities. In Britain extreme examples of this trend – such as that discussed by Church (Chapter 12) – can be
explained in terms of government policy: local planning authorities have
been stripped of jurisdiction and replaced by development corporations
imposing far fewer restrictions on the private sector. But in general the
power of commercial interests is based on other factors (Bristow, Chapter
10; Tweedale, Chapter 11). Despite the proliferation of revitalisation
schemes, in many ports the supply of land available for redevelopment
continues to exceed demand. Equally, the deal that developers are frequently able to offer – a package based on their track record elsewhere –
may well be attractive to an authority burdened by dereliction, yet with
little experience of rejuvenation. Also, many advanced countries have
recently pursued public expenditure control policies which have restricted
the capabilities of cityport authorities to spend heavily on rejuvenation.
Ports still need developers. Thus the model envisages that strategy evolution, associated with an increase in the number and influence of interested
parties, may well lead to a situation in which the cityport authority is
obliged to concede more than it would wish to the private sector. While
much is often made of private-sector/public-sector partnerships, demand-

led planning may also be an appropriate summary of the philosophy underpinning many schemes.

The results of strategy evolution as a consequence of interaction between interested parties can be represented as an outcome continuum. The extremes of this continuum are, on the one hand, schemes tightly orchestrated by public authorities to serve social goals relating to downward transition in maritime quarters and, on the other hand, projects in which commercial interests are overwhelmingly dominant. As with the conceptualisation of redundant space, it is proposed that outcomes can be generalised in terms of a frequency distribution, and that this distribution has shifted significantly through time. Because cityport authorities have been primarily concerned with derelict port land, and because the private sector has generally required prime waterfront sites where redevelopment is not complicated by the presence of a local population, revitalisation with a strong social orientation is rarely encountered. Rotterdam's commitment to inner-urban housing is an exception proving the rule. Almost equally rare are schemes in which market forces are allowed virtually unfettered control, despite examples such as Hong Kong (Bristow, Chapter 10) and the much-publicised London docklands. Between these extremes, public-sector/private-sector coalitions, a phenomenon common in other urban development contexts, have consistently provided the norm (Fosler and Berger, 1982). The outcome in physical terms has often been the waterfront revitalisation stereotype encountered, and commented on, so frequently in earlier chapters: marinas, other water-based leisure activities, museums, heritage buildings, restaurants, desirable housing and – especially in larger schemes – perhaps hotels or a conference centre. It is this norm, however, that has shifted as waterfront-revitalisation strategies have evolved. Despite examples of attempts to limit the power of capital (Tunbridge, Chapter 5 and Destor *et al*, Chapter 6) private-sector pressures, in some cases coupled with limits on the ability that cityport authorities have to intervene, have induced a significant shift in the curve towards commercial dominance of rejuvenation. Clearly, this shift is closely related to fundamental issues raised in Part III: the proliferation of stereotyped developments, the offspring of commercial dominance and emulation that does not consider appropriate alternatives; deep disquiet over the commonplace neglect of social objectives; and the view that 'success' in waterfront revitalisation should be more stringently defined.

Towards a research agenda

Models frequently serve a retrospective purpose, in as much as they attempt to extract controlling processes and dominant trends from complexity. But they may also be prospective, and in this sense the model of waterfront revitalisation may be employed as a basis for future research. Clearly, with respect to investigations in individual ports, it may be treated as a framework to identify those aspects of redevelopment that typify, or contrast with, experience elsewhere. Beyond this, however, the argument advanced suggests an agenda for research into revitalisation processes in general, research which should in turn contribute to further refinement of the model itself.

One issue arising at an early stage in revitalisation is the nature of the filtering process which distinguishes areas considered suitable for redevelopment from those destined to remain fallow. As has been emphasised, the recent growth of revitalisation has by no means exhausted the supply of redundant space, but does this simply reflect the demand–supply relationship, or are there types of abandoned waterfront that are the victims of specific handicaps? So far as strategy initiation and evolution are concerned, clarification is necessary – both of the balance of power between public authorities and private investors, and of shifts in that balance as revitalisation progresses. To what extent have social objectives set by authorities subsequently been eclipsed as commercial influences have become more powerful? In addition, the efforts of other interest groups – such as local communities and environmental groups – to influence strategy development must not be overlooked. It is apparent from earlier chapters, that, albeit with exceptions, such groups, to date, have usually had little success in achieving significant policy modifications. Here, therefore, a central concern is to explain the relative failure of these groups. Does the fact that revitalisation acts to improve dereliction – and is therefore seen by the public and the political and business communities to be environmentally beneficial – weaken the power of groups which question the nature of 'improvement' or its socio-economic consequences? Equally, the contribution of emulation to equifinality, the tendency of processes to converge towards a common outcome, deserves investigation. To what extent, for example, can recurrent themes in revitalisation be attributed to the expanding activities of developers, to the influence of 'leader' cityports such as Baltimore, Toronto and London, or to more general learning processes?

Although it is necessary to refine understanding of the processes of change on the waterfront, the evaluation of revitalisation must also be given high priority. Questions raised by a number of contributors, but especially the issues highlighted in Part III, underline the conclusion that assessment should become a priority for studies in this field. Opportunities for assessment are provided by many aspects of waterfront revitalisation, but a distinction between physical and socio-economic outcomes can usefully be drawn.

In the physical context, it must be recognised that today's urban-design decisions are creating environments for the next century, and perhaps beyond. Arguably, therefore, analysis of these new environments should concentrate on whether current design preferences are creating coherent, appropriate, and appealing environments which future generations are likely to consider valuable additions to the urban mosaic. Clearly, work in this field is prey to the dangers of subjective analysis, but it is equally clear that many design professionals are uneasy that current practice may be neglecting long-term considerations in the interests of ensuring rapid, impressive, change (Ardill, 1988; Gardiner, 1988). Evaluation of physical outcomes must also recognise spatial issues. Is revitalisation generating ever-sharper contrasts between reviving port areas and their surrounding maritime quarters? In what circumstances does the renaissance of abandoned docklands overspill to initiate change in these quarters? In this connection, physical issues are inseparable from social questions: does proximity to revitalisation schemes offer benefits for the local community, or is it inevitable that this community will suffer gentrification, rising property prices and the infiltration of services unsuited to the community's needs? The question of impact over-spill is, in turn, related to a major physical-planning goal noted earlier and adopted in many cityports: the reintegration of the abandoned waterfront and the city. How frequently, how effectively and by what means reintegration is attained are all subjects for investigation, as is the contribution of public and private investment to the reintegration process, a point underlined by Edwards (Chapter 8).

Economic evaluations may usefully focus on both short- and long-term considerations. In the short term, the major question is the valuation of the abandoned waterfront as an asset. As the model has indicated, the progress of revitalisation has ensured that redundant space – at least in older port areas – is no longer regarded as valueless. In this situation it is appropriate to seek to establish to whom the benefits of real-estate development have accrued and are accruing. What is the balance of gain between developers, the port authority and the city authority? Ultimately, however, economic evaluations must depend on the long-term contribution made by re-development to the cityport economy. Given the magnitude of redundancies generated by ports and port-related activities, the scale and nature of direct employment creation must feature prominently on the research agenda. So, too, must indirect benefits, particularly with respect to employment supported by linkages between activities in the revitalisation areas and firms elsewhere in the cityport. Less obviously, but very importantly, it is necessary to establish whether revitalised waterfronts are essentially city-oriented – that is, whether they simply interact with the cityport by providing local opportunities such as housing, recreation facilities or office development. City-oriented schemes will produce benefits, but their potential is likely to be much less than if revitalisation taps markets external to the city and therefore generates external earnings. Clearly, the potential to appeal to external markets will depend partly on the local resource base. Historic cities such as Portsmouth (Chapter 3) may be well placed in this respect. Yet external market exploitation may also depend on local initiative to develop, for example, conference centres and associated hotel growth. Thus this research issue does not simply relate to the scale of external earnings generated by specific projects. From the planning viewpoint the fundamental question is that of how external markets can be identified and exploited to sustain cityport growth.

This review of research opportunities is in many ways an argument for interdisciplinary evaluation of waterfront revitalisation as a new and important dimension of urban development. Architects, planners, geographers and economists – these and many others may work towards this goal. Emphasis on physical and economic research opportunities, however, must not be allowed to obscure the human dimension of change on the waterfront. Past cityport prosperity has been heavily dependent on the labour of maritime quarter-communities which, as earlier chapters have repeatedly stressed, now find themselves economically stranded by port retreat. Evaluation of progress in revitalisation cannot, if it is to be comprehensive, avoid the reality of this downward transition. Yet the studies presented here demonstrate that social goals are low on the agenda. Of all the examples discussed in earlier chapters, only one – Rotterdam – provides evidence of sustained commitment to the needs of formerly port-dependent communities. As ports and peoples have been separated by retreat, two sets of problems have been generated, but only one has commanded action. How this has happened, and how a better balance may be achieved, are urgent issues which must not be ignored.

References

Ardill, J. (1988), 'Docklands "disaster" attacked by planner', *The Guardian*, 21.4.88, 3.

Clark, J., Wilson, C. and Binder, G.L. (1979), *Small seaports: revitalisation through conserving heritage resources* (London: Bowker Publishing Co. for the Conservation Foundation).

Fosler, R.S. and Berger, R.A. (eds) (1982), *Public–private partnership in American cities: seven case studies* (Lexington, Kentucky: Lexington Books).

Gardiner, S. (1988), 'Towering range', *The Observer*, 3.4.88, 39.

Gilman, S. and Burn, S. (1983), 'Dockland activities: technology and change', in T.S. Gould and A.G. Hodgkiss (eds) *The resources of Merseyside* (Liverpool University Press).

Healey, P., McDougall, G. and Thomas, M.J. (1982), 'Theoretical debates in planning: towards a coherent dialogue', in P. Healey, G. McDougall and M.J. Thomas (eds) *Planning theory: prospects for the 1980s* (Oxford: Pergamon), 5–22.

Hoyle, B.S. (1986), 'The transformation of the port of Southampton', in J.J. Charlier (ed.) *Ports et mers: mélanges maritimistes offerts à André Vigarié*, (Caen: Paradigme), 171–88.

Lindblom, C.E. (1973), 'The science of muddling through', in A.K.F. Faludi (ed.) *A reader in planning theory* (Oxford: Pergamon), 151–70.

Pinder, D.A. and Husain, M.S. (1987), 'Innovation, adaptation and survival in the West European oil refining industry', in K. Chapman and G. Humphrys (eds) *Technical change and industrial policy* (Oxford: Basil Blackwell), 100–20.

Richardson, S.L. (1986), 'A product life cycle approach to urban waterfronts: the revitalisation of Galveston', *Coastal Zone Managemet Journal*, 14, 21–46.

Slack, B. (1980), 'Technology and seaports in the 1980s', *Tijdschrift voor Economische en Sociale Geografie*, 71, 108–13.

Index